Gardening
for
Everyone

Gardening for Everyone

Edited by Roger Grounds

with contributions from
John Turpin
John Parker
Ken Smith
Michael Gibson

Special Feature:
Terrariums and Dish Gardens by
Conrad B. Link

Westport Corporation • New York, N.Y. 10010

ACKNOWLEDGEMENT
The publishers would like to thank **Garden News**
for making available a number of photographs for
reproduction in this book.

Horticultural Consultants: Francis C. Stark, Professor and Chairman,
Department of Horticulture, University of Maryland, and Conrad B.
Link, Professor of Horticulture, University of Maryland.

Note: The horticultural consultants have checked botanical terms
against Bailey, *Standard Cyclopedia of Horticulture,* and other
sources, but have used as the final authority Bailey and Bailey,
Hortus Second. Some botanical terms named by the authors have
been retained even if they appear in none of our sources.

The original of this book was published in Great Britain, primarily
for British gardeners. The British flavor of the text is unmistakable,
but we have endeavored to adapt the cultural and hardiness recom-
mendations to the United States, with no inconsiderable bias toward
the Mid-Atlantic region.

The chaper on *Terrariums and Dish Gardens* is written especially
for this American edition by Conrad B. Link; photography in this
chapter is by Melvin C. Brennan.

Contents

Introduction

When you buy a house the chances are you will also make a garden. The family, the house, and the garden together make one entity — the home. If you take pride in your house, you will also want to take pride in your garden.

Your garden is yours and yours alone; you may do with it what you wish. You may leave it to become a wilderness — in which case it will probably reproach you as might an undusted living-room; or you can try to make it attractive — and it can become a rewarding hobby. There is, of course, a middle road, the making of a garden that gives the maximum of pleasure with the minimum of effort, and most people will aspire to that.

There is no mystery about gardening: there are no secret, rustic incantations to make things grow. Successful gardening is simply a matter of deciding what you want to do, finding out how to do it, and then doing it, preferably in the right sequence and at the right season. This book is not a comprehensive treatise embracing the whole of horticulture: its aim is to show every gardener, whether keen or reluctant, how to achieve a garden that is colorful and fruitful with the minimum expenditure of time, money, and effort.

Whether the garden is a handkerchief-sized plot or a couple of acres, an established garden or merely the bare earth the builders left behind, this book gives you the information you need to make it attractive. If the simple, practical advice given here is followed, even the most unpromising site can be made into a place of beauty and enjoyment.

It is often said that what the keen gardener is striving to do is to recreate an earthly paradise, trying to create his own private Garden of Eden. And in this age of noisy machinery, jangling telephones, whirring computers, aggressive competition, and frayed nerves there is indeed a need for some such dream; perhaps that is why gardening is now the most popular of all hobbies. But there are other reasons, too: a garden can be more than just a background to living; it can be a challenging and rewarding pastime. Apart from the pleasures of growing flowers larger and more colorful than your neighbor's, there are also the rewards of growing fruit and vegetables both cheaper and more tasty than those you can buy in the stores. Gardening is indeed all things to all men.

Roger Grounds

The Modern Garden

There has never been such an exciting time for gardeners as the present. The modern garden is the outcome of centuries of evolution and development. All that is best from the past has been kept; all that is least acceptable to modern ideas has been discarded. Gardens may not be as large as they were in the past, but they are vastly richer in the means to make them more beautiful and easier to maintain.

The gardens of New England and England, of San Francisco and Canberra, have been enriched not only by the treasures brought back by the brave plant-hunters of the early years of this century from the rain forests of the Andes and the slopes of the Himalayas, from the cold clime of Kamchatka and from sunny South Africa, but also by the highly skilled labors of plant breeders. There has never been such a wealth of plants from which to create colorful and fruitful gardens. Precisely the same is true of garden design, where one can draw not only on the best ideas of the great traditions of American and European garden design, but also on the design of gardens from such countries as Japan, with its very different traditions.

This is a far cry from the stuffy gardens of the Victorians who surrounded their villas with miniature "alpine" effects, displays of ferns, and winding tiled paths. They were happy in their suburban grotto-gardens, while their country cousins laid a less restraining hand on nature and perfected the "cottage garden," which to this day remains an ideal that many would like to recreate.

All gardeners must be influenced by the past, which lives on in the gardens of great country houses and to a large extent in public parks, and do their best to merge the traditional with the taste and requirements of today. To this end there are available aids of which our forebears never dreamed. And those who supply us with plants and seeds will tell us that we have an ever-increasing appetite for novelty and improvement in all kinds of garden plants!

The gardener, too, has changed with the times. Even in the present century there was a clear distinction between those who tilled the ground to provide essential produce for the kitchen and table and those whose station called for the employment of one or more gardeners. Social and economic changes have brought home and garden ownership within the reach of most and at the same time eliminated or reduced the size of gardens. There are now few professional gardeners attached to private gardens, and landscape contractors have taken over this function, doing work for many homeowners during the season.

It is hardly suprising, therefore, that today every man is his own gardener. And man includes woman. Women's liberation came early in horticultural matters. Perhaps it has always been considered "safe" for the "fair" or "weaker" sex to pick flowers and arrange them, but there was one Victorian lady who was made of sterner stuff — and gardening has never been quite the same since. Her name was Gertrude Jekyll. She designed, made, and wrote about gardens and was of equal stature to her contemporary, William Robinson, whose effect on modern gardens has been equally great. Mainly through their writings, a new "middle class" of hobby gardeners of both sexes was encouraged to garden creatively, tastefully, and colorfully.

There is no such person as the average gardener (no two have quite the same approach), but if we were to seek today's typical gardener we would find him or her looking after a suburban "front and back" in which up to two-thirds of the area is devoted to lawn and the rest mainly to flowers, roses, flowering shrubs, and possibly some vegetables. Our gardener will be equipped with an armory of aids, some traditional, others very modern. It has never been found necessary to alter the basic design of digging tools, and the spade, fork, and hoe are likely to be with us as long as there is earth to be cultivated.

The lawn mower was developed by the Victorians, who also used shears and pruners, sprayers and simple garden chemicals. Conservatories for the protection of tender plants were known from earlier times in England, and their development into modern greenhouses with efficient heating systems has been a steady evolution. The mechanical aids in today's garden will include a lawn mower powered by gasoline or electricity, and perhaps an electric hedge-trimmer. Electricity may also be used in the greenhouse to heat the air and a propagating bed — and even to control the movement of ventilators and shading blinds.

Most modern gardeners will also be familiar with sophisticated garden chemicals to fertilize soil and control plant troubles. They will know the difference, if they are wise, between total and selective weed

Vegetables play just as important a part in the modern garden as flowers. They not only save money, but are very satisfying to grow.

killers, between contact and systemic insect-control products, and they will realize the value of the *protective* application of fungicides. The biological value of keeping a compost heap will be appreciated, and some will also be able to test their soil for plant-food status as well as relative acidity/alkalinity. For those who don't, these things are easy enough to learn.

Not only a trained scientist can be a successful gardener today: the above summary serves merely to illustrate the progress of gardening. Those who supply us with aids are also obliged to supply full instructions on their safe use.

Technical aids must always be seen in proportion; a good gardener is never gimmick-conscious. He will welcome labor-savers with gratitude but will remain healthily skeptical of "miracle" products. What really counts is accumulated experience with plants and soil, constant trial and error in their management, and the patience to proceed at the pace of nature rather than with the haste of modern man.

Elements of the Modern Garden
Let us look more closely at the components of a pleasing and useful garden. As was said earlier, there is no set formula, but some features have been noted that are common to most. A garden without flowers is unthinkable, at least for the area that can be seen from the house, and until recently the design was not complete without a lawn — often two. Today, however, paving and other hard surfaces are no longer restricted to paths and service areas.

Imaginative use is being made of preformed slabs, cobbles, granite paving stones, and stone chips as labor-saving groundwork, relieved by formal beds and perhaps a pool or statue. Such modern garden design is particularly appropriate in the context of the "town house" terrace. This architectural approach has brought with it a new interest in the form and texture of plants, which accounts for the growing sales by nurseries and garden centers of miniature evergreens and compact shrubs with gray, silver, and variegated foliage.

Gardens are not just there to work in; they are there to enjoy as well. Outdoor furniture like this is an asset to any garden.

However, for the majority a green lawn remains a restful contrast, with improved machines to take the drudgery out of mowing — and there are even powered edging machines to give that clean finish without much effort. The balance of herbaceous border flowers, bedding plants, and bulbs depends much on personal preference — though most of us will pack in as many of each as space, time, and ready cash allow. Selection and management of these flowers is covered in later sections. Flowers need no general words of commendation, but it can be said that flowering shrubs still remain relatively overlooked, while ornamental trees come lower still in the garden-maker's list of priorities.

It is true, of course, that for a couple of weeks in spring our gardens may be gay with golden-yellow forsythia, pink cherry, barberry, and the very showy azaleas and rhododendrons — followed very much later by an autumn blaze of berries from *cotoneaster* and *pyracantha*. But this is just to scratch at the surface of the treasury of flowering shrubs and small trees, as later chapters will show. The rose is regarded as a shrub and is justly a firm favorite. Yet it is so easy to be wooed by those who wish to sell only hybrid teas and floribundas, to the exclusion of the informal beauty of the shrub roses and the delightful older varieties that clothe walls, fences, arches, and doorways so well.

Generally speaking, shrubs will look after themselves if kept in proportion by restrained pruning. Fruit trees are ornamental as well as productive, but newcomers to gardening tend to avoid them because it is said they need such careful training. This is true up to a point, but most grown for garden planting today are propagated on rootstocks that impart a dwarf habit and slow growth and they do not get out of hand. Berry fruits are easy to manage, and the new gardener may want to plant some strawberries. A row of raspberries or grapes can make a useful and quite attractive screen between ''kitchen'' and ''pleasure'' areas.

Recent times have seen a renewed interest in home vegetable growing. Rising food prices are one reason, and another is an awareness that food from the garden is fresher, better flavored, and perhaps grown with fewer chemical aids than produce bought in a store. Vegetable gardening has cast off its gloomy cloth-cap wartime image and become an interesting and rewarding pastime. Consider allocating an area to a rotation of ''salads,'' ''roots,'' and ''greens.'' Lady gardeners in particular need no persuasion to grow herbs, which are charming in growth and piquant in the pot: it is best to allocate them a special bed near the kitchen or even to maintain them on the windowsill in pots or a box.

Soil, Site, and Climate

Soil, site, and climate are some of the elements of the garden; their disposition is our next consideration. The gardener must be a realist and respect the limitations of any site while at the same time using all his resources to overcome problems. For example, on a windswept hillside there will be constant damage to all but the lowest-growing plants until a screen is provided to break the prevailing wind. This may be in the form of a lattice fence, a hedge, or a group of trees — and must be considered a priority. The more tender shrubs must not be grown in exposed northern districts, and extremes of dryness in a sunny location or shade cast by buildings or trees will limit the growth of a wider range of plants.

Other considerations are the size, shape, and slope of the site, and these aspects will be covered in detail later. A little, but not much, can be done to counter the influence of local topography and climate on the garden, but the native soil is another matter altogether. Its type will certainly influence the character of the garden, but no gardener worth his salt will admit defeat because he is presented with inhospitable clay or sand. Again, the degree of acidity or alkalinity will influence what can be grown — the rhododendron tribe will never be happy in a lime-rich soil, and hydrangeas will be pink rather than blue. Slight acidity suits the majority of garden plants, while the inclu-

12

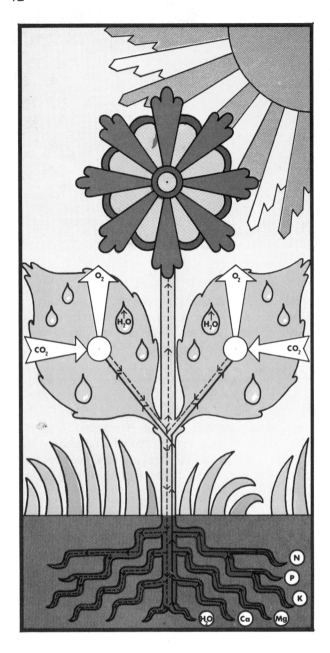

Diagrammatic representation of how a plant lives.
Photosynthesis is the key to plant life.
This is the process whereby the chlorophyll
(green pigment) in the leaves absorbs energy from
sunlight and uses it to convert carbon dioxide
absorbed from the atmosphere and water
absorbed by the roots into carbohydrates, from
which the plant cells are built. The stems carry the
nutrients absorbed by the roots to the leaves, and
also foodstuffs to all parts of the plant. Finally, the
leaves give off oxygen and water vapor to the
atmosphere as a by-product of photosynthesis.
[O=oxygen, CO_2=carbon dioxide, H_2O=water,
N=nitrogen, P=phosphorous, K=potassium,
Mg=magnesium, Ca=calcium]

sion of peat, organic matter from compost heaps, animal manure, and acidic fertilizers will all ameliorate excess alkalinity.

Making and Remaking Gardens
The need to make or remake a garden comes about in the following ways. An existing garden can no longer be tolerated and requires major changes to make it acceptable. A house is acquired with an existing garden that must be improved, or a new house with a barren site is taken over. In the first two cases it is likely that some permanent features can be salvaged and a new design planned around them. Ground left by the builder is an empty canvas on which the gardener can create an original picture.

In all cases the pleasant task of garden-making begins on paper — graph paper — on which a scale plan is drawn. The larger the paper, the easier and more accurate the draftsmanship. Start by measuring the outside perimeter of the house. Then choose a scale that will enable the whole site area to fit on the paper: 5 or 10 feet to the inch is often employed. Some rudimentary surveying equipment is required. The basics are a tape measure; a couple of long lines of cord or wire; half a dozen stout, pointed stakes about a foot long; an equal number of 4-foot stakes or canes; and a large, right-angle triangle made of wood. Take as a base line a wall of the house that faces the greatest part of the garden. Run lines at right angles from this wall until they meet the boundary of the site. If the line of sight is impeded, set up canes along the line so that each is exactly in front of the previous one when viewed with the eye close to it. Transfer these maximum distances to the graph paper, marking the boundary points with dots.

From points along these initial lines (marked by canes) run "branches" at right angles until these lines reach other garden boundaries. Measure the distances and transfer them to the plan. If the garden is on several sides of the house, these house walls must be used as new base lines to make further right-angle measurements. When sufficient dots have been made on the paper they can be joined to make an accurate perimeter plan of the site. Also measure and mark the location of any tree or other permanent feature that is to be retained.

Draftsman's tracing paper now is useful. Pin a sheet over the graph paper and sketch in possible positions for certain major features — paths, borders, lawn, vegetable garden, pool, greenhouse, and so on. Over this can be placed another sheet of tracing paper on which variations and other details can be marked in a different color. In this way a picture of the future garden can be built up and changed until the ideal is achieved. Aim for simplicity and seek a balance between straight lines (as for paths) and sweeping curves (for lawn and border edges). Bear in mind that an "artistic" design of little beds in grass, or winding paths, may look nice on paper but to translate it into spadework and concrete mixing can be a herculean task at the outset and require constant edging and maintenance. Instead, allow for a larger lawn area than you might think you want, and include a large, sweeping border instead of scattered beds. Later it will be much easier to cut into the grass area to make another feature (or put additional shrubs in a big border) than to erase items from an overly "busy" layout.

While still at the planning stage, some design principles should be noted. To create an effect of greater distance make a focal point, with a tree, sundial, or seat for example, at the end of a converging vista, and let a path "disappear" behind a hedge or trellis. Conversely, to shorten a long site, divide the garden into self-contained areas. For example, a circular lawn near the house with a low wall on its far side will concentrate interest on its pleasing proportions so that the eye is less distracted by the length of garden beyond. Most garden perimeters are rectangular, so try to break the rectangle by curving the edges of lawn and borders.

Above all be realistic: design for easy management (none of us gets younger). Have good access paths for the mower and other heavy tools; this may mean a slope instead of steps. Consider bringing the vegetable area and greenhouse near the dwelling house if ease of access is more important than eye appeal. And remember that you may want to supply electricity to the greenhouse or even have a hot bed. By the same token, it is pointless to place a shed at the rear of the plot and tramp the whole distance for every item that is kept there.

Groundwork

Give plenty of time and thought to these early deliberations: they can save much regret and work later. However, the time has come to put theory into practice and make first contact with the soil. If the garden is on level land there should be no need to move soil in any quantity unless it is to relieve uniform flatness by creating undulations. An artificial mound must often be raised for a rock garden, and it can be an economy to plan this in combination with a pool: the excavation for one making the elevation for the other.

On a site where the main garden falls away from the house, a primary task could be to make a terrace against the house, which may require some fill. The fall of a site can be broken at any point by building a low wall of stone or brick, moving some soil to the higher level at the same time, and interrupting the wall with a couple of steps. Gardens that slope toward the house present drainage problems and for that reason are not often found. But if the nature of the site demands such an arrangement, banks and ditches will need to be provided for the natural flow of surplus water away from the house.

A level site is generally preferred for the lawn,

Different plants have different garden uses. (a) *Celastrus orbiculatus,* though ideal for a pergola, takes some years to show itself to any effect. (b) Brooms are ideal short-term plants for filling gaps while more permanent plants get established. (c) *Halimium occimoides* is a gambler's plant, inclined to fade away.

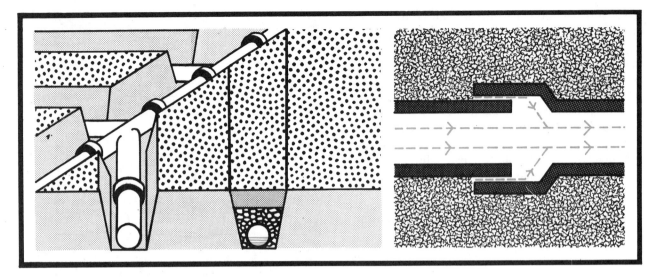

Drainage This is the traditional herringbone pattern used when laying drains. The outlet to the drain is at the top of the diagram.

although a slight slope will assist drainage and lawn management. Some soil movement is generally necessary, and a cardinal rule is to preserve the valuable topsoil, which during excavation may get buried and replaced by less-fertile, less-friable subsoil. Therefore, shovel away as much topsoil as is practicable from the area of soil movement, and keep it heaped nearby.

A slope can be leveled in three ways: by adopting the lowest level and removing all soil above this; by adopting the highest level and importing soil; by choosing the intermediate level and removing high ground to fill low ground. Unless dramatic changes in level are required, the third alternative requires the least effort and soil movement.

Here is one way to level a site. Cultivate the ground roughly and move soil (with the precaution of reserving topsoil that might get buried) until the site is roughly level by eye. Final adjustments are made with the aid of pegs, a mallet, a plank about 6 feet long, and a spirit level. At a central spot in the area being leveled, knock in a peg until it is flush with the ground. Knock in another peg the same distance from the first one as the length of the plank, and adjust it until the plank spanning the two pegs is level according to the spirit level placed on top. The second peg may then be proud of the ground or slightly sunk, so soil must be added or removed accordingly. Proceed in this way across the site, moving soil with a rake. Finally distribute evenly any reserved topsoil that remains.

While still at the early design and soil-moving stage, it is most advisable to investigate whether artificial drainage is required. Free percolation of excess rainwater from the region of plant roots is a prerequisite of healthy growth. A light, sandy soil will have no problems in this respect: indeed, it may require the addition of water-holding organic matter. But the drainage of even a light surface soil can be impeded by an impervious lower layer. A heavy clay soil will inevitably drain slowly, and the gardener must judge by studying his soil after rain to see whether puddles remain on the surface and constitute a drainage problem.

Put in drainage channels at an early stage. It is hard work, but it may make the difference between pleasure and dismay in future gardening activities. To conduct water, there must be a gradient. If the garden slopes, then take advantage of this to run channels to a ditch or dry well at the lowest point. On a level site the channels themselves must cut more deeply into the ground as they cross the site to the chosen outflow point. Remember that standing water can be useful in the right place: a low-lying area can make an excellent bog garden.

Otherwise drainage water should be discharged into an existing ditch or into a stone-filled dry well that is dug as deeply as possible at the lowest point. Tile drains are the most permanent, laid end to end in a narrow trench about 2 feet deep and surrounded with 3 inches of pea gravel. The alternative is to dig a similar trench and pack it with a 9-inch depth of stone in place of tile drains. A single drain across the site is rarely sufficient, and a herringbone pattern of branches about 15 feet apart, falling to meet the main drain, should ensure adequate drainage on the most difficult land.

Soil Management

A little more can be said at this stage about the different types of soil that have been mentioned in passing and of how the gardener can analyze them in order to understand better their physical and chemical potential for plant growth. To discover the main constituents of a soil an empty jar is all that is required. Dig a narrow hole with a trowel, and remove a slice from the side to a depth of 3 to 4 inches. Crumble this into the jar. Pour in water to cover the soil, and shake the contents well. When this is left to settle, the heavier constituents will fall to the bottom, and the lighter parts will form narrow bands above. This will give an indication of the proportions of gravel, sand, silt, clay, and organic matter present. Generally speaking, the coarser the particle size is, the easier the management of the soil will be.

Simply by sight and touch you can ascertain if a lump of soil sticks and smears (clay); has a gritty texture (sand); or feels like talcum (silt). Best of all is old meadow land, where root penetration by grasses, the manure of animals, and the activity of earthworms have created a deep, crumbly, fibrous loam.

Chemical soil analysis is best carried out with the help of a soil-test kit, which can be purchased from a garden store. First stage testing is for acidity or alkalinity. This is generally done by shaking a sample of soil in water and dipping specially treated paper strips into the solution. The color the strip adopts is then compared with a chart showing the degree of acidity or alkalinity. An extreme of either will be problematic — but is not often found. A neutral or slightly acidic reaction is best for general-purpose gardening.

More sophisticated soil-test kits enable the plant foods present to be analyzed. Most states provide a soil-testing service, however, through the County Agricultural Extension Agent.

We have now opened the door to the complex and controversial world of the soil and the additions that man incorporates. There are three major plant foods — nitrogen, phosphate, and potash — commonly referred to as N, P, and K. An analysis on a fertilizer package will usually show the symbols P_2O_5 and K_2O for phosphate and potash. There are several other essential elements needed by plants, such as calcium, iron, magnesium, manganese, and boron. There are enough of these in most properly managed soils. Nitrogen encourages green growth, while the others play vital roles in making roots and strong stems and in swelling fruit or giving flower-color.

How are these food elements supplied? Under natural conditions there is a cycle by which plants and animals contribute their debris to the soil. This debris is rich in plant food as well as being organic material that improves the structure and health of the soil during its decay into humus. When man cultivates a garden he inevitably interrupts this natural cycle and makes great demands on the food reserve of the soil. He will tend, for example, to keep ground bare around clumps of flowers and shrubs so that little vegetation returns below ground. He will try to grow several crops of salads or other vegetables from the same site in a year, and he removes grass clippings when the lawn is mowed.

It does not take long for the soil to become deficient in plant food, and when it does, the quality of the

Types of paving Paving materials with different textures give a garden character. Combinations of modern materials such as concrete with traditional ones such as granite paving stones are very effective.

garden deteriorates. The best way to repay the debt to the soil is to add cow manure, which contains nitrogen and other plant foods and is useful in improving structure. The next best thing is properly to add rotted leaves and plant waste, which we call compost. Useful additional soil improvement comes from turning under the winter weeds each spring. But this natural feeding is not enough for an intensively cultivated garden, and N, P, and K should be provided by modest applications of artificial fertilizer. Additional calcium comes from spreading limestone (but only if the soil is neutral or acid). Peat has no food value but improves structure and makes soil less alkaline.

Lime is also scattered on heavy land to improve friability. The transformation of heavy clay into friable loam is the dream of all gardeners unlucky enough to be stuck with the former, and in recent years a range of "miracle" products has been offered as a cure. They will do what is promised of them — but in time, and at a price. Another material for the same job is gypsum, which has been known and used far longer than the alginates, of which most of the clay-loosening products are composed.

Older than all these materials is nature's own way of creating a surface tilth — by the combined effects of winter freezing and thawing, which shatter lumps into ever smaller pieces, and by the drying effect of winds which furthers the crumbling process. This is true of all soils that form clods when wet, and the gardener should not be anxious to break these down when he carries out autumn digging after clearance of summer flowers and vegetables.

It cannot be over-emphasized how vital is the addition of decaying organic matter to the soil for the health of the garden and its easier management. The effect is cumulative. The humus so provided enriches the soil and also "opens it up," so that water and air pass more freely. Thus, it dries and warms up more quickly in the spring, and growth is not delayed. Organic matter attracts earthworms which help to bury it, and by their burrowings they aerate and drain the soil further. Such a soil will have a balanced ecology.

Friend or Foe
A word now about friends and foes in the garden — especially foes, which can be controlled with a great array of chemical weapons these days. The foes you face are the insects that wish to share the fruits of your endeavors (there are also larger creatures, such as birds and mice, which are not being considered here); fungal spores which alight and develop on plants when conditions are right for them; and weeds. Friends occur in the insect camp, notably among the ladybirds and parasitic wasps, and in the soil are found the helpful centipede (which is more active than the harmful millipede), certain burying beetles, and the invaluable earthworm. Any damage done by birds is surely compensated by their activity in searching

out pests, including slugs and snails.

Before resorting to chemical controls, be sure that other approaches have been tried. There is no substitute for cleanliness in the garden. This concerns such points as removing all trash and litter for composting or burning and avoiding dense, damp tangles of growth, which are breeding grounds for pests and diseases. It means attending to hand weeding, cutting back dead growth, digging out the last remains of food crops — and keeping tools clean. It is attention to detail, for which there is another phrase — a green thumb.

But when troubles are rife, as will be the case from time to time in every garden, then use modern aids before epidemic levels develop. However, do not get carried away just because a suitable spray is at hand. It may be just as easy, cheaper, and at no risk to the environment if, say, some caterpillars are picked off by hand, or a patch of weeds is pulled out of the lawn rather than spot-sprayed.

Protection and prevention is obviously wiser than last-minute action to combat a big build-up of trouble. There are insecticides with limited persistence in the plant's sap stream so that pests arriving the day after spraying will be controlled. These sprays are called systemic. The same property will soon be introduced into fungicides, but in the meantime these materials are best sprayed on to susceptible foliage, such as that of the rose, ahead of possible infection so that a protective barrier is formed.

The technical word for weed killer is herbicide, and here, too, there are innovations of great value. For use on the lawn there are selective herbicides that will destroy broad-leaved weeds but will leave grasses unaffected. And there are newer ones which if sprayed on clean ground among woody plants prevent fresh weed growth without injury to the shrubs.

A Look Ahead
As this survey of a garden in the making draws to a close, it may be of value to stand, in the mind's eye, at an upstairs window that commands a view of the whole garden. Time has raced forward and a composition on paper has matured in reality. And now the seasons of the year unfold in the garden below. First we are presented with the winter scene. The color green is well distributed, with the lawn in one plane and the specimen evergreens standing sentinel for the vertical dimension. A good number of the border and rock-garden plants also are evergreen, and one notices the emerald bark of shrubs like *Kerria* in a sheltered position. Even those modest silvery shrubs, such as *Elaeagnus* (Russian olive) have become important. The golden privet takes on a new value. There are pink flowers among the bergenia leaves that spill from the border's edge onto the path, and the *Hellebore* is carrying a dozen or more white or purplish-white flowers. You may compliment yourself that the garden pool, kept free of ice, is a great attraction for birds

The modern garden Paving, and the use of shrubs and perennials
that can be relied upon to keep down most of their own weeds,
make the modern garden easy to maintain.

in winter. A final delight is the low beech hedge which really does hold its petrified golden leaves until sloughed off by emerging new ones.

The calendar pages fall away, as it were, and early spring bulb flowers sparkle in the rock garden. The ever-glossy leaves of the camelia contrast with the precious buds, and the bursting of forsythia, cherry, and azalea precedes a fresh green tracery. Delicate April gives way to profuse May and June, with a cavalcade of color. Fruit trees and bushes have flowered, and the strawberries are reddening. There are already fresh lettuce and radishes to eat, and the first pulls from the rhubarb are especially sweet. Tulips are past, but lilies continue to delight. Borders fill out until no soil can be seen, while the roses are presenting their second flush. The beans and beets and carrots add color and texture to the vegetable garden.

A red-gold tinge in the leaves of the vine on the wall signals that we have passed into another season. Roses remain, dahlias join them, and chrysanthemums follow closely. Green tomatoes may be picked for use after frost has killed the vines. Late butterflies cluster on the clump of stonecrop and sleepy wasps come and go between the apple and the pear trees. September sun ripens onion skins to parchment, but sudden gusts bring down the first leaves — a timely reminder that these must be gathered for composting. Among fallen leaves the pink trumpets of colchicums peep (these are like large crocuses), and there are garlands of berries on the firethorn and cotoneasters.

The daydream at the upstairs window fades with the shortening days when weekend daylight must be used in order to complete clearing and digging. But leave some spadework for winter, when activity makes the hands tingle and breath hangs heavy in the crisp air. This is when the gardener takes stock, ponders over the seed catalogs, and hopes the roses he has ordered do not arrive during a cold spell. The year has ended, but not for a gardener with a bright, frost-proof place were pot plants are being raised, brought to flower, or rested. He may also be counting the days until the hyacinths in bowls are ready to be brought from their dark cool ''plunge'' bed and introduced into the January living room as the first offering of a new spring. But many of these things may still be mysteries to you: the following chapters will initiate you.

1

2

3

4

Color through the year
1 Christmas roses. The earliest herbaceous plants to flower, usually in January or February.
2 Camellias. These flower from early March into May. 3 Roses. Many modern roses will flower for five months of the year. 4 Autumn color. The last great burst of color before winter.

Techniques of Gardening

As with every other worthwhile activity in life, you only get out of gardening what you put into it. This does not mean that having a garden with a riot of color all summer long must be back-breaking work, weekend after weekend, year-in and year-out. It does mean that a job done once and done well — even if it is hard work at the time — will save a tremendous amount of hard labor later.

As was mentioned in the introduction, there is no secret to success in gardening; it is simply a matter of finding out what must be done and then doing it, preferably in the right order. The matter of doing it in the right order is particularly important when it comes to carving out what are, in effect, the foundations of the garden. Unless this is done well, the garden will never flourish, and no amount of work in the years that follow will ever make up for lack of preparation at the initial stage. The matter of doing things in the right order is probably of more importance at this stage than at any subsequent sequence of operations.

Surveying the Site

The first step in making a garden is to survey it. This is not a difficult operation: you need not be a chartered surveyor, nor do you need complicated instruments. Basically, all you need do initially is to walk around your garden and determine what you want to do with it and what the problems are going to be. You will need to take reasonably accurate measurements of the dimensions of the garden, so that you can draw up accurate plans.

In the garden of a newly built house this is usually not difficult. However, if you have bought an old house with an established garden, the problems may be more complex. Established gardens are basically of two types: those that have been maintained in good order and those that have been neglected. With an established garden that has been maintained in good order, it is wisest to continue maintaining it in good order for your first year. This will enable you to find out what is already in the garden before you decide to make any changes. If you have acquired a neglected garden, a lot of clearing will be necessary before you can survey the site, possibly even before you can establish the exact boundaries.

Site Clearance

Clearing the site is an essential operation in all gardens, old and new, but the problems of each are rather different.

With old, overgrown gardens the first step is to clear away the undergrowth. Only when this has been done can you establish the boundaries and the lay of the land. The simplest way to clear the overgrowth is to use a rotary mower and then to use a saw and pruning shears on any scrubby growth.

The problems that face those who have taken on a garden surrounding a newly built house are rather different. It is quite possible that the builder will have removed all your topsoil and left you with only the relatively infertile and intractable subsoil. In this case you will have to buy topsoil, usually at considerable cost. The topsoil should not, however, be brought back into the garden until all grading and changes of level have been made. Where patios, paths, and drives are to be made, no topsoil will be needed.

Even if the builder has left your garden with its original topsoil, the chances are that he will also have left you with quite a number of other things — such as broken bricks, large slabs of concrete, and broken bottles. You may also find that he has buried pieces of plaster, metal, roofing, sheets of plastic, and other materials incompatible with fertility and good drainage. These all should be removed. When large slabs

1 Lilies need a woodsy, well-drained, preferably lime-free soil.

2 *Leycesteria formosa* will grow well on any fertile soil.

of concrete occur, these must be broken up with a sledge hammer or levered out of the ground with a crowbar or pickax. The concrete rubble is worth retaining somewhere on the site if you are contemplating laying a drive, paths, or a patio. It will save having to buy stone for drainage.

Soil

To the non-gardener, earth is just earth. It is when you want to start growing things in it that it begins to take on more importance.

Soil is made up of two basic types of material — mineral and organic. The mineral part is the result of vast geological forces that have, with the assistance of weathering over an immense period of time, broken down basic rocks into finer and finer particles. Basically, therefore, the type of soil in any garden will depend largely on the type of rock from which it has been broken down. The organic part of earth is called *humus*. Humus is the sum of all the decaying vegetable and animal matter in the soil. Within the structure of the soil it forms a kind of sponge which retains water and enables plants to acquire essential nutrients from the soil.

There is a third component of soils that is often forgotten: it is known as the soil population. This is made up of a surprisingly large number of creatures, some of them beneficial, others destructive, which live in the soil. These include not only the obvious creatures, such as earthworms, but also a very large number of microorganisms. The extent of the soil population will depend largely on the amount of humus in the soil. It is the function of these microorganisms to break down dead creatures and vegetation and release the plant nutrients locked up in them so that the plants can use them. Thus, the overall fertility of any soil depends on the ratios in which these various elements are combined.

Basic Soil Types

Gardeners recognize a number of different types of soil. Each has its own peculiar advantages and disadvantages.

LOAM   Loam is the ideal soil in relation to structure, and it contains some clay, some silt, and some sand. It feels smooth without being gritty or sticky if rubbed in the hand when sampled moist. Neither is it powdery. A light loam has more sand in it — more than

3 Autumn color is most pronounced in many plants.

4 Hydrangeas will grow on any soil, but most will be pink on alkaline soils and blue on acid soils.

5 The Japanese cut-leaf maple prefers a soil slightly on the acid side and shelter from cold winds.

6 **Day lilies** grow best in fertile soil with plenty of humus and in full sun.

two-thirds. A heavy loam has more clay — more than one-third. A medium loam has just the right texture and retains water and food well. It warms up quickly in spring, enabling plants to get a good start. If it becomes very acid, it will need dressings of lime, and it is best to add small amounts of lime at regular intervals rather than wait until the soil becomes too acid. Humus-making composts and manures will be needed, as well as fertilizers.

SANDY SOIL Sandy soil is non-sticky even when wet, and those who are used to heavy soils often envy gardeners with sandy soils, because the latter are so easy to dig or hoe. But it is a hungry soil that needs a lot of manure, peat, compost, etc., and fertilizers. It warms up quickly in spring for early sowings.

CLAY SOIL Heavy and cold, clay soil is sticky to the touch when wet and binds up into unbreakable lumps in dry weather. Improvement of drainage, as mentioned below, will help. Supplemental fertilizers will also be needed. More liberal liming will be necessary.

PEAT A dark, spongy soil, peat is often very rich in plant foods. If it is the fen peat type it will need good drainage and lime, as it is invariably too acid. Peat

soils should not be over-limed, however, as this upsets the chemical balance of the soil.

STONY The proverbial infertility of stony ground is due to the fact that all the moisture runs out of it so quickly. However, a few stones in the soil may actually help to retain the moisture. It is, in any case, almost impossible to remove all the stones, since more seem to surface to take the place of those removed. A far more positive approach is to add plenty of moisture-retainers and rich humus-makers, such as compost, manure, etc., together with plenty of fertilizers.

Drainage

Paradoxical though it may seem, plants and people have a lot in common. Both need air and water for survival, but both need them in the right proportions. Thus, although everyone would admit that it is necessary to drink water in order to stay alive, the same people would also admit that it is not necessary or even desirable to drink all the time, nor would they like to drink stagnant water. Precisely the same applies to plants. They need a soil that is moist but well-drained. Very few plants can live with their roots

7 *Cornus kousa* 'Chinenis' needs an acid soil and some shade to give off its best.

8 Hostas do best on a rich soil that will not dry out in summer.

perpetually submerged in stagnant water. Air is excluded from a waterlogged soil, and plants need air at the roots in order to live.

Soils in which these adverse conditions exist are badly drained soils, and steps must be taken to improve the drainage. Good, deep digging, dealt with later in this chapter, will usually achieve all that is necessary, but sometimes it is necessary to take more drastic steps and introduce drainage pipes. The method of laying these is dealt with in the preceding chapter. However, the decision to lay drainage pipes should be made before undertaking the next task, so that the two can be done together.

Site-Leveling

Grading is probably the major task in any garden. Therefore, if it is to be done, it must be one of the first tasks to be undertaken. If you start with a sloping site, you may have to level it; certainly some level areas will improve the general appearance of the garden. If you start with a level site, you may want to introduce into it some changes in level to relieve the monotony of a single-level garden.

The first operation in any site-leveling or change of level job is to remove all the topsoil from the area to be leveled. Of course, if the builder has already done this for you, it saves some trouble. The topsoil, which is the upper layer of soil, is usually darker than the soil below. It may vary in depth from a few inches to a few feet. The subsoil, which lies below the topsoil, is lighter in color and less friable.

To determine the levels of a sloping site, use thick bamboo canes of different lengths, a thick straightedge about 6 feet long, and a spirit level. Put a peg at the highest point of the garden, and place a stake about 6 feet from it, making the top of the stake level with the peg, with the help of the straightedge and the spirit level. The distance and height of the stake will then give you the angle of your slope. In this way the whole garden can be covered by a series of stakes. To make different levels and slopes, place other stakes beside the marker you used to map the slopes. With these other stakes you can work out absolutely horizontal lawns by using the spirit level and straightedge, or you can devise new angles of slopes by making the other stakes fall short or rise above the marker stakes.

The best way to get a completely flat surface is by the "cut-and-fill" method. After removing the topsoil, you then remove the subsoil, transporting it from higher levels to the lower levels, until the desired new level has been achieved. You then replace the topsoil, or import some, as the case may be, and level off with pegs and a spirit level.

According to the way in which the pegs are worked out, this method may be used either to level an entire sloping site or to convert the sloping site into a series of terraces. Similarly, higher areas can be created in the garden, as can sunken gardens. Where there are changes of level, measures must be taken to ensure that the levels remain constant and do not slip away through erosion and natural settling. If the change in level is not great, a gentle slope can be covered either with grass (which may be difficult to mow) or with a shrub or mixed border or ground cover, or a retaining wall can be constructed. Walls may be of either dry stone construction (which is useful in assisting drainage) or bonded brick. In either case, the walls should be built on a firm foundation of concrete and should be sloped back slightly against the level above them. An alternative is to use the change of level to create a rock garden, but it is usually necessary to use fairly substantial stones for this purpose. Techniques of dry-stone walling and bedding-in rocks are dealt with in detail in the chapter on rock gardens.

Having created changes of level, it is then obviously necessary to create a means of passing from one level to another. This will necessitate building a sloping path or a flight of steps. The techniques of building these are dealt with in detail in the chapter on Fences, Hedges, Paths, and Edgings. At this stage it is merely worth bearing in mind that not only will you and your family want to pass from one level to another, but also that you will have to move such things as lawn mowers and other equipment from one level to another.

Marking the Borders

Having leveled the site or created new levels in it, the next step is to mark the borders, working strictly from your plan.

When marking beds and borders, it is useful to have a right-angled frame for getting the corners square. This is easily made by taking three pieces of straight-edged wood and screwing them together so that they form a triangle, one corner of which is a right angle. Curves and circles are marked with a fixed stake with a line attached to it, and another stake, the whole device being used in the same way as a pair of compasses.

To mark out an oval bed, decide on the length and width. Using a radius of half the length, make two curves or arcs from the two extreme points of the width. Insert a stake where these two curves intersect.

There will be two points at which the curves intersect, so insert a stake in each point. Then take a line that has a loop at each end and is exactly the same distance as the length of the proposed bed. Secure this line with the loops over the two stakes, and with a third stake score a line in the ground, keeping the cord taut all the time. This will mark a perfect oval of the prescribed length and breadth.

Making a Lawn

After leveling the site and marking the beds and borders, the next operation is laying the lawn. This operation is dealt with in another chapter.

After the lawn has been laid, begin digging the beds and borders in preparation for planting. If an area is being devoted to vegetables, that section can be dug just as soon as you move into your house — provided, of course, that you are not contemplating any subsequent earth-moving operations in that part of the property.

Digging

The purpose of digging is to break up soil to admit air and to allow ready drainage through the soil particles. Also, a soil that is well-aerated and which drains freely is one in which a useful soil population can thrive.

Digging is generally regarded as a back-breaking chore. However, if you do it steadily, only digging at one time an area you know you can cope with, then it is one of the most rewarding and satisfying of all gardening operations. It is rewarding because you can lean on your spade at the end of the afternoon and see a patch of ground that not only looks good, but really is good, and in which you know your plants will thrive.

The type of digging you do will depend on your analysis of the condition of the soil. At this stage you will not be too concerned with the refinements of soil-testing and finding out what fertilizers need to be forked into the surface of the soil. You will be more concerned with the problems of drainage and the soil structure and type, as discussed above.

If the topsoil is thin or the area has already been dug to the depth of two lengths of the blade of a shovel, it will only be necessary to give the ground a plain digging. *Plain digging* means digging a trench one shovel deep and turning over the next strip of soil into it, and so on. The soil from the first trench is taken to the end of the plot being dug and is used to fill the trench made by the last strip of soil to be dug. Manure may be left on the surface of the dug ground in the fall to rot down into the soil.

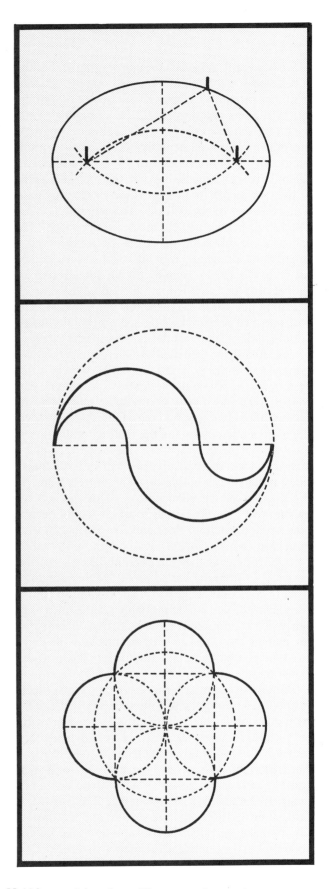

Marking out borders All you need to make a right-angle are three pieces of wood screwed together, the ratios of the sides being 3, 4, and 5. For circles and elipses, all you need is a piece of string attached to a peg.

It is generally agreed that rough digging of this kind is best done in the fall or winter so that the action of frost can penetrate the uneven surface of the ground left by digging and thus provide that crumb structure which the gardener is ultimately seeking. Digging at this time of year is particularly beneficial to clay soil.

Double digging enables you to improve the drainage of your soil, because it reaches two shovel depths, or over 18 inches into the soil, which in many cases will be down to the subsoil. This subsoil is never lifted, but manure and compost and other fertilizers can be forked into it, and it can be forked over to improve the drainage. You work across a wider area, say 2 to 3 feet, and begin by taking out a trench one shovel deep of this width at one end of the plot and wheeling the soil to the other. Or you can divide the plot into two narrow lengths and work down to the bottom and back, so that the earth you have taken out of your first strip is returned to the ground in the space left by the removal of the last strip, which in this system will be adjoining the first one. When you have forked over and dug in compost or manure in the bottom of the first trench to the depth of a shovel, you dig a second trench behind the first, carefully turning over the sod so that the grass and weeds are placed upside-down. Alternatively, you can slice off the top like a turf and lay it upside-down in the trench and just dig the rest of the earth onto it. This method will enable you to examine the roots of weeds such as bindweed, dandelion, elder, nettles, couch grass, and buttercup, which must always be removed from the soil altogether, as they are perennial and some may grow again from the buried roots. Double digging is usually done only on new ground. If you use a rotary tiller instead, you would probably set the tines to cut fairly deep and go over the whole area. Then spread the manure, etc., and go over the area with the digger again in the transverse direction, to work in and break down the manure.

Ridging is a similar form of digging, except that it results in exposing the soil more to the frost's action by increasing the amount of surface with ridges. It is very useful for heavy clays. As before, a shovel-deep trench is dug and removed to the other end of the plot. The trench should be about 2 feet wide. Starting at one end, the next three shovelfuls of soil, one behind the other, are turned over into the trench. The first will be farthest away, the second next to it, and the third on top, to make the ridge. Or some prefer to lay the first shovelful in the center and the other two at an angle to each other over it, also making a ridge. The plot is made into a line of ridges in this way.

Manures and Fertilizers

Nowhere is the analogy between human beings and plants more true than in the matter of food. Human beings need many different kinds of foods and they can take them only in a certain form. Some foods are needed more than others at certain stages of life, and so on. All this applies to plants in different ways. Although most plant foods are simple elements which the plants turn into more complex ones, whereas in human food processes a reverse situation applies, the food needs of plants are exacting and must be studied if the best results are to be obtained.

Just as human beings need differing foods for various purposes, so do plants. The three major plant foods — nitrogen, which feeds the green parts of the plant; phosphorus for the roots; and potassium for flowers and fruits — are known under the general heading of NPK, which are the distinguishing letters from their chemical formulae. The humus-makers carry the food, and the fertilizers are the food itself. Top-quality stable manure carries enough NPK for most plants in its natural state, and the other humus-makers also carry these foods in varying degrees. Generally, however, it is necessary to supplement the humus-makers with fertilizers in order to provide the amount of chemicals that plants need. A short answer to the question of what the gardener should do to feed his plants would be as follows: give them plenty of animal manures and humus-makers, as described above, plus a general fertilizer containing nitrogen, phosphates, and potash, i.e. balanced NPK, and you can be assured of good crops, brilliant blooms, and a generally healthy garden.

Some of the above fertilizers are organic, some are inorganic. The terms are much overworked. If sufficient humus is worked into the soil, inorganic chemicals will not be harmful if used sensibly. Organic fertilizers are of animal or vegetable origin; inorganics are from minerals in most cases and are sometimes known as "artificials." A third class are known as "organic-based," which are artificially mixed organic and inorganic fertilizers. Since the term artificial might be applied to much of the pretreatment of organic fertilizers, the terms seem a bit loose. To some people the term organic as applied to dried blood — which is a product of slaughterhouses and will contain its due measure of the chemicals that were included in the animals' feed — may seem misleading.

You can buy ready-mixed compounds of NPK in varying proportions or with other chemicals added to suit the needs of various types of plants. Balanced

Plain digging
The purpose of plain digging is simply to turn over the topsoil and aerate it.

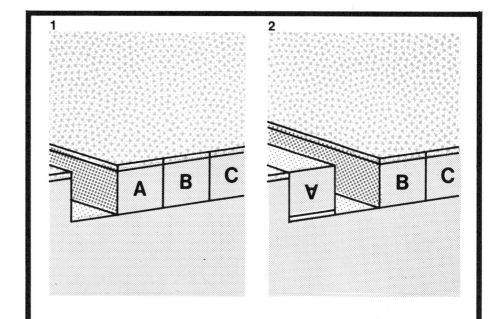

Double digging
Double digging is needed when preparing new ground for planting, and it involves incorporating manure into the second spit.

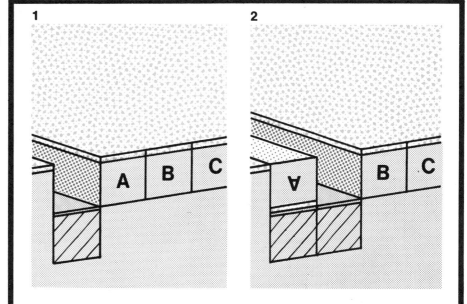

Ridging
This is used only on very heavy clay soils.
The point is to expose the largest possible area of soil to the crumbling action of wind and frost.

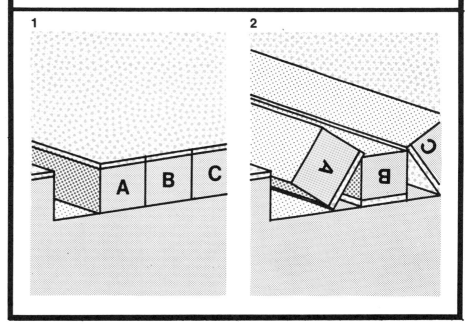

Ligularias and liatris, like most hardy perennials, need a slow-acting fertilizer

NPK Table

Nitrogen	Sulfate of ammonia	Top dressing on growing plants	1 oz./square yard
	Nitrate of soda	Top dressing, quick-acting	½ to 1 oz./square yard
	Hoof and horn (expensive)	Base dressing before sowing	4 oz./square yard
	Dried blood (expensive)	Base dressing at sowing or after	1 to 2 oz./square yard
Phosphate	Superphosphate	Base dressing before sowing or planting	1 to 2 oz./square yard
	Basic slag	Autumn or winter before sowing or planting	4 oz./square yard
	Bone meal	Autumn or winter before sowing or planting	2 to 4 oz./square yard
Potash	Muriate of potash	Base dressing at sowing or planting	1 to 2 oz./square yard
	Wood ashes	Base dressing at any time	6 to 8 oz./square yard

NPK in equal proportions for general garden use might be marked 10-10-10. An NPK compound fertilizer marked 10-5-5 would have 10% nitrogen, 5% phosphates, and 5% potash.

Other known chemicals required by plants include calcium, magnesium, boron, iron, manganese, copper, molybdenum, zinc, and sulfur, but only in minute amounts. All but calcium and magnesium are known as "trace" elements because only traces of them are needed in the soil.

Soil Testing

One of the most important aspects of soil balance which has not so far been considered in great detail in discussing the soil is the pH. All garden soil is either acid or alkaline, and the degree is measured on what is known as the pH scale from 0 to 14. Thus, below 6-5 the soil is termed acid, and above 7-5 it is alkaline. Some plants, such as Erica (below 5-5), hydrangea, blue (below 5), and rhododendron (below 4-5), thrive on acid soils; others, such as brassicas and lilac, prefer more alkali in the soil. An acid soil is easily balanced by introducing lime. An alkaline soil with a very high pH is less easily corrected with additions of peat, compost, sulfate of ammonia, or sulfur. The amount of lime needed depends on the type of soil as well as the pH, because heavier soils need more than others to correct acidity.

The simplest way to find the pH of your soil is to take a soil sample to your County Extension Agent. These agents will usually advise how much limestone you need or what corrective action is needed.

Compost

Traditionally it was the practice to dig more plots on the garden each winter, but on established gardens a method of compost cultivation enables you to cut down almost entirely on digging. Properly done it can be most beneficial to crops and can be an advantage on thin soils or soils that have a lot of stones; hillside ground with steeply sloping ground and very fast-draining soils will be able to retain moisture better.

The basis of it is an adequate supply of compost materials and a correctly constructed compost heap. On small gardens the supply of dead vegetation can be very small indeed and unsuitable for composting, and a reasonably sized heap, preferably $3 \times 3 \times 3$ feet and the bigger the better, should be made. Smaller-sized heaps than this should be covered with plastic, preferably black and thick, or they will not heat up enough to break down the compost. The plastic should be loosely held down with bricks to permit some air to enter the heap.

Compost is a soft, brownish-black substance that looks rather like peat, but it is richer in plant foods. Good compost that has been thoroughly matured has no perceptible smell and is quite clean and free from disease. Frames to hold the compost can be bought or made to roughly correspond to the size of heap you intend to make. Compost heats to over 150°F (65°C) and this kills diseases and weed seeds and even the roots of some perennial weeds. But the sides of the heap will not be quite as hot as the center, and while the compost drawn from the center can be put on the garden at once, the compost at the sides may not have broken down sufficiently. It usually takes up to six months for the compost heap to heat up and break down its contents, somewhat less time in warm summer weather.

Moisture and air are needed as well as warmth, and if you use a plastic sheet to help the heating process you should not put it on until construction of the heap has been completed.

A simple arrangement of boards and posts can be built to hold the compost or wire netting which can be detached from the posts when the heap is completed. Boards and wire netting permit air to reach the heap, and ventilation can be helped also by the inclusion of sand in the same way as the inclusion of such substances helps to aerate the soil.

The heap should stand on open ground, which can be dug slightly and covered with a little lime. Everything organic can go in (even small pieces of newspaper will rot) — vegetable waste, leaves, grass cuttings, etc. It is best to leave out sticks, leaves poisonous to other plants, grass mowings that have been in recent contact with selective weed killers, and perennial weeds such as bindweed and the roots of bermuda grass, buttercups, etc. Light material should be well mixed with heavy and the heap well tamped down, because air pockets will prevent proper heating. In very dry weather it will be necessary to water it. The heap should be built in layers, with materials that will help to break it down. Remember you are using bacteria to make a chemical reaction. For every 6 to 9 inches of compost sprinkle on a dusting of fertilizer. Cover this with a layer of soil an inch or more thick. Lime can be used if desired. There are also several kinds of compost activators which accelerate the breakdown of the compost. If you use these you must follow the manufacturer's instructions carefully. Do not rush the completion of the heap. You will find that when you have put what seems like half the garden on the heap it sinks down to about half when composted. The time it takes for the compost heap to mature depends on how well it was constructed.

Planting

After you have prepared your soil, you are ready to start planting. The success or failure of any plant will depend to a very large degree on the thoroughness with which the soil has been prepared, but correct planting is almost as important. There are different points to bear in mind when planting different types of plants. Bulbs require different treatment from trees, and shrubs require different treatment from annuals. For this reason the techniques of planting a particular type of plant are dealt with in the chapters dealing with specific types of plants. In general, however, there are two important rules: plants should always be planted firmly and should always be planted to the correct depth.

Having done the basic creative work of leveling the site, laying the lawn, and preparing the beds and borders, you next turn to those techniques concerned with the maintenance of the garden.

Weeding

In an established garden where the weeds are among growing crops and shrubs and flowers, the use of weed killers is not simple. Here foliar weed killers, such as those based on the chemical paraquat, should be used. These are absorbed by the leaves of the growing plants and kill all plants on whose foliage they fall, so considerable care must be taken to make sure that these weed killers do not come in contact with the leaves of the plants you want to grow.

Annual weeds and those spread by seed can be easily discouraged by hoeing regularly. Rhizomatous and other types of perennial weeds should have their roots pulled. Selective weed killers are useful for killing brushwood or weeds in rough grass and should be used in dilute form for this purpose, according to the instructions.

Weeds with runners over ground, like the creeping buttercup, should be dug out or treated with paraquat.

Pre-emergent weed killers are applied immediately after sowing seeds of cultivated plants. They will keep the plants, when they emerge, free from weeds for a couple of months or more. However, they must be used carefully or they may affect the seedling.

Lawns are cleared of weeds by various types of selective weed killers.

Hoeing is an effective way of keeping down small weeds around the plants and keeping the soil texture in a state in which plant foods can continue to break down and the roots can continue to get air. Its disad-

vantage is that it tends to cause the surface of the soil to dry out, and so it is useless among surface-rooting plants such as rhododendrons and azaleas, where the same effect can be achieved by mulching.

Irrigation

Watering is generally needed in most places in summer, as plants should always have a reasonable amount of moisture. Never water sparingly, because this attracts the roots toward the surface of the soil, where they may subsequently dry out. When you water, give the plants a thorough drenching and fully saturate the soil. Rain gauges can be purchased which will tell the amount of rainfall there has been, giving a rough guide on how much water should be given artificially. Beware of watering acid-loving alkaline plants with tap-water.

Propagation

Nothing is more pleasant than to spend cold winter nights looking at seed catalogs and sending off a list of plants to your favorite seedsman. Visions of bright colors fill the ''inward eye,'' and it is true that while a colorful garden and a well-filled vegetable plot can be had by buying bedding plants and seedlings from the nurseryman, the cheapest and most interesting way of doing this is to start with seed. It is among the annual flowers that you will be looking for next season's brilliant display, although you will probably order some biennials and perennials for planting later in the spring or summer to provide color in the succeeding season or as permanent background flowers.

Seeds are of little use without beds prepared for them, and by following the instructions earlier in this book you should have the soil well broken up by spring. It is not too late to dig in the spring; it just means you will have to tamp the soil down with your heel instead of having the slow action of the winter weather do it for you. Light soils are warmer, so on sandy beds you will be able to sow quite early. They dry out easily, too, and are easier to work, but if you have quick-drying soil it might be good to put a little moist peat in the seed drills. Seeds need moisture, air, and warmth to germinate, and it is necessary to break the soil down to a fine tilth by using a rake, which will help to get rid of large stones and weeds as well.

Bedding plants probably produce more color per
square foot than any other type of plant. They show to best effect
against a dark hedge or background of trees and shrubs

De-horning a pear tree. Operations like this can look difficult but are really quite simple.

Clay tends to be colder than sandy soil, and it is difficult to work when cold and wet. You must wait for the right moment to get it into condition and consider carefully when to sow. If you sow too early you may lose the seed through the cold. Some gardeners cover the beds with clear plastic about two weeks before sowing to provide enough extra warmth for the seeds to germinate. Sowing times are later in the north and on higher ground.

Cabbage seedlings as they can be bought from the nursery, ready for planting. Those in the lower flat have cupped leaves and should be avoided.

Seedage

In general there are two ways of sowing seed out of doors — broadcast or in drills. When sowing broadcast, seed should be mixed with fine sand and allowed to dribble out slowly though the fingers held fairly close to the ground. Sowing in rows, or drills, may be done in the same way, using finger and thumb only and making sure you keep to the line of the drill, which can be scratched in the soil with a dibble or broom handle. Pelletted seeds are easier to sow because they are large enough to be placed one by one, and each is covered by a capsule of food which gives the seed a good start. Mark the rows with labels.

Cover the seed with fine soil to about twice its own thickness. It is best to have some fine soil ready rather than rake over the soil around the seeds, as the rake may collect all the seeds into one spot. When planting in rows, if you mix some fine soil with peat to cover the seeds, the rows appear as a dark line and mark where you have been sowing. Larger seeds, such as peas and beans, should be sown more deeply — about 1 to 2 inches. If your garden is subject to the depredations of birds or mice you can soak the seed in a mild solution of repellent substance.

In general, sow as thinly as possible, water *before* sowing, and mark the labels with a pencil that will withstand the weather.

Starting seeds under heat indoors has many advantages. Not only is the range of plants you can cultivate greatly increased, but you can have colorful garden flowers earlier. By the time the soil has warmed up enough for sowing outdoors, the indoor plants will be ready for hardening off and planting. You do not necessarily need a greenhouse to do this. A heated propagating unit on a table by the window getting the most light will do.

Seeds may be raised indoors in boxes such as those used for market plants, or in plastic trays or earthenware pans. When heat is involved and the gardening is done indoors, hygiene becomes important, and all "utensils" must be cleaned with warm water and a weak disinfectant.

Pots and receptacles with large drainage holes must be lined at the bottom with flat stones covered with a layer of coarse peat or sterilized fibrous loam. The soil is then used to fill the container and firmed down lightly to within half an inch of the rim. If you use an unsterilized compost from the garden you risk having soil-borne seeds, diseases, and pests destroy your efforts. It is far better to buy a reliable ,proprietary potting soil.

Summer pruning of apple trees.

The soil should then be thoroughly soaked by standing it in a bowl of water. When the water has permeated to the surface, remove and drain. Then sow the seeds and cover with a sheet of glass and brown paper tucked in under the edge. Turn and wipe the glass regularly. Some seeds have been found to germinate well by tying a plastic bag over the whole box, and it is also possible to hold a plastic bag over a pot rim with an elastic band, keeping the seed away from the light until it germinates. Once the first leaves appear, remove the brown paper and prop up the glass, or remove or loosen the plastic bag so that light and air can reach the seedling. If seedlings are left in the dark they die.

While the plants still have their seed leaves they can be pricked off into other boxes of potting soil. When pricking off always be careful to hold the plant by the leaf and not the stem, which may look more robust than the leaf but is most delicate. Plant labels of metal, wood, or plastic are useful for lifting seedlings. Every seed tray or pot should be clearly labeled.

Once the true leaves have formed, it is time to move the plants into a richer potting soil, carefully firming around the seedling each time it is moved. Water the seedling with a fine hose or gentle spray and make sure the soil is always moist and that the temperature and ventilation are adequate. When moved, they should be given more moisture, extra warmth, and

Loppers are used for pruning any branch that is too thick to be cut with shears.

Eucryphia billardierii
a dainty,
narrowly erect
evergreen, suitable for
mild climates.

less light for three or four days. Avoid drafts, and repot seedlings that were started in late winter or possibly earlier.

Before planting out, seedlings must be hardened off, either by increasing ventilation in the greenhouse or by transferring them to a frame that can be propped open. At all times care must be taken to see that they are protected from excesses of climate. These may include too much heat from strong spring sunshine, as well as frost and cold at night, when frames may have to be closed and covered. Strong wind and heavy rain may also result in fatal damage to the young plants.

By the end of May or the beginning of June most plants should be in their final positions in the garden.

Softwood Cuttings

These are stem cuttings of various kinds, including those taken from herbaceous plants in late winter, spring, or early summer. Many shrubs can also be propagated from cuttings taken around July.

Usually a longer piece of stem than necessary is taken and trimmed with a sharp blade just below a joint (node) or leaf bud. They are trimmed just below a node or bud because this is a vital point from which new roots will develop. Dip the cutting in a weak solution of fungicide and then dip the tip in a suitable hormone rooting powder. Shake the excess powder back into the tin and set the cutting in moist soil or a mixture of half sand and half peat in a 6-inch pot prepared in the usual way, with good drainage material at the bottom.

The cutting should be about 6 inches long and have the lower leaves removed, leaving about four pairs at the top. The hole into which it is inserted should be about a third of its length, and the soil should be carefully firmed. Water it and insert thin stakes around the pot so that they protrude about 9 inches. Cover it entirely with a plastic bag and secure the bag with a rubber band around the bag, pressing it against the stakes, not the pot. This allows water forming on the inside of the bag to run back into the medium. When new leaves appear you can be certain that the cutting has rooted. Remove the bag but keep the plant in the pot until it has made reasonable roots. Then repot it into a larger pot or transfer it to open ground in the growing season. If you use propagating boxes, cuttings may be rooted on a large scale and potted when rooted.

Hardwood Cuttings

These are also stem cuttings, usually taken in late September or early winter. Unlike softwood cuttings, which are generally rooted in warmth, hardwood cuttings may be propagated in a cold frame or in the open garden. The cuttings are cut from the parent plant just below a lateral bud or with a heel of the old wood attached. A heel is a strip of the bark and old wood from the main stem to which the cutting was attached. Hardwood cuttings, as the name implies, are taken from woody plants. The length of hardwood cuttings should vary according to the size of leaves and twigs: short twigs and leaves, short cuttings, is the rule. Generally the size of the cutting varies between 6 and 12 inches.

Many evergreens like the *Rhododendron beuravoides* shown here are most easily increased by layering. This rhododendron is grown mainly for the bright fox red felt on the underneath of its leaves.

Some plants, e.g. clematis and verbena, are best increased by "internodal" cuttings; that is, a cutting taken about halfway between joints. As with other types of cutting, all but the top four or five pairs of leaves are removed, a special hardwood-rooting hormone compound is used, and the cuttings set in pots or boxes in 4 or 5 inches of rooting medium. In open ground a slit is made in the ground by rocking a shovel back and forth, and the bottom is lined with sand. Masses of cuttings may then be inserted about 3 or 4 inches apart and about one-third of their length deep, and firmed. Frost sometimes causes cuttings to be lifted, and they must be firmly pressed back into the ground.

Division
This is the easiest of all modes of plant propagation. Merely lift the plant to be divided out of the ground and divide it into a number of small pieces. With herbaceous plants, each root section must have at least one good bud on it. Much is made of the use of two forks back to back for dividing plants. In practice, an axe or knife or bare hands perform the task more easily, except in the case of delicate fleshy roots, such as those of peonies, when wounds should be dipped in a mild fungicide to avoid infection. Single-rooted or single-stemmed plants are obviously not suited for division.

Layering
This is one of the most natural forms of propagation, as some plants do it for themselves without any prompting from man.

Strawberries layer themselves naturally, and the gardener helps this process by pegging down the strawberry runners in pots of peaty compost sunk in the soil around the plant. Hairpins are often used to peg them down. When the layers have rooted well, the connections are cut and the new plants can be planted anywhere.

Many drooping plants, such as rhododendrons, may be layered by making a small notch or shallow cut with a knife on the underside of a branch near the ground, then pegging it down and burying it under 3 or 4 inches of sharp sand and good soil. Remove the leaves of the underground section and use a secure peg such as a metal tent peg with a hook wide enough to hold the branch. The soil around the layer must be kept moist. This is often done by placing a slab of stone over the layering point. Plants that may be so treated include carnations and pinks, lilac, heathers, winter and summer jasmine, chaenomeles, cotoneasters, wisterias, and chimonathus. Layering is usually done in the fall and throughout the dormant period.

Leaf Cuttings
These are very useful for propagating house plants. Chose healthy leaves, and if you have a mist propagation unit you will be able to carry out this operation far more successfully, because moisture and heat are essential. Covering with a plastic bag as described under soft cuttings and keeping the plants in a warm temperature on a shaded window sill is quite satisfactory. *Begonia rex* will root if pieces of leaf are laid on

sand after making light cuts across veins on the undersides. It is better to peg down the leaf with hairpins on a sandy compost in the case of plants like streptocarpus. Christmas cactus (*Zygocactus*) and similar plants may be propagated by inserting the cut leaves in the side of a pot filled with sandy compost. African violets *(Saintpaulia)* and plants like peperomias may be started by detaching a complete leaf and stalk and inserting the stalk in a hole made with a pencil in a mixture of half-and-half peat and sand, or peat and vermiculite. Gloxinia is also easily started this way.

Root Cuttings
These are made by taking small sections of roots, about 2 inches, and inserting them in deep sand so that the top of the cutting is just below the surface. Root cuttings are generally started in the fall and kept in a frame or unheated greenhouse over winter. In spring top growth should have started and they can be potted.

Budding
This is a method of propagating chosen varieties of woody plants, such as roses, by attaching a bud onto a vigorous-rooting stock of the same family. Most of the roses grown in gardens are cultivated varieties growing on vigorous stocks like *Rosa canina,* the Dog Rose.

Using a razor-sharp knife (as in all propagating by cutting), cut a shallow slice of the selected bud and bark from a fresh, vigorous shoot which has been previously cut off the variety to be propagated. Remove the wood from beneath the bud, but make sure the base of the bud is not disturbed, as this would ruin the whole operation. On the chosen stock make a T-shaped cut (in the case of roses this should be at or just above soil level), cutting down to but not into the wood under the softer bark. Open the T-cut slightly and slide the piece of bud and bark down to the base of the "T". Tie up with raffia to make sure that the growing surfaces of both plants are firmly touching. Budding is usually done in summer, and a shoot should form on the stock by the following spring, when other growth may be cut out altogether in favor of the new shoot.

Grafting
This is a more advanced technique than most of those so far discussed and is sometimes done to add other varieties to established fruit trees in the interests of pollination or to renew life in aged trees. It can be done by experts on soft-tissued plants with the aid of moisure and warmth. Grafting is usually done in spring, when the rising sap makes success more likely. The pieces to be grafted onto the stocks are "heeled in" in a V-shaped trench, firmed in the previous autumn. The trench must be in a shady position to ensure that the pieces (scions) are more dormant than the stock that is to receive the scion.

Whip and Tongue Graffing
This is best done when the stems of stock and scion are both about ½ inch in diameter. The stock is cut off about 6 inches from the ground with a sloping cut and slit vertically. A scion with four buds is cut below a bud to match the cut made on the stock, with a slit tongue to fit the slit in the stock. The joint is made with as much as possible of the growing layers under the bark of the two plants meeting. The joint is tied firmly with raffia and covered with grafting wax.

Crown Grafting
This type of grafting is eminently suitable for renewing old trees. The main limbs are cut back to about 2 feet from the trunk in January, and in April another 2 inches are cut off. Slits about 3 inches long are made in the bark of the branches. Thin, tapering wedges are cut in the young scions that are to be grafted on, and these are fitted into the slits so that the growing layers under the bark meet. Wax is used to seal the union.

There are a number of other forms of grafting adapted to various types of situations, such as stub grafting, used for renovating old stocks but not cutting the tree back as far as in crown grafting, and bridge grafting, which is used for repairing damage to bark.

Large Garden Design

Gardens may be regarded in two ways: as a fill-in to the architecture, such as spaces that the architect or builder didn't fill, in which case the plants are an afterthought; or as places in which to grow plants. For the true gardener, the plants come first, and the design of the garden will largely be determined by the type of plants he wants to grow and the amount of time or effort he is prepared to put into maintaining the garden.

In spite of these very different ways of approaching garden design, the basic precepts remain the same. There are certain basic rules that pertain to the design of all gardens.

As land gets scarcer, gardens get smaller. Anyone with a quarter of an acre or more of ground has a large garden by today's standards.

Most fortunate are those who have a *new* garden to create in an area of that size, because undoubtedly, when you start from scratch you can have a better,

cleaner, more modern outlook from your house, with the wide range of plants and materials now available.

If you are taking over an established plot, especially if it is fairly large, the chances are it will be cluttered with overgrown shrubs, darkened by high trees, laid out and fashioned with cracked and weed-infested paving, an ill-placed rockery, and a dirty pond. If that is the case, you have your hands full.

Whether you are starting from scratch or replanning an existing garden, the same basic principles apply.

Much depends, of course, on your situation: the type of plot, its overall shape, and where the house sits in relation to the main part of the garden. It is impossible to produce a single blueprint that can be applied to every garden. In the end the choice of styling must always be your own.

Basically, in the design of gardens we will be looking for: (1) a pleasant and interesting outlook from every window in the house — an outlook that

Many new houses are built in the gardens of grand old houses. If you are lucky enough to have a garden with a wall like the one shown here, you will find it makes an excellent background.

blends with your house and is entirely compatible; (2) the creation of vistas, giving your garden a sense of distance, space, and depth; (3) the inclusion of special features, such as rockeries, ponds, pergolas, and terraces; (4) the element of surprise, discovered by visitors as they walk around your garden; (5) where the situation lends itself, an air of mystery, which can often be created by dividing the garden into two or more sections, each in a contrasting design.

Above all, your garden must suit your own special requirements and the amount of time you will be able to spend on it. Gardeners often set out with a vision of their dream garden but end up with a nightmare, simply because they have given themselves too much to do.

It is important, therefore, to establish truthfully in your own mind the type of garden you really want. Try to imagine how you want it to look in five years' time, for you can be sure everything will not be completed in a season or two. Once your intentions are clear, stand back and take a long, hard look at the scene before you.

The way your garden will look eventually is not the only factor — far from it. Study how the land lies in relation to all points on the compass. Make a note of the general aspect, of shady or especially sunny areas; check for wind tunnels and particularly exposed places; look for damp and waterlogged patches. All these are vital when you are deciding where to locate your flower beds, where to put screens and windbreaks, and where to build your ''sitting out'' areas. With a larger garden, which may not be particularly well protected from the elements, these points are vital. Make a thorough survey, and take notes on your findings.

Next, give some thought to the features you might eventually like to include — a pool, patio, arbor, terrace, or rockery. Again, draw up a list so that you can sketch them in on your master plan — even though you may not be able to start work on them for a season or two. One word of warning: do not try to include every possible style and feature in one garden; the result will be that each detracts from all the others. Confine yourself to two or three really good ideas, and work on them.

Planning

After studying the site and listing the main features desired, it is time to start planning. Equip yourself with a thick pencil and several sheets of graph paper (you will need several, because planning is a progressive development).

Scale accurate dimensions of your house and garden boundaries. Then begin the design itself. This is usually best done in three stages.

Stage one consists of a rough plan on which to map out paving and terracing around the perimeter of the house and also the general area of the lawns. Try to nominate a focal point, perhaps a large tree or shrub

midway down the back garden. If there is no focal point, you will need to establish one. Designing a garden is like painting a three-dimensional picture, and you will find it helpful to have some object on which to take your bearings in order to arrive at a design that has balance and is in perspective.

On stage two of the plan, add the dominant features, such as trees and shrubs, walls, terraces, and arches, that will provide and establish the outline of the garden proper.

The third stage is mapping out your flower beds and the paths that will take you around the garden, and drawing in the special effects.

As the plan progresses, remember to refer regularly to your notes and take into account all your garden's advantages and disadvantages.

The Design

There are many varied ideas about styling a garden. There is also a lot of talk about landscaping, which to many people — and even to some reputable landscape gardeners — means getting the site as level as can be, laying a good lawn, and surrounding it with a flower garden and trees.

Styling a garden is an individualistic thing: it can be compared with the way you furnish your house. It will reflect your own personal taste. Your living room suite — by some coincidence — may be the same as your neighbor's. But the way you place it in your living room will be completely different. The same applies to your garden: the plants and features may be the same as your neighbors, but the way you combine them will be different.

Creating an original garden is more difficult on entirely flat sites than it is on what initially appear to be difficult sites — those with dips and mounds and slopes. These natural contours can be used — and even exaggerated — to create sunken gardens, terraces, rockeries, miniature streams, and so on. If you had thought of grading and leveling your rough plot — bear this in mind before beginning to flatten it.

Level sites present something of a problem in creating interest. The special effects and vistas have to be created rather than adapted from natural resources, and this requires good planning and an appreciation of the use of colorful subjects.

An ultra-modern garden with clean-cut shapes, colorful patios, and terracing will look completely out of place around an older-type house. Similarly, a brand-new house seems to call for bright materials and a light and airy surrounding.

Whether your choice in design is for a fairly open style or for a ragged ''back to nature'' look, much will depend on your needs and may be governed by the age of your house.

Whatever your choice, it is important that when you look out from the house there is an immediate impression of space and light. Therefore, the central area of the first part of your garden is best kept open:

trees and shrubs should be kept away from windows. The exceptions to this rule are climbing shrubs, like clematis and honeysuckle, which can be trained close to the walls and need not overshadow the windows.

It is also worth noting here that the roots of trees and hedges and even some of the more vigorous shrubs spread far and wide. They will very often throw up suckers that could ruin asphalt drives or patios, and they should be planted well away from your property. Willows send their roots in search of water, and, if the cement becomes weak, they could find their way into cracks in the drainage system, causing leakage and blockages.

On your plan, you will naturally start at the house and work outward. It is often best to aim at a paved area around as much of the house as possible, and certainly at each entrance.

A fairly substantial patio is usually called for at the rear, and this may be built with steps up or down to the garden itself, according to your site. The use of steps is always more interesting than going straight onto the lawn.

Many forms of paving are now available. Slabs come in a wide range of sizes, colors, textures, and finishes, and the design possibilities are limitless — the choice is yours.

Perhaps the easiest way to plan your patio and paved areas is to map out the design on a separate sheet of paper, using colored pencils for the right effect. The patio may require edging, either with a low wall in brick or stone or perhaps ornamental cinder or concrete blocks for a higher type. Again the choice is wide, but, as with paving, it is important to be thoroughly satisfied with the design before starting the job.

The next stage is your lawn. For most people this is the central feature of the garden — yet it is often the most neglected, ill-considered area in the whole garden. It does, after all, require the loving care that you will lavish on your favorite flower. It needs the same close scrutiny in selecting the variety of grass most suited for the wear and tear it will get. The commonly held view that lots of grass makes a garden easy to run is nonsense. It will need mowing once a week, sometimes twice, during the seven-month growing period; it will need treating for weeds, fertilizing, aerating, watering — and so on. If you establish a huge lawn entirely out of proportion with the size of your garden, you will have nothing but a well-tended paddock.

Variations on a theme. There are many different ways of designing a garden. None of them is "right." It is all a matter of personal taste. The four examples shown here are all pleasing gardens, but each has its own character.

The shape of the lawn will have a substantial effect on the general view of your garden. A slim lawn will make the garden look longer, a shaped lawn will take the eye around with it and will give the impression of size.

Do not be afraid of unusual shapes. You might try a zigzag effect, for instance, repeated on a parallel basis on each side of the lawn, or, instead of running the grass area and general garden aspect from end to end, i.e. north to south or east to west, consider a diagonal approach, laying the lawn across the garden, corner to corner.

Circular lawns also can be extremely effective, and double circles are even better, one in the foreground of the garden, the second in the far part, linked by paths and a covered archway.

Alternatively, to achieve a definite contrast between the first and second garden, use a circular shape in the foreground and a rectangular or octagonal shape in the second section.

As you draw in the second part of the garden, remember that at least some of it must be visible in the general view from the house, and not entirely cut off — one section from the other.

The development of two or more sections to the garden is one of the techniques of designing a medium-sized garden, and it really does offer tremendous scope for originality.

Where it is possible to establish a series of gardens on different levels, the use of steps can be extremely effective. These help continue the line of the house into the garden and give the illusion of greater space.

Glades
Another suggestion for the far section of the garden is a pleasant, peaceful glade — a feature that is easy to make and to maintain. Furthermore, glades may be made on level or sloping ground and may be small or large.

The glade will consist of a lawn bordered with shrubs and trees planted well apart so that the form and beauty of each subject can be seen and appreciated.

Try to keep all the subjects you plant in proportion. Choose only trees and shrubs that are entirely suited for medium-sized gardens.

Backgrounds
When the general format of the garden has been established, it is time to think of backgrounds.

The list of trees and shrubs, ornamental and flowering varieties, is endless, and it really is somewhat pointless to recommend any specific type for an unspecified situation. The general principle is to add height and depth to the perimeter of your garden without shutting off natural landscapes, and this can be achieved, even if it is necessary to install fencing or hedging, by careful and imaginative planting. There could be a continuous line of one particular type of

tree, with lower decks of bushy shrubs, banking down to the low-growing plants of the border.

Elsewhere in the garden — space permitting — you will want an assortment of trees and shrubs, but be careful in locating trees. The charms of young weeping willows may become trouble in years to come, when the trees reach maturity.

You may wish to plant trees or shrubs close together as windbreaks or as a screen for outbuildings. In this case you will probably find that slim, columnar conifers planted in groups of three or four are most suitable. One other word of caution: quick-growing trees remain quick growing — and could cause embarassment as the trees mature.

The technique of repetition with tree planting is widely used. This means planting a columnar conifer, for instance, on each side of steps leading from one garden section to another or on opposite sides of the lawn.

Before you do any planting in the general run of the garden, look out from the windows of your house to ensure that vistas are not being spoiled and that unwanted shadows will not be cast over the garden or house in future years.

Permanent Features
The introduction of stone into any part of the garden scheme should serve a definite purpose — to raise or break levels, or to make a wall leading to steps. Above all, it should fit in with the general character of the garden. Flagstone paving, terraces with balustrades, flights of steps, dry-stone walling, and stone-pillared pergolas are delightful features of gardens where they fit in with the environment. However, one must guard against losing beauty and aesthetic charm by the indiscreet use of stone. Try to give it an atmosphere of age.

Stone can also be used effectively for raised beds, which can be real eyecatchers. There are also numerous possibilities for low walls, alpine gardens, and surroundings to pools.

Paths
The construction of "service" paths — i.e. those that lead from the house to other buildings — the greenhouse and so on — should be carried out at an early stage of the new garden, probably at the time the house is built.

The paths that take you around your garden can be left until later, but it is best to get most of the messy construction work over with before the garden begins to take shape.

Paths can be effectively used to help in the creation of vistas. They can lead in curves or straight lines to your inner gardens and special features. They can turn unexpectedly to reveal a rockery screened from the general view.

There should be as few main paths as possible; try to avoid having them give your garden a formal look.

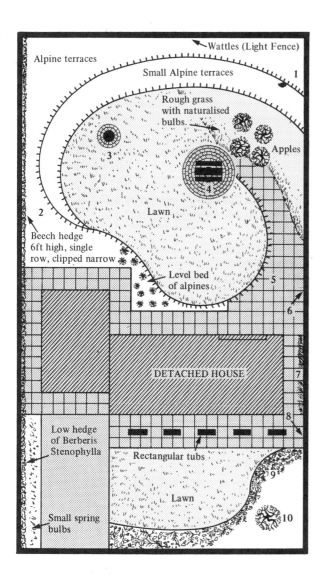

Alpine terraces

Wattles (Light Fence)

Small Alpine terraces

1

Rough grass
with naturalised
bulbs.

Apples

3

4

Lawn

2

Beech hedge
6ft high, single
row, clipped narrow

Level bed
of alpines

5

6

DETACHED HOUSE

7

8

Low hedge
of Berberis
Stenophylla

Rectangular tubs

9

Lawn

10

Small spring
bulbs

Key
1 Terrace face, highest point. **2** Height decreases. **3** Brick circle
with sculpture. **4** Patio table with seats, brick concentric circles. **5**
Barbeque area. **6** 6-ft overlap fencing. **7** Narrow bed of ferns. **8**
Ranch fencing continued to end of house. **9** Bedding plants. **10**
Tree.

Borders and Beds

The extent of your borders and beds will depend on
personal choice. Some gardeners will want large areas
for special-interest plants like chrysanthemums,
dahlias, roses, delphiniums, and so on; others will
want to restrict their floral displays to perennial borders backed up by a profusion of colorful annuals.

When selecting and designing your floral displays,
remember that formalized beds can act as a striking
contrast to the ragged look if you have the facility for a
divided garden.

Rose gardens should in general be designed on a
formal or geometrical plan, such as a circle or rectangle, and there are numerous other plants that lend
themselves to this sort of treatment.

Peonies, for instance, could be given a border or
bed to themselves. Asters, in all the many shades, also
make good single-subject beds.

Another unusual element in the design of beds and
borders can be achieved by massing flowering plants
of a single color together so that you have whites,
blues, reds, oranges, and so on — all in separate beds.

To help cut the amount of work involved, a number
of shrubs can be included in flower borders. They can
also be used to create a sense of depth in borders if you
build up a bank of flowers, from tiny dot plants to
tallish shrubs, interspersed with lupins, hollyhocks,
and delphiniums.

Try to choose summer-flowering shrubs to blend
with the flowering times of your herbaceous plants.

As with trees, the repetition of particularly outstanding plants in a herbaceous border helps with the
overall design effect.

Replanning an Old Garden

Creating a new garden from an old one can be more of
a headache than starting from scratch. The plot may
be cluttered and untidy and possibly badly neglected.
Once-proud trees and fine shrubs may be overgrown
and out of shape and condition. Herbaceous plants
may be overcrowding one another so that they cannot
be seen. Rose beds will be a tangled mass . . . but
somewhere under that dank, matted undergrowth lies
a garden.

Somehow you must determine which parts of the
garden you want to keep and which to discard. You
may be tempted to clear the lot and start over. But that
would not be a wise move. The gardener who was
there before you — despite his possibly strange think-
ing on design — probably lived with that garden for a
number of years. So don't ignore the lessons he may
have learned from it. A tree here or there may have
been planted as a vital windbreak. He may have discovered acid pockets in the soil, or waterlogged,
boggy ground, and these factors may have had some
bearing on the plants.

Before you contemplate a mass razing operation,
take a good look around and try to discover the garden
that existed before and the reasons your predecessor

had for his various planting schemes. Clear the ground of weeds, being careful not to injure too many plants in the process. Walk around, covering every inch of the garden, and try to establish the original plan — it may become apparent, once you have cleared some of the debris.

Only then will you be able to decide which sections you wish to retain and which you want to revamp. Then you will be able to incorporate established features into the new plan.

The order of priorities in which you tackle a neglected garden is entirely different from that of a new garden. Never begin by embarking on any major constructional work, such as reshaping rockeries, reestablishing a water garden, or building a patio. These are all jobs for later . . . much later. While you were engaged on these time-consuming jobs, the already-neglected living parts of the garden would become even more difficult to reclaim.

The first task is to bring the growing sections back to life. This may take a whole season, and, while you are engaged in this reclamation, your overall plan will begin to take shape. The trees and shrubs you decide to keep can be pruned into shape so that you can get an idea of your backgrounds and color schemes. Beware of overpruning, however, in the first year. Too-drastic cutting may be more than these already-neglected plants can stand, and they will die.

Front Gardens

With a quarter-of-an-acre plot or more, it is likely that you will have a fair amount of space to play with at the front of the house. This is not an invitation to use elaborate schemes. Front gardens — unless they are on especially awkward sites — should be simple, with enough shielding with trees and shrubs to afford a degree of privacy from passersby.

There should be a fairly open outlook from the windows. Properties of all ages can be set off admirably with a "clothing" of climbers for the front wall. The view should be attractive both from the house and the road.

The lawn area can be used to shape the garden, and it is probable that your drive and paths will also have some bearing on this factor.

The use of trees and shrubs can also be effective in establishing the shape, and remember the repetition ingredient, which is particularly useful at the front with, for example, columnar conifers on either side of the drive.

Try to avoid the use of hedging on the boundaries. In gardens of this size they tend to emphasize the enclosed look. Some sort of barrier, such as ranch-fencing, picket fence, or heavy chains between posts, is far more effective, supported by some imaginative plantings of trees and shrubs.

Small Garden Design

By comparison with the lavish way in which the planning and design of larger gardens are approached, the smaller plots that are so much more familiar these days present special limitations—and a special challenge.

The house itself will necessarily influence the style of the garden, both back and front. Boundaries are more visible and confining and need special attention.

Another factor that will affect design is the growing needs of a young family. It is seldom a satisfactory compromise to allow a young son to use two precious shrubs as goal posts, and yet, the needs of budding football and tennis players and the like in the family must be catered to, and this is far more difficult in a small garden than in a large one. The damage done by pets, particularly by dogs, is also far more noticeable in a small garden than in a large garden.

The smaller the garden, the more important it is to answer two vital questions: What do you want from your garden? How much work do you want to put into it? The really enthusiastic flower man may want to turn over large spaces in a somewhat confined area to his pride and joy. A retired couple, on the other hand, may want a pleasant haven that does not require hard labor.

Design is also affected by the enforced factors in the development of large housing estates. Many developers have what can only be described as a mania for complete uniformity with open-plan fronts and squared-off backs—often with the same fencing.

It is therefore necessary to look closely at the problem of ''clothing'' or hiding these boundary fixtures—which can give the owners of smaller gardens a real ''don't fence me in'' phobia.

You may also be faced with hiding a neighbor's cabbage patch or washing line—clearly visible through a chain-link fence. And, of course, you will want to achieve some degree of privacy.

At the same time, if the garden next door is an established one, it would be well to take account of those of your neighbor's plants and trees that are visible from your garden—and use them in drawing up your own planting schedule.

These will all need your attention in deciding where you are placing taller trees and shrubs which affect the outline of your design. One word of caution: forest trees are generally not advisable in these confined areas; there are many subjects more suited.

An evergreen shield of *Cupressocyparis leylandii* is an ideal subject for a background. It can be pruned to the desired height. Where wind is not a problem, *Chamaecyparis lawsoniana* will make a

A garden need not be dull just because it is small. Indeed, some very exciting effects can be achieved. The important thing is to avoid trying to have too many different features.

good 8-foot screen and is easier to control for height.

Once you have established your needs, the planning can begin. There is no single answer or master plan that can be applied to a thousand and one different situations. The basic principles, however, remain the same.

The outlook to the garden is likely to be confined to the front and back, with little or no side garden. It may be a long, narrow plot or a short, wide, one. So the task of creating a sense of space and distance, and of establishing pockets of interest which are not immediately visible at first glance, becomes more difficult.

As with the creation of larger gardens, it is necessary to draw up a plan of the design. To say, as some do, "I will plant as I feel fit," without working to a basic plan, often produces a garden that is not only unsightly—but also means more work in the long term. In fact, the more thought you put into planning on paper, the less hard work you will have to do in the garden in the long run.

Before beginning to plan the garden you need to look closely at the site and assess to which points of the compass the garden is exposed. Open aspects, for instance, will require screening and breaks from the biting winds, from north and east. It is also important to take into account which points of the garden will be put into shade by buildings or trees. This is not to say that you should avoid causing shaded areas—these can themselves help add depth and beauty. But you should exploit those situations that you find in your garden.

Westerly exposures are favorable to plants that are in the "hardy" classification. Southern aspects are to be used for plants that crave the sun and are suitable for all the most popular plants, such as roses, dahlias, sweet peas, vegetables, and so on. Sites facing the north are more prone to lingering frost pockets and generally lower temperatures. Easterly aspects will get biting winds. Bear all these points in mind as you draw up your plan.

Note, too, other problems such as poor drainage, wind tunnels, and so on, so that remedial action or precautionary measures can be taken as the garden takes shape.

As already explained in the section on larger gardens, it is usually desirable to have a paved area around as much of the house as possible, with paths leading off to outbuildings, gates, and so on. These will be installed before the major part of the garden development gets under way.

You can leave the "walking" paths—those that take you around the garden—until after you have established the basic plan of the garden.

Looking out from the house, a focal point is necessary as you prepare to paint the garden picture.

At a suitable point about three-quarters of the way down the garden, perhaps at a curve in the lawn, try to establish a fixture that draws the eye—a specimen

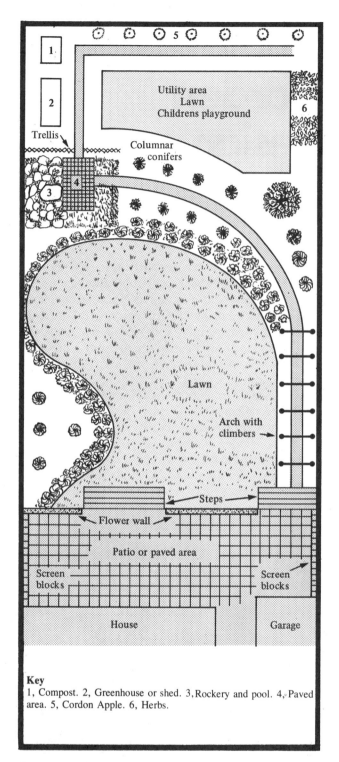

Key
1, Compost. 2, Greenhouse or shed. 3, Rockery and pool. 4, Paved area. 5, Cordon Apple. 6, Herbs.

Some modern gardens tend to be rather long and narrow. The plan shown here shows just one way of breaking up the length of the garden. The screen of columnar conifers breaks the garden effectively into two small gardens. In spite of this, a sense of distance is achieved because it is possible to see through the conifers to the garden beyond.

shrub, for instance, like a magnolia, a maple, or a group of medium-high conifers; or perhaps a pergola or an arbor or portico. It is around some feature such as this that the rest of the garden can be created.

Even with smaller plots the aim is to give the

impression of space. In general, try to round the corners of the boundaries, softening the harsh, fenced-in corners with flowering shrubs or with a screen or pergola hiding a vegetable patch. At the other extreme, do not fall into the trap of cutting out too many island beds in the lawn. They merely tend to destroy any sense of space that might be created by the lawn. One or two bold island beds are all that a small garden can take.

So what is the design solution to the formal rectangular plot, of say 100 by 60 feet, which is about the average size of new gardens today?

After establishing your focal point, the major item to consider is the lawn. It creates what garden designers call the open center—a usually level area of quiet, around which the garden can flow. The greenness of the grass acts as a background to the color of flowers. Avoid square or rectangular lawns. Try to create a lawn with pleasant curves, perhaps accentuated at a convenient point by a row of small, slow-growing conifers, or a selection of low-growing shrubs that will tend to hide part of the garden. The curved lawn will lead the eye away and save some of the features for a second look.

The front part of the lawn should be kept open, to give the impression of space. The curve is perhaps best brought in at about the middle of the lawn, with a mixed border and shrubs cutting well into it—but not entirely hiding the remaining part of the garden. It may even be possible to create a second garden, part of which should be visible from the first. But this, of course, becomes more difficult in smaller plots.

If you follow this plan you will have, from the house looking out, first an open space, then an eye-catching feature midway down the garden, with perhaps a path curving around one side of the lawn, part of it going beneath a pergola.

You will need to draw in on your plan at a fairly early stage—usually after deciding the shape of your lawn—the permanent features such as a rock garden, a pool, or a pergola. You can then lead your paths to and past these features and try to hide part of them from the general view from the house so that the element of surprise is introduced. Consider also using these fixtures to hide inescapable garden eyesores——such as compost heaps, which are bound to be more clearly visible in the smaller garden. A trellis can be used effectively to hide eyesores and to divide small gardens, but do try to use it to train plants that give some sort of year-round foliage. A huge trellis full of sweet peas looks marvelous in summer. And a bank of runner beans even has its merits for looks and as a shield. But both look awfully bare in winter.

Imaginative planting of individual or small groups of conifers and shrubs will also help to hide part of your garden from first glance. The division of the garden into two or more sections, or terraces, is the aim in most design. But, of course, this is not always practicable in smaller gardens. Try it if you can.

The pitfall to avoid in trying to make your garden look larger than it really is, is not to overdo the creation of these vistas or overcrowd your garden with tall and bushy subjects and special features. Simplicity is often the rule with confined spaces. Do not try to have more than one or two features, or you will end up with a cluttered mess which will be the complete reverse of your intentions.

A curve cut into the lawn, for instance, may not be entirely feasible with a wide, shallow lot. Try to get away from the formal look imposed by the boundaries by making the lawn circular or oblong, perhaps with an island bed in the center.

Color Content

Let us now progress to the borders and beds. Again, it is impossible to suggest anything other than in general terms. But in planning, try to aim at a mixture of subjects that will give you year-round color—not necessarily in flowers, but with foliage and berries too. This is important because the careful and imaginative selection of brilliantly hued plants and colorful blooms can do much to enhance the look style, and dimensions of the garden.

It has already been suggested that you should use a background of evergreens to provide the outline to your garden. These will act as a foil to the color of your flowers. The grays of lavender, rosemary, and senecio, for instance, contrast beautifully with the red berries and apple-green leaves of the taller shrub *Skimmia foremanii* or *Pernettya mucronata*, with a choice of white, pink, lilac, and crimson berries. Attention to these contrasts can help in creating depth on the perimeter in what could well be a fairly narrow bed in front of a fence.

Borders can bring out your artistry. The underplanting of bulbs and bays of dwarf plants at the foot of evergreens and individual shrubs is a good way of establishing a herbaceous border. Although the shrubs can thrust forward to the edge of the border at regular intervals, it would be useless to plant dwarfs farther back than the middle of the border. The planting of groups of dwarfs partly hidden by taller plants is another way of creating surprises in small gardens.

Where the planting area near fences is small, use the fences themselves to help provide the backdrop to your design. There are many climbing plants that can be used for this purpose. Clematis is an excellent choice—and there are sufficient varieties to provide a long flowering season. Vigorous, fence-hugging climbing roses 6 or more feet high are also excellent. Fences like this are also most suitable to accommodate fruit trees on a small scale—with horizontal or fan-trained pears, plums, or peaches.

Changing Levels

Differing levels quite often occur, even with modern developments where the builders—for their own convenience—try to get the ground level and graded.

Gentle slopes upward or downward are commonplace, and there may be one particular part of the garden that has an incline or change in level. If you have a slope—use it. It is a bonus to be exploited.

Sunken Gardens

If you are faced with an entirely flat garden, it could well be helped by creating a change in the levels—and one of the most effective ways is a sunken garden. Certainly, it will mean some hard work, but that's all part of the enjoyment of gardening. Sunken gardens can be used at both the back or front of the house. Again, a separate plan of this is advisable.

The base of the sunken garden is most likely to be in flagstones, reached by a single set of steps from the main level of the garden. The wall could be used as a rock garden, and it should be wider at the base than at the top. Use the topsoil from your excavation to fill in around the stones. Plant the surrounding area in the same way that you would a rock garden. The effect can be magnificent.

Bog Gardens

Waterlogged areas of your garden can be turned to your advantage with a bog garden, where you can grow many strange and beautiful flowers. It can be a fascinating addition to your scheme, perhaps sited at a point where its discovery by visitors is a pleasant surprise. Any low-lying place where water collects naturally on the surface is suitable for growing plants that may not thrive elsewhere.

In many cases very little special construction is required, although you may have to introduce some clay to hold the moisture. Alternatively, where an entirely stagnant water situation exists, you may have to dig down about 2 feet to provide some bottom drainage, which can be achieved by putting in a layer of old bricks or porous rocks.

If your bog garden is in the shade, all the better, for moisture will be saved. But shade is not vital if the plant roots are in damp ground. There is a wide range of suitable plants for this situation, such as *Macleaya, Lysichiton, Aruncus,* and *bamboos.*

Shaded Areas

In designing your gardens, the planting of tall subjects or the erection of fences and buildings must be treated with care so that you can control shade and the casting of shadows. However, do not try to eliminate shade altogether. We are prone to over-emphasize the sunny aspects of the garden and neglect the advantages of shady or sheltered spots. Shade in the garden has an important part to play, particularly in the summer, when heat may need tempering. Many gardeners tend to overlook this and consequently have suffered plant losses. Many of our flowering shrubs and plants prefer shade rather than full sun, and they will need shade at the hottest time of year to prevent scorching of foliage and flowers.

In your planning consider well the habit, form, and height of the various subjects you wish to plant, graduating them from front to back, placing in the open those that like the sun and underplanting in shaded areas those that thrive better in cooler, moist situations.

The use of shade itself can be taken into account when you are weighing the possibilities for adding depth to your garden. And of course it can also be used admirably for sitting areas.

Children in the Garden

A family with young children will want, initially, a garden to play in rather than to look at, so the design can be a progressive one to allow for additions, restyling, and planting when the children are older. They will want a fair-sized lawn to set up wickets and goal posts. So the outlook and view from the house will naturally be an open one, probably throughout the garden.

The creation of vistas can still be obtained in this garden, as can attractive beds, special features such as a rock garden, raised flower beds, and a good range of trees and shrubs. Pools of any sort where young children are to play are generally rather risky.

Beds of tender plants will need to be kept well away from the lawn, and the trees and shrubs you choose should be fairly sturdy.

The beds can still be carved out to give your lawn an attractive shape. It is best to use low, sturdy shrubs as a ground cover close to the lawn.

Paving and Patios

Formal or informal, paving is an aspect of the garden that can make or mar the finished result. Of all forms of paving, concrete slabs are by far the most convenient and offer the greatest scope for imaginative design. The range of slabs available is tremendous——different sizes, colors, textures, and finishes—and the design possibilities are increased almost limitlessly by the possibility of combining concrete with other types of paving.

Regular patterns, of more or less formal design, are easy to create. Many makers of precast paving slabs produce useful leaflets containing a variety of patterns, with an indication of the number of slabs required.

Patterned walks, patios, and other paved areas can be designed to suit the particular situation or the gardener's individual taste. Perhaps the easiest way of going about the job is to buy a large pad of square-ruled graph paper and a box of colored pencils. Using measurements taken on the site, the area to be paved can be drawn out roughly to scale and a whole range of possible patterns sketched out and considered before ordering the paving slabs.

It is particularly important when planning the paving pattern to be thoroughly satisfied with the design before the job. Concrete paving, properly laid, will

The traditional herbaceous border has largely given way to island beds in which the plants can be viewed from all sides. Such beds can be adapted to gardens of any size provided the plants are kept in scale.

Here a rock garden has been used to create interest. Although the rockery itself is fairly level; the plants grown against the wall of the house give it a sense of height.

last a very long time, but a design that is over-bold can become tiresome very quickly, even though it may look delightful at first. It is generally, better to under-play contrasts in color or texture rather than to overdo them. Use one or two closely matching colors or textures for most of the work, with contrasting areas used sparingly for accent. This will usually be more satisfying in the long term.

Laying paving is not difficult. The ground should be dug out to the required level and well compacted. If the ground is soft, roll in a layer of slag or stone and finish off with a level layer of sand.

Set out string lines to keep the edges of the slabs in line and then start at one end bedding the slabs. Leave ⅜ to ½ inch space between the slabs and bed each slab. Tap each slab down to the required level with a wooden mallet until there is no tendency to rock. Joints can be filled with mortar, which should be rubbed to a slight hollow with the thumb or a short wooden rod. As an alternative, slabs may be spaced more widely—about 2 inches—and the gaps filled with strips of turf or seeded with a close-growing plant: camomile is attractive and hardy and the fragrance as it is stepped on is a pleasant bonus.

Another inexpensive, and quite attractive, path or patio can be obtained from used bricks. These can be obtained from a local junk yard. They can be laid to any pattern and are quite durable. They also should be laid on about 3 inches of sand for solidity. Beware of one danger, however: smooth, hard-surface bricks tend to become slippery during wet weather.

The permanency of concrete rules it out for many people. But for various reasons it may have to be your choice of material for patios or paths. If nothing else, concrete is durable. It will last almost indefinitely; it is resistant to weather; and if the job is done well it should never need repair. Another advantage is its versatility, and nowadays the range of color and finish available is quite extensive.

For large areas, such as a patio, it will probably be best to buy the cement ready-mixed. Alternatively, for a small job, you can buy the materials in dry form for your own mixing.

Garden Steps
Steps in the garden can be both functional and used as a design feature. They can be used to continue the lines of the house and the patio into the garden itself. They can help in the creation of distance by using them to link one part of a garden to another. On plots with changing levels, they can help induce the element of surprise—by leading to a fish pond, a rose garden, or some other special feature that is not readily apparent in the general view of the garden. A variety of materials can be used. Flagstone, slabs, concrete—even logs—or just plain grass.

Pergolas and Walkways
There is a place in some gardens for a pergola: at front or back doors, or over the patio a pergola can be

beautiful with a clematis or honeysuckle, or perhaps a climbing rose.

In smaller gardens, the construction can be quite simple. The easiest form is one made entirely of treated wood. The uprights should be set 2 feet deep and can take the form of a lean-to at the side of the house, or as a walkway.

If you want to be more ambitious, try a stone or brick piered construction; the piers can be 2 or 3 feet high, with soil around the top for planting, or the piers can go right up to the cross-members. The cross-members should protrude at least 1 foot over the uprights or piers. Remember to treat all lumber in preservatives.

Walls, Fences, and Hedges

Your choice of boundary barriers should be well considered—a bad choice will undoubtedly ruin your whole design. Fences and high walls tend to foster a "fenced-in" feeling. Nevertheless, they are often unavoidable, particularly when a barrier is required.

The rustic look for rear-garden fences seems to be fashionable these days, and perhaps for that very reason it would be worthwhile to attempt to look for something more original. Ranch-fencing can look attractive in the right setting, and there are some new lines on the market now in concrete fencing. For patios and high shields close to the house, screen blocks can be used to good effect, particularly when they are used with various kinds of stone. These modern materials can give your garden that extra bit of finesse and professionalism. Another reason for liking screen blocks is that they can eliminate one of the major problems caused by high barriers—that of creating airless areas in the garden, which are conducive to pests and disease.

It is vital that a garden is able to breathe. Air movement is essential to all plants and assists in the moisture movement from the leaves. The moisture is taken up by the roots. If this movement does not exist, the whole atmosphere can be damp. Lawns may take hours to dry out after a shower; frost pockets may occur; disease can become prevalent. These are some of the dangers that can arise when we attempt to enclose our garden entirely for absolute seclusion. So in locating your boundary barriers, try to make sure that air movement is not unduly affected.

If you decide upon a hedge rather than a fence or wall, give considerable thought to the type, and if at all possible, run paths beside them. There are two reasons for this. First, when clipping the hedge, it will be easier to collect the debris; second, most forms of hedging require a good root run, and this can be detrimental to other subjects in the nearby border. A quick-growing hedge remains quick-growing and at the peak time of the year will need cutting more often than hedges of less-vigorous growth.

Additional information on hedges and fences is given in a later chapter.

Another variation on the small garden theme. It is often little details, like the wrought-iron gate and the oil jar shown in the picture above.

Garden ornaments can also add a lively interest to a small garden. For example, a sundial placed on a paved area can create a delightful air.

Unusually Sited Gardens

Awkward Sites

Considering the amount of work involved, gardens on more or less level sites are at a distinct advantage over those on awkward sites. However, the design possibilities of many awkward sites are far more interesting than those of level sites. Thus, an awkward site may be a blessing in disguise.

In these days, with the general scramble for building land, houses are being built on plots that even a decade ago would have been considered unsuitable. Gardens on sharply sloping hills are not uncommon. To the ingenious gardener, no site is too difficult to beautify. Fascinating gardens can be created on such unpromising sites as old quarries.

The basic design principles for awkwardly sited gardens are the same as those for level gardens, but there are a number of special considerations to keep in mind.

Terracing comes to mind immediately when we think of gardening on slopes, and in many cases it may be necessary. If your plot provides the scope for such a development, this is good. However, before undertaking a terracing project be quite certain that terracing is the answer. Try to envisage the completed job.

There is seldom any problem with terracing a site on a slope falling from the house. The main point to bear in mind is that part of each terrace going down should be visible from the top. Where possible, elements of surprise should be incorporated along the paths down.

Some sites, however, do not lend themselves to this sort of approach. This is especially true when a slope rises rather steeply immediately from the house. Whereas a falling slope has much in its favor, a rising slope, visible from your windows, can give a confining impression — unless, of course, you are on a

Lenten roses thrive in positions too shady for most plants.

hillside where the sheer expanse takes the eye up and away.

A short, wide plot, for instance, that may have a boundary fence at the top of the slope, or a shield of trees, is not for terracing. You would not be able to create the vista you desired. A different, less formal approach ought to be applied here, perhaps with a selection a small gardens within the whole garden, i.e. rock gardens, and even a falling stream — all reached by a winding path accentuated by specimen trees and shrubs.

Terracing on gently rising slopes is quite permissible, since a sort of rolling, undulating impression can be achieved with banks, rather than strict walled-in sections. However, try to hide the linking features, such as paths and steps, since these tend to emphasize the fall to the house and thus shorten the vista.

We tend to think of an entirely symmetrical layout for terracing, but this is not necessarily the best way to approach the problem. Terraces can easily be curved or slanted. Curving may even be necessary in order to follow the natural contours of the site.

Naturally, a long, gently rising upward slope is better for the creation of vistas, but a downward slope offers more scope for surprise elements, and with both it is important, before you begin your plans, to consider the exposure.

Terraced sites on hillsides can present severe exposure problems, and it is necessary to know how your site will be affected by winds, frosts, and rain. You can then choose your plants accordingly and build in some shielding features where desirable. If your slope is in the back garden, the front part of the terracing will be in the form of a patio, with steps to the garden proper. Alternatively, the terracing may go traversely and not be immediately connected to the house, in which case linking paths will be necessary from the flat area around the house to the rising or falling grade. On larger plots, consider emphasizing these entrances to the terracing with covered walkways or conifer-lined paths, for instance.

A lawn on gently rolling sites can be extremely attractive — even on steeper banks, if you have the right type of mower. However, it is vital that slopes be free of hollows or bumps — otherwise you will get scalping of the lawn. They should be eliminated by lifting the turf and scraping or adding earth accordingly.

Hillside Gardens

Hillside gardens may at first seem to be an almost impossible hurdle to establishing anything like a normal garden. Quite the reverse is true. Unless they are bounded by tall trees on all sides, such gardens will invariably get sunshine for part of the day, and if they face anywhere within the southern arc of the sun they will catch more than their share of it.

In order to accommodate plants, however, it will be almost essential to terrace the site, so that the growing areas can be made a less acute angle than 30 degrees. If they are steeper it will be difficult to stop soil erosion and enable efficient cultivation of the ground, especially if vegetables, fruit, and annual plants are grown.

The use of winding paths toward the top, interconnected with broad, terraced crosswalks, is perhaps best. They will give many levels to the garden, with attractive views from up and down.

If the house is old, soft brick or stone looks better for terrace walls than bright, reconstructed stone or concrete blocks, although the latter is ideal for modern properties.

One of the best types of stone for terraces is random-squared, in which the blocks are of different sizes. This is also the most expensive. On the other hand — poured concrete may be cheap, by comparison, but it is very permanent and not very attractive.

Part of the fun of making a hillside garden is the gradual fitting of the constructional features to the landscape, so they must be flexible enough to accommodate changes as you progress. Moreover, apart from having a rough plan, it is almost impossible, without skilled advice, to visualize what the best layout will be, of both plants and materials, when you start.

Any excavation to provide level areas will provide useful soil for beds, and soil is often a rare commodity on hillsides. Avoid gravel and bricks for the sloping paths as they are much too slippery, especially in winter. Asphalt gives a good grip, and so does ribbed concrete or rough stone.

The real answer for connecting a hillside garden, however, is steps, and very beautiful layouts can be made, with curving steps, flanked by low retaining walls, topped by cavities for plants; perhaps in other places the use of dry walls, filled with plants, can also be a special feature.

Rock gardens can also be built in the intermediate spaces between levels — waterfalls, too — and on the various levels of terracing, wide bays can be created here and there to break the general line. If you like pergolas for climbing plants, these can be erected along the terracing.

Generally speaking, the garden must be constructed from the bottom up, and not the reverse. If the ground slopes right to the roadway or boundary at the bottom, then in order to make the first terrace — which may be the lawn and patio — you will have to bank-up the boundary line as you proceed with the excavated earth and then face it with wall, bricks, or rocks. However, you should sink a drainage pipe into its face, otherwise water which drains down the hillside will be trapped behind and may eventually create problems.

Always look for the best way to dispose of excavated soil without carting it far, and remember that one square yard of stone weighs about 200 pounds.

You can make some steepish grass banks if the soil

In new housing developments, where there is a distinct tendency for all the houses to look rather similar, many people have an urge to do all they can to make their own garden distinctive. Here effective use has been made of a difficult corner site. The finished result would be a joy in any setting, and the envy of one's neighbors!

is reasonably firm and sodded rather than sown, but they will be difficult to mow.

You need at least 6 inches of soil for grass and at least a foot of soil for plants. Adequate terracing will be needed around the house to allow for the moving of garden materials, for the provision of seating, and so on.

The terracing walks and the steps up and down link the whole scheme. Rather than have large drops in stepping, try to descend diagonally or in curves — and set plants in the steps or paving in some places. Many carpeting plants give a very pleasant scent, and this is a means of saving valuable space.

Small specimen conifers and foliage plants are particularly attractive in hillside gardens: they give that vital three-dimensional effect. Trees, however, should generally be sited toward the top or to one side.

Ornamental features can be added as you progress, and there are many choices of materials. Cast concrete, slabs and stone laid in concrete, slabs laid on sand, broken slab paving, brick paths, asphalt and bitumen, blocks, bricks and dressed stone, screen blocks, dry stones, and cobbles all have their merits. Avoid using loose stones as these need a good deal of maintenance, especially when weeding.

If you have grassed banks, do not construct quick changes in level or steep humps or hollows, or mowing will cause scalping or missed parts.

The hillside and banks allow enormous scope for the establishment of mixed plantings of carpeting plants and low shrubs, with erect shrubs and small weeping trees here and there for accent and contrast. Brooms, *Cistus, Hypericums,* dwarf conifers, Japanese maples, and no end of other plants can be used. Remember that the plants can be just as attractive from below as from above. Rambler roses can look very effective pegged down on slopes, as can climbing roses tied to a low wooden trellis. Many other kinds of trailing and climbing plants lend themselves to being grown along the slope.

Hillside gardens should allow the maximum planting of climbers against fences and walls and on the house, and the free use of window boxes and tubs and urns near the house can establish immediate interest from close range. Generally, put such features as tall walls, hedges, arches, and pergolas toward the side of the slope — to allow a more or less complete view from top to bottom, broken only by the various compact features at each level.

Level terraces can be either paved or grassed, and provision may also be made for pools, fountains, and waterfalls; these are particularly enhanced on a hillside garden. Raised beds are also especially appropriate — linking one level to another and bordering pathways.

Hiltop Gardens

Planning and making a hilltop garden is one of the greatest tests of a gardener's ingenuity. The main priority is to provide shelter against gales for yourself and the plants in the garden. The first job, after initial planning of the layout, is to establish trees, tall hedges, and other kinds of windbreaks, such as wall bays for climbing plants.

It is not until later, when such trees are established, that the main plantings of herbaceous plants, roses, shrubs, and bulbs can take place, although naturally the time this can be done depends a lot on how exposed the actual location is in relation to the worst weather.

Much depends on the position of the house, how near the hilltop it is, and the location of the other features. But if one can picture them like chessmen, their positions interchangeable, then suiting their relative positions to the actual site will be much easier.

The first area to consider on a hilltop site is the area surrounding the house — the house garden. This should be sheltered with trees, or even a high wall, if the weather can get too rough. If the hill slope is steep, it may mean that you could provide only a flat area of ground on one or two sides.

Even if you have to construct it, this flat area is necessary, because not only does it make the house stand out as a feature but it will provide sufficient level space for siting the garden shed and patio, which need to be close to the house. You do not want to transport garden equipment and sundries long distances up and down slopes.

The patio will be a main feature, perhaps with a low wall along it, planted with the most suitable plants of the season, and adequately shielded. It can have, at the hillside end, an arch-covered ornamental gate, leading toward the next feature, the hillside garden. The patio might also have alcoves for sitting in during less favorable weather, and part can be covered overhead.

Steps, curving or straight, will lead from the patio to the lawn, which, to accommodate the slope of ground, will probably have to be partly excavated at one side and perhaps built up at another. An ornamental retaining wall could be built at the junction of the patio with the lawn, and this can be planted with rock plants in cavities left for the purpose.

The lawn can still have the usual flower beds in or around it, with accentuating specimen trees, and will presumably connect to a path leading to the hillside garden.

The hillside garden will have a path that winds through it and will pass through rock outcrops, partly made as planted rock gardens — rocky bluffs for carpeting or hanging plants and low conifers to contrast with the tall trees that will give the main area shelter from gales in winter.

Plenty of scope will usually be available for informally locating rock edges, water cascades, and green clearings among shrubs and trees for a garden seat — perhaps among rhododendrons, with low shrubs carpeting some parts. It may also be possible to construct other surprise elements and shielded seats to enjoy the view.

The actual summit, of course, will be the pièce de résistance. It will need to be partly clothed with trees and shrubs to keep off the wind, possibly to the southwest and the north and northeast, with views to the other points of the compass.

A short avenue of grass or steps, flanked by hydrangeas, conifers, or other plants, can lead to the hilltop itself, where you might like a flat circle of ornamental bricks or paving, with an island bed, and low walls around the edges, with seating set in them.

The hillside garden and hilltop provide endless possibilities for sun-lovers and shade-loving plants.

If you wish to grow fruit and vegetables, it would be best to locate these somewhere in the shielded house garden.

Retaining Walls

There are many materials available for walls. For low walls, of not more than two or three courses high, a light foundation of rubble tamped into the soil will be adquate footing.

More generally in terracing, the wall is to be built in loose ground, and you will need to dig down below the freezing zone to provide a foundation of at least 3 inches of concrete. With taller walls you will need a foundation of up to 6 inches of concrete, again set in the soil below the freezing zone.

Where the wall is to retain a large amount of soil or hold back a fairly extensive terrace, you will certainly need a double course. A cheap brick or concrete block can be faced with the better quality material. The cavities along the top of double walls can either be capped or filled with some of the wide variety of plants suited to this type of situation.

Where you must dig into the soil for foundations, you will also need to insert a damp course about 6 inches above soil level. Weep holes for drainage are vital, too, and should be left at intervals of about 6 feet along the base of the wall. To assist drainage on the retained side, crocks or cinders should be placed in the soil close to the weep holes.

Dry walls are generally not suitable for retaining walls on steep slopes, unless you are a real professional at building them. However, you could try your hand at a low one for raised beds or a slight terrace effect. Dry walls more than a foot high should be

A well-kept vegetable garden **top.** The garden is situated on a hilltop and the hedge is essential to protect the crops from wind damage. **Below.** The herbaceous peony is a long lived perennial. It grows and flowers best in fertile soil in full sun.

given a backward slant of about 1 inch per foot in height.

For solid walls, which are most suitable for terracing, the main point to remember is the absolute necessity of maintaining line, level, and plumb. Adequate mortar joints and the need for piers or other forms of support are also vital in long walls that have to retain a large amount of soil. Line, level, and plumb are assured by regularly checking with string line, spirit level, and plumb line.

For concrete block work, mortars made with ordinary cement and sand are too strong. Using slightly weaker mortar of masonry cement and builders' sand — not concreting sand — in a one-to-five proportion will ensure that any cracks that may develop through settlement or temperature changes will follow the mortar line and will not crack the blocks. Then you can re-point as necessary. Mortar joints should be made about ⅜ of an inch thick for blocks, and the blocks should be laid to "bond," with staggered vertical joints as with brickwork.

Steps in Terracing

Creating steps requires that extra bit of expertise at the best of times, and in terracing they may present more problems than is normal. Quite often, the situation will call for steps from a fairly high drop, which must be constructed in a way that they are entirely safe for those walking on them.

Numerous materials are available, but for a difficult site the choice is fairly restricted — either completely flat-surfaced slabs or heavy timber. Concrete could be used, but it is so permanent that it is seldom recommended for steps.

From a high drop the steps should not be too steep; each step should have a few inches more than the normal length, and with extra-long or curving flights, a regular "landing," perhaps with a seat, may be useful. The treads should not be less than about 16 inches, and the risers about 6 inches. Begin the construction from the bottom and work up.

Also give some thought to the wings of the steps, particularly on hillside sites. These side walls can take a variety of attractive forms. You could use cavity walls for planting, stone, or formal brickwork capped for finish. If you do decide to plant the walls lining your steps, do not use plants that are likely to grow down to the steps themselves. This could be dangerous.

Specialty Gardens

Town gardens may seem unpromising, but they can be made a little oasis of rest and retreat.

Town Gardens

The town garden in the strictest sense is usually so small as to be barely a garden at all. It can be a depressing sight, particularly with older properties where the previous occupants had no interest in trying to make a garden in such a restricted and confined area. However, properly planned town gardens can be real gems.

Probably the best approach with these gardens is to treat them as another room to your house, which is what they really are — a room without a roof. The choice of style, layout, and planting must be an entirely individual matter.

The functions of your garden, because of the smallness, must be given priority. You might, for instance, want to turn the whole site over to a special interest. You may wish it to serve as a play area for children as well as providing some of the basic pleasures of gardening; or perhaps you would like an entirely paved garden with a background of climbers, highlighted with container-grown plants.

There are many things to take into account as you develop the design and, as with larger gardens, it is best to work to a plan.

Every inch of space will count, so take your time and use it well. First and foremost, look out of the windows and make a note of the eyesores that are now in existence, and also bear in mind those you may be adding, such as a garden shed. Mark them in on your plan and try to work out ways of screening them. There are many ways of doing this, even in confined areas. Climbers over lightweight trellises, or trained over plastic netting, can be most appropriate. Something more sturdy may be called for in some instances. A narrow strip of tall ranch fencing could be used, with a suitable climber trained over it.

The importance of color in a small area cannot be stressed strongly enough. A mass of dark shades will be boring and unattractive. You will need as many color highlights and contrasts as you can fit in. This ruling can be applied to fixtures as well as to growing things. A dark wall usually cries out for treatment. You are certain to be using it for training climbers, or even cordon fruit, and for a good part of the year those plants are going to be just one color — a green and brown that will be barely noticeable against the dark wall. So try to give the wall some color — paint it with cement-based paint in one of the large range of pastel shades now available. Approach it with the same sort of feeling as you would in choosing the color scheme for your living room, with wall colors to match the furniture.

As for the design itself, the layout must be a fairly simple, basic one; perhaps simply a lawn surrounded by a steepish bank of plant life. Any fancy work with paths or arbors is usually out of the question, since features like this will overemphasize the smallness. Paths should be confined to the basis of communication, without unnecessary curves. It may help to introduce a feature that will act as a focal point, perhaps a sundial or birdbath in the center of the lawn, or a rock feature cutting in from one corner. But do not do anything that will spoil the initial open area, which is really quite necessary, and remember that too many special effects will ruin your artistry.

There is no reason why there should not be some pleasant curves in the lawn, and this will help create the illusion of space and depth. Where possible, surprise elements and an air of mystery in some shady corner can be created.

A fair-sized sitting-out area, either immediately outside the house or in a secluded corner, is usually called for, and perhaps a covered construction can also be added, with climbing plants. Note any wind tunnels that may exist. These are usually more prevalent in small sites than in larger gardens. Terracing and introduction of steps and raised beds may be necessary on changing levels, and these will all give additional scope for colorful planting.

For the remainder of the garden, the choice is yours. Use your imagination and let simplicity, color, and function be your guides.

Three final points of advice on town gardens. First, the rear garden of an older property is often cluttered with rather ugly buildings of one kind or another. Get rid of these if you can, and thus have more space for gardening. Second, soil can often be poor in these confined spaces. It may require a few loads of peat,

Gardens by the sea are less affected by frost and plants like *Amaryllis belladonna* may thrive there.

Plants like the glamorous agapanthus shown here can be grown in pots to decorate town or roof gardens during the summer.

manure, or other luxuries before you start planting. Third, try not to make your garden too permanent. Consider a basic plan, but with features — like ornaments, statues, container-grown conifers and plants — that can be changed around every so often to relieve the monotony.

Gardens by the Sea

Harsh winds, sand, salt, spray, and even tides — these are the hazards that the seaside gardener must overcome to be successful in his endeavors. Seaside gardening is a constant battle against nature, yet it is a battle that can be won by careful planning and the selection of suitable plants. There are many native shrubs, trees, ground-cover plants, and perennials that are by nature adapted to seaside conditions.

By the sea, you may be perched high on a cliff or, at the other extreme, close to the water. Perhaps you are sited slightly inland, where the full force of coastal elements is not felt, but whose presence will still be much in evidence.

With a sea view, you may wish to make this a principal part of the design, and very high outlines will not be required on that aspect of the garden. At the same time, you will need to establish relief from the wind and spray and ward off the reflected glare from the water. Whether or not you have an open aspect, a special emphasis on screens and windbreaks will be necessary — not only for yourself, but also for the less-hardy plants you will want to grow.

Study closely the general needs and maintenance of the garden itself. Soil, for instance, will need improvement in most seaside gardens. It may be sandy, silty, stony, or clay-like in texture and will need regular additives of peat, fertilizers, and manure. There will also be a moisture problem, and regular mulching will be necessary. Soil depths will be shallow, particularly on sloping ground, and it will be necessary to establish ground cover to prevent further erosion. These are factors that will prove all important as you begin to draw up your plan.

In spite of all these disadvantages, seaside gardens have one great advantage over inland gardens: the great body of sea water has an ameliorating effect upon climate, and frost is later in seaside gardens. This means that you can grow a whole range of less-hardy and exceptionally beautiful plants that could not be grown outdoors farther inland.

The basic design elements of locations, vistas, garden division, surprises, and mysteries blended with the natural landscape remain the prime object, but the ways and means of achieving them are obviously affected by the "built-in" requirements of seaside locations.

If you are a complete newcomer to seaside gardening, observe the local conditions carefully. Note how your neighbors are gardening. Talk to them and your local garden center about the area. Learn all you can about the extensive problems your garden is likely to present before making any elaborate plans.

You will probably find, for instance, that they recommend gray- and silver-leafed foliage plants, such as *Senecio laxifolius,* which have elements of silky hairs on the leaf surface as a built-in protection against salt and blown-in sand. There are many other plants they could recommend. Willows, sea buckthorn, and tamarisk have narrow leaves which stand up to the wind. Yucca, sea holly, yew, cotoneaster, hydrangea, buddleia, and black pine also do well on seaside sites. You will need all this information quite early in your planning.

Once you are satisfied that you know enough about local conditions, make a start. The windbreaks will be your first line of defense — and do not begin by believing that high, closed barriers will solve the problem. Recent experiments have shown that wind can be just as much of a problem whistling around the lee side as on the facing side. So, if you plan to erect a fence, do not make it absolutely solid; choose ranch or wattle fencing, or one that allows the wind to filter through.

The better way, perhaps, is to take a lesson from nature and erect a living screen of trees and shrubs, depending on the size of your garden. For young hedging it would be well to plant it beside a framework of wire neting — so that it will not blow away. Planting will need to be somewhat closer than normal to allow for a thinning-out by wind-pruning.

Fuchsias. In frost-free seaside gardens these will often form large evergreen shrubs.

Witch hazel, *Hamamelis mollis,* a shrub for all gardens. It flowers in the dead of winter.

Once the perimeter offers protection to the remainder of the garden, you can begin to introduce the less-hardy plants.

These protective planting schemes cannot be recommended too highly. They will help combat the distortion and devastation that can be caused by high winds carrying salt spray, which is deposited on the plants to dry into crystals, which are beneficial to few plants.

Another design feature that may require special attention is the patio. This should be developed with a view in mind. If a natural landscape exists, take full advantage of it. Therefore, your main sitting-out area can be at the back, front, or side of the house, according to the view. It may require screening from the elements by concrete blocks, and low air currents can be kept out by a cavity wall of 2 or 3 feet in height. You could also consider building alcoves into the patio for additional shelter on particularly windy days.

Rooftop Gardening

Many older buildings — and quite a few modern, tall apartments — lend themselves to rooftop gardening. If you are planning a roof garden, it is wise to get expert advice — just to make sure that the roof is structurally sound and will be able to stand not only the weight of the garden but also the regular tread of human feet. Once that is established, you can begin planning.

The size, lavishness, and luxury of your roof garden will depend on your pocketbook. If, for instance, you are able to call in specialized assistance for structural additions, perhaps designed by an architect, your garden in the sky can be quite spectacular. There will be scope for a wide range of features, like archways, sheltered areas, water features, an aviary, special lighting, furniture, and even a miniature greenhouse, all of which can be built in lightweight materials if necessary.

The first thing to remember is that the garden will be entirely artificial and that all your materials will probably have to be carried up several flights of stairs or in an elevator. Bear this in mind as you begin your planning. As with all garden-design situations — work to a scale drawing.

The design itself will have little resemblance to ground-level planning. There will be few landscape features to take into account, apart from other buildings and passing clouds. There will be no need to establish privacy, although you will require screens for shade, not only for yourself but also for the plant life. The rooftop will be scorching in the heat of summer, and your soil beds will not have the natural power of conserving moisture.

The rooftop can also be fairly desolate, so you will need to establish shields around the edge of the roof to screen your garden from a somewhat bleak outlook and also to form a resistance to the wind, which will also be more noticeable.

Take note of existing structures, such as a protruding chimney breast or elevator towers for developing secluded alcoves. It is important at an early stage to examine the roof wall. Most flat roofs will have a wall of reasonable height, but for safety's sake this may require additional building to make it at least 4 feet high.

The walls themselves can be used as an extension of your gardening space by clothing them with climbers and hanging baskets. They will probably be of bare brick — so before you put in the plants, paint it all with cement-based paint, available in many pastel colors. This will have the effect of illuminating the green foliage that will be growing against it. A white wall will highlight the various container-grown trees and shrubs close to the wall for additional windbreaks. This sort of perimeter arrangement of climber and container specimens will help add a degree of depth to the garden. Banking schemes can also be used against walls. Taller conifers, for example, can be grouped as a background to a row of more prostrate shrubs.

The beds should be long and narrow, and, with imaginative planting, some really excellent features can be achieved. Island beds can be used well but generally need a fairly open area to set them off. Also try to establish some focal point that attracts the eye as you enter the garden: a specimen tree or shrub, or perhaps a pergola clothed with climbers around a protruding structure. To sum up, the basic design will follow these lines: a central focal point, a logical, rather formal arrangement of beds whose low line will be interrupted by occasional prostrate trees or shrubs, and a backdrop or shield of climbers and taller specimen subjects. Additional windscreens and shade can be effected by building a fairly sturdy trellis on the wall or parapet surrounding the garden.

Beds will naturally be contained in wooden structures, light concrete blocks, or brick, and you should place a layer of heavy-gauge polyethylene beneath each bed. They will require regular water throughout the year, so some sort of piped watering system should be installed or hoses must be available.

If space allows, a screened section for your tools, compost, and supplies will also be useful. Soil may be in short supply, so supplies of peat, humus, and lightweight substance such as perlite or vermiculite should be available on the roof.

The floor of your roof can be "paved" for a patio area or a path. Some lightweight concrete-based patio tiles which would be suitable are now on the market.

Large areas of water are usually out of the question because of the weight factor, but you might consider a small water garden with either a polyethylene or fiber-glass pool.

Although there will be plenty of year-round heat on the roof — scorching in summer from above and comfortable from heat rising from the building in winter — you may wish to install a greenhouse for additional interest. There are several all-polyethylene, lightweight models available that are ideal for this situation — but they must be properly anchored to the roof to withstand high winds.

Grass can be grown on the roof with varying degrees of success, but you will require 4 to 6 inches of a lightweight soil mixture and a good supply of water and constant maintenance.

There are simulated lawn carpets, rather expensive, but entirely trouble-free and eminently suitable for the roof.

Gardening from an Apartment
A new craze is sweeping North America among frustrated gardeners who have little space for outdoor gardening. Cellars and basements are being fitted with powerful lamps and heat for underground gardening.

Many sorts of plants can be grown under these conditions — ranging from tomatoes to geraniums. It is a sort of glasshouse without glass. If you have a cellar — consider an artificial garden. Your local electric company will advise you on the lighting requirements.

Some basement apartments have tiny courtyards available for container gardens and perhaps one or two trees. Certainly, warmth is usually no problem in the belowground-level sites. As with aboveground apartments, windowsills, doorways, staircases, and balconies can all be utilized.

The big problem with gardening in containers is not so much scale, but the selection of suitable plants to fill them. The most important aspect is the space available for roots. Some urns and boxes, while charming to look at, are impractical in this respect. Another important consideration is the provision for drainage. A generous layer of rocks and a suitable potting soil are essential.

Today garden centers, garden shops, and nurserymen stock a wide variety of containers. Some are expensive, others comparatively cheap, but usually almost every purse is catered to.

Wooden tubs can be round, like the old type of beer barrel, or square, with either vertical or sloping sides. The most durable are made of redwood and do not require painting. Cedar also stands up well to the dampness of soil. All plants, of course, grow well in clay pots, and there are scores of sizes and shapes available, some plain and others ornamental. A range of terra-cotta pots, well designed and in an attractive color, are now on the market. There are also ranges of fiber-glass containers that simulate lead; and modern reproductions, convincing in color and finish, are obviously far less expensive than the handsome eighteenth-century lead ornaments that decked the gardens of yesteryear. These fiber-glass containers are lightweight, strong, and durable and do not in any way hamper plant growth.

Planting can be permanent or seasonal. Boxwood, bay trees, cherry laurels, *Yucca, Skimmia, Viburnum tinus, Mahonia japonica,* and other similar shrubs are all useful subjects.

Potentillas in shrub form, camellias, azaleas, and rhododendrons are excellent in containers located in shady areas but will require protection or shelter from cold winds. Hydrangeas and hardy fuchsias need full sun. Variety and color must be the aim, and bulbs on their own or combined with bedding plants are ideal for this. Seasonal planting is relatively easy, as there is a wide choice, starting in early spring with spring-flowering bulbs.

Hyacinths are particularly attractive in containers of all kinds, as they are perfect in form from any angle, and their range of pastel colors and pleasant scent make them a triple treat. Daffodils and tulips of all types do well in containers and provide a spring-like splash of color; the shorter-stemmed varieties and miniatures are particularly effective.

Pansies and violas can be interplanted with hyacinths; muscari and scilla are most effective with daffodils, as are *Mysotis* and wall flowers with tulips. Imaginative gardeners can plant crocuses with hyacinths for continuous bloom through March and April.

Lilies are splendid subjects for containers, yet few gardeners seem to cultivate them this way. By choosing a particular type and variety, containers can be made to produce superb shows of lilies from June into

Town gardens
Paving is an essential part of almost every town
garden. Many different types of paving are available.
All paving shown here is of some type of concrete.
Alternative materials include stone paving slabs,
granite paving stones, brick, and even wooden blocks.

Courtesy the Cement and Concrete Association

the fall.

Herbaceous plants such as double daisies and polyanthus can be added to containers planted with bulbs for spring color, while pelargoniums, petunias, nicotiana, heliotropes, and alyssum can be depended on for high summer color.

Short-stemmed bedding dahlias in a host of colors will flower from July to October in containers, and even shorter-stemmed anemone-flowering dahlias are excellent subjects for window boxes. For something really different, try the 8- to 10-inch tall anemone de Caen and anemone St. Brigid in containers for endless numbers of bright flowers from June into August.

Tomatoes can also be grown in window boxes or tubs in full sun, and for a Christmas effect, miniature conifers can be used.

One of the secrets of success with gardening in containers is proper watering. Never overwater, but do not let tubs or pots dry out completely. Gardeners should also remember that plants in confined space exhaust nourishment. Bulbs need no fertilizer, but all containers should have their soil renewed or partially renewed at the top. If this is impossible because of permanent plantings, nourishment should be replaced by applications of complete fertilizers.

Whatever the plantings, town gardeners, particularly those with rooftop or balcony containers, will find that fiber-glass or plastic containers are particularly useful because they are light and therefore easy to lift and move.

Cottage Gardens

With more and more old country properties being renovated, the cottage garden has taken on a new importance. It is certainly the right type of garden for many older houses.

To many people, a cottage garden is simply a chaos of colorful plants. This conveys the general impression that there is no planning involved and all you need do is sow seeds all over the place. The facts are very different. The chaos is actually highly organized, and the successful cottage garden is invariably the outcome of careful observation. It is worth having a quick look at the origin of the cottage garden.

Throughout the long, settled period of the reign of Queen Victoria, gardening flourished in England as it had never flourished before. The big houses, employing vast staffs, from head gardener to pot boy, set a standard of excellence never seen before or since. And for the first time smaller houses had attractive gardens, with correspondingly smaller staffs, right down to the cottager who often made his garden from plants and cuttings given to him by his more wealthy neighbors and employers.

During the latter half of the nineteenth century gardening was the main interest of the British people. There were then few other forms of entertainment for the countryman. There were no radios, televisions, motion pictures, motorcycles, and no automobiles.

The garden offered recreation — and profit — to the farm-worker or anyone employed in rural industries. It would often be a glorious mixture of flowers, fruit, and vegetables — each plant being cared for individually, to make a complete picture of considerable beauty.

One reason for the success of the cottage garden was that the proud owner was able to devote all of his time to the study of his plot — largely because he had little else to do. This is much more important than we realize today, for some plants will grow successfully in one place, even in a small garden, but will be a total failure in another. The Victorian cottager, sitting quietly on his broken chair outside his front door, smoking his pipe and contemplating his plot of land, was able to observe and remember the behavior of different plants in different places and, as a result, to grow them all to perfection.

The basic design of the cottage garden was usually so simple as to be no design at all — merely a straight path from the gate to the front door, with two plots on each side. But there would often be certain features in many cottage gardens that would dominate the scene.

An old gnarled apple tree — a Bramley seedling, perhaps, or something similar — would be the largest single specimen. This would provide blossom in the spring, fruit for preserves and jellies, apples for apple pies, and — a trick that sums up the cottage garden — a home for a climbing rose.

The art of topiary — clipping trees into peculiar shapes — came back to large gardens in the Victorian period with the revival of formalism. This, too, strayed over into the cottage gardens — a clipped hedge decorated with the occasional peacock, or large clipped specimens, either simple mounds of yew or box, perhaps with a figure on top, would be placed at an appropriate point to form a solid basis for the design. Similarly, there would be two or three large shrub roses or ornamental shrubs.

The rosebush might be the thornless "Zephirine Drouhin"; the old large white, "Frau Karl Drushki"; or some long-forgotten hybrid — like the variety now known as "Rubrotincta," a single Damask rose with a white flower margined with red and having a delicate scent.

The shrub could be something very common — *Kerria japonica "Flore pleno,"* or it could equally well be some little-known, exotic plant — perhaps a *Hammamelis* or a *Viburnum,* given to the skilled cottage gardener as a cutting.

There is no catalog of "Cottage Garden Flowers." Even so, there are certain plants that have come to be associated with the style, although it would be better to describe many of them as "Tea-Cozy" flowers, the sort that are seen on elementary embroidery designs and on colored calendars.

Yet these do give the effect of old-world cottage gardens — hollyhocks, for example, are singularly appropriate, although they may be difficult to grow

Gardens like this are a thing of the past, yet one can
learn a lot from them, especially about blending
the colors and setting out bedding plants.

because of the prevalence of rust. Again, although of comparatively recent introduction, clarkia, godetia, and nasturtium are easy annuals which give a good show, need little skill, and fit into the picture.

Curiously enough, there are some plants that will grow very well in small gardens but are totally unsuccessful in larger areas, where they might be somewhat lost. The Madonna Lily, *Lilium candidum,* is the best example, for it grows really well only in a small space.

Sunflowers, the big brash yellow "frying-pan" annual types, are also typical — because the seed can be put to good use. Also, the runner bean was originally grown as a decorative plant — and tripods of scarlet runners are very much in the cottage-garden tradition; so, too, are sweet peas, both the annual kind and the everlasting pea, *Lathyrus latifolius.*

The cottager realized the decorative value of vegetables. The beautiful glaucous foliage of nearly all the brassicas — the cabbages, cauliflowers, sprouting broccoli, and so on — is as attractive as the much-admired hosta, if it is regarded with an eye that has not been conditioned by false values of rarity.

These are some of the elements of the cottage garden. But it is not something that can be ordered ready-made from a landscape gardener. It must depend entirely on the thought, care, concentration and skill of the owner. Given that — it is one of the most beautiful and satisfactory styles of gardening in the world.

A plant that looks good in a small garden is *Pieris japonica* 'Variegata'. The variegated leaves are attractive at all times of the year. The plant needs an acid soil and some shade.

Labor Saving Gardens

Throughout the previous chapters it has been stressed that a well-planned garden is a garden that is easy to maintain.

It is not good to plan an elaborate plantsman's paradise totally beyond your capabilities. Bear in mind the amount of time you will be able to devote to your garden; otherwise your dream could soon become a nightmare!

It is possible to have a trouble-free, light-work garden of pleasing design. Most of the basic garden-design principles that have already been mentioned will still be applicable. You will still want, no doubt, a patio, lawns, and a selection of trees and shrubs. It becomes a question of substituting less-troublesome features for those that require year-round maintenance.

Larger paved areas than would normally be the case can help, and choice of materials for paths and so on will also affect the amount of work required through the year. Gravel paths for example, require regular maintenance. Stone, asphalt, or concrete would be better. Wood chips or tanbark may also be appropriate.

Pools can be left to their own devices for long periods of the year and require only occasional tending. Huge rockeries can be tedious, but again the amount of work they entail is largely controlled by the type of plants you use. Lawns are trouble-free for five months of the year, apart from the raking of dead leaves; but for the remaining seven months they will require attention.

Perhaps the major part of the work in a pleasing design can be eliminated by careful selection of plants for borders and beds. There is a good deal of work involved in growing, planting, and the general maintenance of geraniums, salvias, antirrhinums, petunias, lobelia, and so on. Try this arrangement as a trouble-free substitute: plant out dwarf shrubs like potentiallas, cotoneasters, dwarf conifers, and helianthemums, and set them out 2 to 3 feet apart. In between them plant a selection of winter-, summer-, and autumn-flowering bulbs. In the center of the bed, plant three or four clematis, choosing varieties to flower at different times of the year. Do not give them any support. Just let them grow along the ground, spreading between the shrubs and pegging down where necessary. You will have a year-round color spectacular that is hard to beat and, apart from one or two clean-up operations, it will be entirely work-free.

There are many other ground-cover shrubs that can be used for planting a less-work border, including *Cytisus procumbens,* a mat of bright yellow flowers in May; *Euonymus fortunei* "Gracilis," a spreading green foliage with silver-gray variegated leaves; *Juniperus procumbens* "Blue Rug," a low-growing conifer; *Sarcococca ruscifolia,* an attractive broadleaf evergreen; and *Taxus canadensis,* a dwarf evergreen.

Ground-cover perennials suitable for filling-in between larger shrubs, thus creating labor-saving borders, include: ajuga, bergenia, hosta, polygonum, pulmonaria, *Sedum spectabile, Stachys lanata,* and *Tiarella cordifolia.*

Trouble-Free Conifers

The increased emphasis on labor-saving plants these days has brought a new interest in dwarf conifers. A well-chosen group of these perfectly proportioned miniature trees can bring joys of trouble-free landscape gardening into even the smallest areas, giving a sense of maturity and serenity.

Blechnum tabulare is one of the most striking of ferns, with leathery evergreen leaves, for gardens in frost free areas.

All the plants shown here are useful,
labor-saving plants
Top, *Cistus* ×
kewensis, a dwarf broom.
Center, a heather garden created almost entirely
from heathers and slow-growing conifers.
Bottom, dwarf evergreen azaleas: these
flower so freely that you cannot see the
leaves for the flowers.

The work involved is negligible after initial plant-ing, since they are not fussy about soil. The poorer the soil, the longer they remain dwarfs. They are rarely troubled by pests and diseases.

A dwarf conifer may be one which reaches maturity when only a few feet high, or it may be a slow-growing type of a larger species or an alpine variety. The garden uses of these little beauties are many.

There is one point to bear in mind. Most forms of dwarfs are dignified little plants, and they should not be made to look ridiculous by thoughtless planting — under large trees for example. Probably the best place for them is where natural scenic beauty already exists, or where it has been artificially created in miniature . . . a rockery or surrounding a pool. They will fit in perfectly, giving the impression of age and maturity that is associated with trees, yet in scale with adjacent materials.

Dwarf conifers are perhaps best used as a feature, rather than dotted in various parts of the garden. Plan your groups carefully so that you get the best from a wide range of color, size, habit, and texture. Take into account the winter colors, which with some species are different from the summer colors.

Pay attention to backgrounds, so that they are not overshadowed by taller garden subjects. One really appreciates dwarfs better when they can be fully seen. Careful positioning is important.

The list of available cultivars is endless. Some of the conical or globose forms are excellent when used in isolation on a small lawn or in tubs on the patio, while the prostrate, mat-forming qualities of the junipers make them excellent ground-cover plants, particularly for covering banks or difficult ground.

For greater versatility, many types thrive in pots and thus have the advantage of portability. They may be plunged in the garden to help the effect of the season and later moved to the patio or conservatory.

Apart from the true dwarf, mini-trees will gradually grow larger, but there is nothing to stop you from moving them to a more appropriate site when they outgrow the first location.

Paved Gardens
One often hears a reluctant gardener, surveying his new site, declare: ''I'm going to concrete the lot.'' That really is not as anti-gardening as it may sound, although it should be emphasized at the outset that raw concrete should definitely not be used for covering any major area of the garden. It is far too permanent, and you must allow for a change of mind later — either by yourself or a future occupant of your home. The best choice for paved gardens is colored slabs. It is wise to choose the more subdued colors.

A paved garden is particularly suitable for a smaller town garden or for a front garden with an island cut out for planting. It can also replace a lawn in the planning scheme of a larger garden and still blend pleasantly with the overall design scheme, which

Right A different approach to the labor-saving garden. Here paving is the main feature, with color provided by roses and trouble-free bedding plants.

Below *Picea pungens* 'Kosteriana', an attractive slow-growing conifer, is just the sort of foliage plant that looks good in a paved garden, or provides an ideal focal point.

would be worked out on the same lines already suggested in earlier sections of this book.

The design of your paved garden will naturally be an open one, with perhaps several areas of ground left unpaved for island beds of shrubs and conifers, according to overall dimensions.

You can also have a wide range of containers and container-grown specimens (as described in the section on gardening from an apartment). These will provide complete versatility, lending themselves to grouping in mass arrangements, siting individually on a repetitive basis to highlight a particular aspect, and enabling you to give your garden a constantly changing face.

It is worthwhile to leave a fair expanse of border around the paved area if this is possible, so that you can plant trees and shrubs that will clothe unsightly walls and fences and give your garden some outline and depth. If a border is not possible, revert back to container-grown subjects, which can be used for a similar effect.

Shaped paved gardens can look attractive, although in general it is difficult to overcome the formal, squared-off look that slabs will present. Indeed, your garden situation may well lend itself to an entirely formal design.

Crazy paving is more suited to shaping and informality, although this must be a matter of choice. Bear in mind the permanence of most forms of crazy paving.

The design possibilities are really endless, but, as with all other types of garden design, try to establish a central feature that will act as a focal point. There are numerous other tricks, such as leaving out an odd slab here and there and planting the ground with creeping annuals, perennials, or scented herbs. Creating terraces — even artificial ones — to get away from the entirely flat look, and using tiny edging walls in a material that blends with the choice of paving, either capped or built with a cavity for planting, is another possibility.

There is no reason why the gardener who chooses a paved garden cannot grow fruit trees and set up a mini-orchard. Obviously, this will be possible with cordon fruit in any border, but, where no border exists, the trees can be grown in pots. There is a good deal to be said for such a plan, because you will have the benefit of a splendid flowering period in spring and the bonus of quality fruit in autumn. And the management of pot-grown fruit trees can be simpler than those grown in the normal way.

One vital point to remember is that pots and tubs should be protected during winter so that the roots do not freeze. The trees you buy should be four-year-old pyramids on dwarfing stock. Apples and pears are particularly amenable to this form of culture, and you might like to try others, such as plums, peaches, and nectarines.

Place apples and pears in the less-favorable locations of your garden. The number of plants you can grow in small areas is surprising. You will need little more than one square yard of space to accommodate each tree.

Do not let the trees bear too much fruit in the first two years. The fruit spurs should be thinned out as they develop. Established tub-grown trees will need repotting every two or three years.

Lawn and Trees

Another labor-saving arrangement that can be adapted to almost any size of garden is one in which the basic ingredients are simply grass, trees, and shrubs. No paths or other constructions or special features of any kind, apart from the patio and normal service paths, are used.

The garden would take the form of a pleasant glade which would be reached from a fairly wide patio at the rear of the house. The glade would be a lawned area in which islands had been cut out for planting individual specimen subjects. The front part of the lawn would be left open except for a pair of conifers or standard roses on each side of the opening leading from the patio to the lawn. Then, there could be an informal arrangement of trees and shrubs, with the smaller, low-growing and prostrate subjects at the front, allowing the outline to rise gently as you proceed down the garden.

There are many subjects suitable for this sort of plan, but avoid any trees that will grow to huge proportions and overshadow the remaining members of your glade family. At the front you could use groups of hydrangeas and hypericum, banking up with magnolia, cherry, crab apple, buddleia, *Pieris japonica,* Japanese maple, Chinese juniper, and so on.

Around the base of each tree, cut out a bed that is the width of the branch span of the tree, since grass will not grow well underneath. The bed can be underplanted with suitable subjects, such as seasonal bulbs.

Lawns

The beauties of a lawn are so self-evident that few people ever stop to ask themselves the point of having a lawn. In fact, there are several points that combine to make a lawn one of the most important features of any garden. In the first place it is green, the most restful color in the whole spectrum: this quiet quality in a lawn is the ideal background for the riotous, exciting colors of the flower border. It is also a way of creating vistas. Smooth-rolling sweeps of grass lead the eye away into the distance. Not only can the lawn lead the eye to beds, borders, and distant trees, it can be the perfect background for features within it. Bulbs planted in the lawn will not interfere with mowing if they are kept to one corner. Specimen trees show up more delightfully when planted in a lawn. Isolated beds in formal patterns and shapes set in a lawn are extremely effective if well kept and carefully edged. Curved edges, provided they are not too sharp, are easier to mow, and curving lawn edges may be used for eye-leading effects or just break up a long, monotonous, straight line.

Lawns are also places where people relax in the sun during their leisure, or where children play. Lawns may be used for games such as croquet, badminton, or tennis. Many people turn over areas to lawns because they just have no wish to do anything else with the space at the moment. Very often they may think they save labor by doing this, and it is true that a piece of grass can be kept fairly neat-looking without much care except mowing.

Your lawn will probably combine several uses. Its shape and position will be decided by such considerations as the layout of paths and access to other parts of the garden. It will be planned to take account of the positions of established trees, the view from the house and road, rock-garden features, ornaments, slopes and levels, and the size of the garden as a whole.

The first thing to appreciate about a lawn is that it is composed of living, growing plants that need care and attention just as with any other living, growing plant. Most of the problems people have with lawns arise from their failure to appreciate this simple fact.

Many troubles that affect lawns can be avoided by thorough preparation of the site, which should always be done properly, even if the ground has already been cultivated. It is always much more difficult to correct a badly made lawn than to see that the soil and drainage conditions are correct in the first place.

The preparations for a lawn, whether by sodding, sprigging, or seeding, are roughly the same. If the site is at a new house the effects of the builders' work, including debris and disturbed subsoil, must be removed before a start can be made. A 3-inch layer of topsoil will be needed for the finished lawn, and where topsoil has been cleared by the builders it may be necessary to buy it. Such soil may also be used to achieve a level grade, as it is likely to make for irregular growth if you denude one area of topsoil in order to fill up a hollow in another. When constructing terraces or making other changes involving considerable movements of earth, it is best to remove the topsoil altogether, make the required levels with the subsoil, and then return the topsoil. Levels are easily made by laying a straightedge with spirit level on pegs set into the ground at convenient intervals.

Good drainage is essential to a lawn, and, according to the heaviness and stickiness of the soil and subsoil, you should consider whether drainage tile may be necessary, either in the form of a single pipeline or with lateral pipes stemming from the main pipeline, which empties into a dry well or, preferably, a drain. In most cases of clayey soil it will be sufficient to work in limestone or gypsum at the appropriate rate after deep digging. If you decide that tiles are needed to make a piped drain, cover them with gravel or cinders below the level of the topsoil.

Ideally, after the preliminary digging, the ground should be allowed to overwinter. This helps to settle the soil and leaves it ready to work in the drier spring weather. However, most gardeners like to get on with tasks, once started, and by hoeing and raking they will break up the clods and level the surface, while watching for weeds. Going over the ground with the heel of your shoe to feel out and consolidate soft spots is known as "heeling." There is no real need to use a heavy roller; a light roller such as may be found on the back of modern hand mowers should be all that is needed. During the soil preparation the surface may be improved with sand if the soil is heavy, or with peat and well-rotted compost if the land is light. Peat may also be included with the sand on heavy soils. Almost any amount of sand or grit, and peat at 7 pounds per square yard, will be suitable for heavy clay; over 14 pounds per square yard of manure or well-rotted compost and the same amount of peat will help light soils. A proprietary lawn fertilizer may also be added at this stage. When you have raked and double-raked and gently firmed out every bump and hollow, you are ready for planting.

Sod or Seed?

The great advantage of sod is that it gets off to a quicker start than seed. Late fall and winter (when no frost is about) are the best times for sodding. It can be done in the spring if there is not too much drought, and even in the summer provided water is supplied adequately in dry weather. Sod is simple to lay, requires less fine preparation of the soil, and is usually more robust against the ravages of weather, disease, and garden pests such as birds. Despite these advantages, seed is cheaper and is easy to obtain at high quality. Even the most excellent sod will deteriorate in places where it was not intended to grow. Seed-sowing is limited to the period of August to September, or spring, or even early summer when the dangers of drought and competition from weeds are greater.

Sodding

When ordering sod, ask for the names of the grasses it contains. These should be fine-quality kinds, such as bluegrass, bents, and fescues for an ornamental lawn. They should be free of weeds and disease. If not regularly thick, put them upside down in a box of standard thickness and slice off the extra soil with a two-handled shear or a carving knife.

Sod may come in 1-square-foot sizes, or 1 × 2 feet, or 1 × 3 feet. Do not pile them, but keep them flat until laid. Keep in mind the pattern made by bricks in a wall when laying sod and you will not go wrong. Do not forget to rake in a final dressing of a complete fertilizer before laying the sod, and use planks to prevent heavy treading on the newly laid lawn. Start from a corner of the site. Use a garden line for straight sections and cut curving edges with a half-moon edger once the turf is laid, using a hose to give good, graceful curves. Make sure the sod is set as close together as possible and topdress with sandy soil afterward to fill in gaps between sod. Further topdressings may be given when growth begins and the regular program of maintenance is being followed.

Seeding

A finer tilth is needed for seeding, and a complete garden fertilizer must be mixed with the raked soil a few days beforehand. Grass seed can be bought ready-mixed, or you can mix your own. You will need about 2 to 3 pounds for 1000 square feet and some in reserve for areas that may need to be reseeded.

Some special dwarf varieties of grass are now available which require less mowing. The following are suggested for various types of lawn. In general, the best grasses — bluegrass, fescues, and bents — germinate more slowly than ryegrass or meadow grass.

Before sowing, rake the site so that the tiny furrows will catch the seed. You can soak the seed in a mild solution of antiseptic to put off birds and mix it with sand to make distribution easier. A distributor may be used, or use rods or lines to divide the site into square yards and sow by hand. The seed should be lightly raked-in after sowing, traversing the lines of the original raking. Do not roll until the seedlings have developed. Do not expect germination for anything from 10 to 20 days. When the grass reaches about 3 inches high, mow it, with the blades set about 2 inches high. When the grass is established, it can be mowed regularly to about 2 inches. Certain warm-season grasses, such as Bermuda grass and zoysias, may be mowed at a height of ¾ to 1½ inches.

Watch out for weeds or alien grasses and remove them while small, without disturbing the sown grass.

Tools for Lawn Maintenance

Though man's ingenuity in devising machines to take over physical labor is boundless, buy only tools that are really useful.

HAND MOWERS   All that is needed unless the lawn area exceeds several thousand square feet, or unless you are a lawn enthusiast who wishes to cut the lawn at least twice a week in May and June (a good practice, by the way), is a simple hand mower. The mower should have a large roller and be adjustable, so as to cut between ½ and 2 inches in height. A grass-catcher is desirable.

POWERED REEL MOWERS   These have a similar type of curved blades to the above, which form a cylinder and cut against a bottom plate, but are powered by gasoline or electric motors. Powered machines are easily able to cut a wider swath than human effort alone will allow, so the blades may be 14 or 18 inches wide, compared to the conventional 12-inch hand mower. Electrically powered mowers are simple to operate, quiet, and do not produce exhaust gases.

A well-made, well-maintained lawn sets off a garden in much the same way that well-polished shoes set off a good suit.

	Parts by weight		
Top quality lawns for sunny area	60%	Kentucky Bluegrass such as Merion, Fylking, or Windsor	
	40%	Creeping Red Fescue	
Children's play lawn	60 to 80%	Tall Fescue such as Kentucky 31	(ryegrass must be mown regularly or it becomes inordinately tough)
	0 to 20%	Kentucky Bluegrass	
	0 to 10%	Perennial Ryegrass	
For shady places	40%	Kentucky Bluegrass	
	30%	Creeping Red Fescue	
	30%	Chewings Fescue	

They are probably better for smaller lawns. You will also need a hand mower for odd corners and verges where grit and stones might affect the mower blades.

ROTARY MOWERS   There is no doubt that rotary mowers, powered by gasoline or electricity, are marvelous for dealing with areas of rough and tall grass. The rotary mower has a horizontal blade that whirls around and chops off the heads of everything that comes within its compass. The speed at which the blade rotates provides its cutting effectiveness, and a hundred revolutions per yard produce a better finish than 50 revolutions. The newest type of rotary mower runs on the "hovercraft" principle and has the special merit of making a close cut and following undulations and banks easily, as well as dissecting the grass into myriads of tiny fragments so that no collecting bag is needed for the mown grass.

EDGE TRIMMERS   Shears are the cheapest edgers and rely not so much on the sharpness of the blade as the perfection of the scissor-like mating of the two blades. The long-handled blades that make a vertical cut are the most useful, although there are types adapted to cutting horizontally. You can also buy electrically operated trimmers with oscillating teeth. Aids to edge-trimming include the half-moon blade which will enable you to recut edges that have lost their definition, and both plastic and metal strip will help to consolidate an edge once it is defined.

DISTRIBUTORS AND SPREADERS   Ranging from knapsack to wheeled designs, these are excellent for distributing fertilizers and solid weed killers evenly in powder or liquid form.

SPRINKLERS   Most lawn enthusiasts end up buying automatic hose-attached water sprinklers, although many types are available.

AERATORS AND DRAINERS   Scarifiers are very useful for freeing the grass from moss and other impediments. The "Springbok" fork, consisting of springy powerful wires, is most useful. Aerating the soil becomes important when it becomes too compact, and special hollow-tined forks working on the soil will pull out cores, leaving it free for air, water, and fertilizer. Spiked rollers achieve the same effect.

OTHER EQUIPMENT   Wheelbarrows with rubber tires are best for lightness and stability. Conventional lawn brooms and rakes are useful, too.

If you inherit an old lawn, it is possible to renovate it without digging it up. Simply water it with a contact weed killer and the top growth will die off within a few days in sunny weather without the weed killer affecting the soil beneath. After about a week, proceed as though aerating it. Do this thoroughly, leaving holes every few inches, and remove the cores to the compost heap. Into the holes brush in a mixture of lime or gypsum and well-matured compost which has been screened. Grass likes a soil which is only slightly acid. Test the soil for acid, and if you find it much below pH 6·5 (see soil-testing), add a little ground limestone to the mixture — up to 4 ounces per square yard. Sand or peat can be added to the mixture, according to whether the soil is heavy or light. Work it well into the holes in the soil and then scarify to get rid of the old grass roots. The surface should then be thinly covered with a mixture of sand and peat with ordinary lawn fertilizer in the prescribed quantity. Lightly rake and sow the seed of your choice.

Diseases

FUSARIUM PATCH   Patches of yellowing dead grass appear sometimes in summer but mostly in spring and fall under conditions of excessive moisture. The patches growing up to a foot in size eventually join up and should be immediately treated with a good fungicide. Prevention is better than cure, so encourage healthy turf and do not overfeed with sulfate of ammonia.

CORTICUM   The grass becomes discolored like straw, with tiny red threads appearing on the grass blades. It is a late-summer to fall occurrence and may be controlled by fungicide application.

FAIRY RINGS   Circles of exceptionally green grass may develop because of the action of certain fungi that feed on the soil, not the grass. They are difficult to eradicate chemically, and the only remedy otherwise is to dig out and resod.

A lawn need not be level to look good. It needs only be green, well mowed, and weed free. *(Courtesy of Suttons Seeds.)*

Fences, Hedges, Paths and Edgings

Fences, hedges, paths, and edgings, together with drives and steps, all serve essentially utilitarian functions. Pergolas, patios, and garden walls, also included in this chapter, are less functional. The fact that something is functional does not mean that it must be unattractive: far from it. Each of these items could easily become an aesthetically pleasing feature of the garden. There are conflicts, of course, the main conflict being that it usually costs more to make something decorative than it does to accept the utilitarian alternative, but this is by no means always the case. An ugly drive or pathway can ruin the appearance of an otherwise impeccably maintained garden, while a well-designed path or drive constructed of interesting materials and in a style in keeping with the garden can greatly enhance its appearance.

It is always important to try to relate the design of a drive or pathway, as well as the materials used, to the overall design of the garden. The choice of materials will be partly a matter of cost and partly a matter of taste. Your house reflects your taste. The same taste will govern the type of garden you will make, and the two will probably coincide, so that the style of the garden will match the style of the house. Again, when it comes to planning a patio or drive, let your taste be the ultimate arbiter in the style and choice of materials. Before making up your mind what to do, see what other people have done, and don't be afraid of being eccentric. If you use styles and materials you like, the chances are that they will harmonize.

Drives

Bluestone, when properly laid and maintained, is probably the most attractive material for drives, and it is inexpensive to lay and to maintain. It is important to stress that the gravel or stone must be laid properly. The object is to achieve a firm surface that will not become a clayey quagmire in wet weather, that will not develop potholes, and that will not be tracked into the house when dry. The first essential is a good foundation. This should be made of a layer about 6 inches deep of builder's rubble or bank-run gravel, well compacted. On normal soils this will provide all the drainage that is needed for a gravel drive, but on soggy soils 3-inch drainage pipes should be laid in a herringbone pattern at a depth of 6 inches. When the gravel is laid, it should be raked and rolled until a firm, even texture has been achieved. The main disadvantage of gravel is that weeds can grow in it, but this really is not a problem, because they can easily be controlled by one of the persistent weed killers.

Many people prefer drives with firmer surfaces,

A good hedge is a real joy, but to look good it must be properly cut and shaped and well fed.

such as asphalt or tarmac, mainly because they believe they are longer-lasting and need less maintenance. If this is to be so, they must be laid as carefully as gravel. When tarmac or asphalt drives are laid over old gravel drives it is important that all loose chippings be scraped off the surface of the old drive, that the surface be re-leveled, and that persistent weeds be killed before the new surface is laid. Both tarmac and asphalt should be laid at least 1 inch thick. The main difference between tarmac and asphalt is that tarmac is laid cold and is porous, whereas asphalt is laid hot and is not porous. Weeds are more likely to come up through tarmac than through asphalt. In either case it is important that the drive is properly leveled and cambered. Unless this is done, puddles will form on asphalt drives, and frost will quickly break up the surface of tarmac drives. Gaps should be left in the edgings for water to drain away into lawns or borders.

Concrete drives are long-lasting, but the glaring white of untreated concrete is unattractive to many people. In addition, such drives are relatively expensive to lay. They should be placed on a solid foundation of bank-run gravel, and the concrete should be laid 4 inches thick. A more attractive and economic proposition is to lay the concrete in two parallel strips for the wheels of a car, and possibly to use some contrasting material for the strip in the middle and at each side. Grass is unsuitable for this strip, as oil drips would soon kill patches and make it unattractive, but pebbles or granite stones embedded in a weak mortar, loose granite chips, or larger chunks of random flagstone are all practical and attractive alternatives. Another possibility is to lay a herringbone pattern of bricks between the strips of concrete and to use parallel rows of paving slabs instead of the concrete.

Paths

The basic principles of constructing garden paths are similar to those for drives, but scaled down. The layer of bank gravel need not be so deep, and if concrete is used, it need be laid only 2 inches thick. It is seldom advisable to make a garden path less than 3 feet wide, and 4 feet is usually better, if you can afford the space. This width allows for the passage of wheelbarrows, lawn mowers, and other garden implements, as well as for the temporary intrusion of path-side plants. It is always a shame to have to cut back one of these plants just as it is coming into flower, merely because it is obstructing a pathway. Except in very large gardens where special visual effects may be needed, there is seldom any point in constructing paths wider than 4 feet. In general, paths should be level with the ground on either side of them, except, of course, where they divide raised beds of a rock garden from a lawn, for example. They should also be flat rather than cambered, as this makes them more comfortable to walk along.

Where gravel is used, a foundation of 3 to 4 inches is adequate on most soils, but on heavy land the

How to lay a path The top picture shows the bedding for the path: *1.* Coarse gravel. *2.* A finer grade of gravel. *3.* Sand onto which the blocks *(4)* should be placed in the second picture shows granite stones being hammered into place with a wooden mallet, a separate level being used to ensure that the path is level. The next picture shows a similar technique being used for laying paving slabs.

foundation needs to be 6 inches deep, and on really badly drained land 3-inch drain pipes should be laid in a herringbone pattern at 18-inch intervals. A layer of gravel 2-inches thick is sufficient. Concrete, when used for a garden path, looks utilitarian, and it is usually preferable to try to find some alternative material. Bricks land in a herringbone pattern look particularly attractive, but the bricks must be sound or they will quickly be broken up by frost. There is a tendency for brick paths in shaded situations to become slippery. The slipperiness is caused by algae. It is a hazard that can easily be cured by watering with a proprietary algicide. Other brick-like materials can also be used to make attractive garden paths. When creating brick, cobble, or granite stone paths it is best to lay a foundation of bank gravel and then a 1-inch layer of concrete. Once this has set, another 1-inch layer of weak mortar should be laid and the bricks or stones embedded in this. Afterward, the bricks or stones can be pointed with a strong cement mixture, or earth can be used and grass allowed to grow up between the bricks. If this is the intention, extra care must be taken in getting the path level, otherwise it will be almost impossible to mow over it.

Paths do not necessarily need to be solid or continuous. Often "stepping-stones" in the lawn or through a rock garden are just as serviceable. Paving slabs, which can be either of the old stone type or of the modern composition type, are the easiest materials for paths of this kind, but there are alternatives. If the stepping-stones are required in the lawn, all that is necessary is to take out the turf to a sufficient depth, put in plywood forms, and lay the concrete *in situ*. Slabs made by this method can be rectangular, circular, or irregular in shape. A similar type of stepping-stone path can be laid between borders, simply placing the stepping-stones on the bare earth. It is important that the ground be thoroughly weeded and dug and then allowed to settle before the path is laid. Random stone flags make the most attractive paths of this type. Once laid, the earth between the flags can be kept clean of weeds by the use of foliar weed killers, or creeping plants can be allowed to establish themselves between the flags.

Flagstone paving is probably the most popular of all materials for paths. Again, either stone or composition paving can be used. Both are long-lasting, although stone is more expensive. To make a lasting path, flagstone should be laid on a firm foundation of rubble and concrete, embedded in mortar, and pointed with a strong cement. If spot plants are to be grown between the paving slabs, holes should be left in the concrete foundation for drainage.

Grass paths winding between borders or shrubberies can look good, but they will not withstand really hard wear. The best grass paths are made from sod, but if seed is to be sown, a considerable proportion of *Agrostis tenuis,* an exceptionally hard-wearing grass, should be included.

Steps

Steps are needed wherever a path passes from one level to another and frequently to provide a means of transition from one level of a garden to another. It is usual to construct the steps from the same material as that used for the path; where the steps do not occur in a path the choice of materials remains much the same. The important thing is that each step should be level: steps that slope away from you as you walk down them are lethal, particularly in wet or snowy weather. If they cover a large enough area to warrant a slope so that surface water will run off, the slope should be sideways, and a drop of ½ inch in 6 feet is adequate.

Edgings

It used to be the fashion to use formal edgings to every path, border, lawn, and drive in the garden. The main materials used were random stone slabs faced on one edge and inserted upright in the ground, brick, tiles, or low box hedges. That fashion has now largely passed, and in general gardens have gained from its passing. There are still, however, places where edgings are desirable — for example, to separate a border from a gravel path or drive. There are a number of possible materials that can be used. Concrete, though not the most attractive, is one of the most widely used. It is serviceable and long-lasting, although harsh to the eye in gardens that are in other ways mellow. Concrete edging can be bought in 4 or 5 foot precast lengths, with rounded edges on the surface that will be aboveground. These precast lengths need to be set in a base of concrete. Brick is far more attractive in most gardens, but the bricks must be sound and hard. The bricks can be laid horizontally as they are in walls, in which case they will need to be laid on a narrow foundation and cemented together with mortar, or they can be laid diagonally, or inserted vertically. Whichever style is adopted, care must be taken to ensure that, where they are to be laid in a straight line, the line is really straight and preferably level. This is most easily done by using a line and spirit level and driving pegs into the ground beside the line of edging to the desired height. It is usually best to use mortar when laying a brick edging. If the bricks are simply set in the soil they are liable to move, and the line becomes untidy.

Tiles also make attractive edgings. These tiles are not of the type used on roofs, but of the type once fashionable in kitchen gardens. They come in a variety of colors and patterns but are usually of unglazed dark-gray brick, either crenellated or with a barley-sugar twist along the top. The easiest way of laying them is to dig a shallow trench, vertical on one side only and kept straight by means of a board, place the tiles in position, and then lay a layer of concrete along the exposed side. Stone slabs, faced on one edge only, also make an attractive informal edging and should be laid in a similar fashion.

Wood edgings are sometimes used. These may be

either of wooden planks or more informally of lopped tree limbs. Neither is as harsh in appearance as some of the other types of edging, but neither is as long-lasting. If planks are used, they should be 6 × 2 inches and should be buried to half their depth in the soil and secured to stout pegs by means of galvanized nails. The pegs should be 2 feet long, inserted on the inside of the edgings at intervals of not more than 6 feet.

Patios

Patios are basically places for sitting out in the garden when the weather is good, and as such are usually paved, either with irregular or formal paving slabs, but there is a wealth of other materials that can be used to provide a variety of surfaces, colors, and textures. From a design point of view, a patio is a link between the house and the garden, and it should reflect the styles of both.

The method of laying a patio is basically the same as that for a paved drive or path. There must be a firm foundation and a 2-inch layer of concrete upon which the surface material will be placed. A patio should always be given a slope, so that water will drain away from the house, and a drop of 1 in 60 is sufficient to achieve this, provided the surface material is laid relatively level. To achieve this drop, the patio should be marked out with wooden pegs driven into the ground to the required depth.

Because patios are often essentially sun-traps, they provide an ideal place for growing tender plants that might not thrive in the open garden. This is particularly true of patios bounded by walls or fences, even if these are quite low. Whether or not you intend to grow tender plants, you will want some color in the patio, and beds and borders should be planned before any concrete is laid, as should the position of any tree that is to be grown to cast shade. If the beds are situated at the foot of a wall, they need to be at least 18 inches wide, as walls tend to create rain shadows; i.e., places protected from rain.

It is not necessary to build a patio on a rectangular plan, although patios are usually fairly formal places and lend themselves to this treatment. They can be any shape you wish, so long as they fulfill their basic function. They are often made more attractive if a number of differently colored materials and different textures are used. Areas of pea gravel set in concrete relieve the monotony of flagstone paving, and so do areas of brick. Garden pools, often with fountains, are frequently incorporated in patios, and the sound of falling water is certainly refreshing on really hot days. Statuary, urns, and tubs of flowers all add to the gaiety of a patio.

Fences

These are purely utilitarian, serving to mark a boundary or to hide some unsightly object. They are usually, by their very nature, unattractive objects, but they need not remain so. Most types of fencing lend themselves to having plants trained against them. Solid fences are ideal to train roses and other climbing plants against, while mesh fences are ideal for growing twining plants. Ivies, including the variegated forms, are excellent for covering north-facing fences.

Of the different types of fencing available, fences of galvanized wire mesh are probably the least durable, although they are not as obtrusive as fences of the more solid variety. Chain-link fencing is very popular and is long-lasting if given some upkeep. It is good for repelling unwanted visitors but gives little screen value. Of the longer lasting wooden types, redwood or cypress fencing is the best: it will last for a lifetime but is considerably more expensive than most of its alternatives. Split oak is more durable than sawed oak. Pine and fir are alternatives, but they need regular treatment with preservatives and even then will not last as long as oak. Interwoven fencing can be bought in prefabricated sections of varying heights and lengths and is usually supplied with posts and fittings. The panels should be fitted between the posts, not on one side only.

Walls

A well-built brick or stone wall, particularly when it has had time to mellow, is a great asset to a garden, but in view of its high cost it is not usually an economic proposition. Fences and hedges usually do just as well in providing privacy or hiding unsightly objects, so the expense can seldom be justified. The average gardener can easily erect a wall up to 3 feet on his own, but he would be unwise to attempt anything higher unless he is an experienced bricklayer.

Low walls, 2 or 3 feet high, are often used to mark the boundary across the front of a garden. They are also useful where something permanent is needed to separate a patio from the rest of the garden. Materials other than brick can be used for low walls, and it is very often a good idea to use local, traditional building materials where these occur. Among such materials are random stone, flint, both either dressed or not, and sea-washed pebbles in coastal areas.

A type of walling rapidly gaining in popularity is the pierced wall, often known as Italian walling. The effect is more that of a screen than of a solid wall, and in small gardens the lightness and airiness of such pierced walls is much to be preferred to the heaviness of a solid brick wall. Manufacturers now produce pierced wall blocks in a wide variety of patterns. Brick may also be laid in an open pattern.

Hedges

Most gardens benefit from having at least one good length of hedge, whether to provide shelter from cruel winds, privacy, a background to a herbaceous border, or quite simply because a good well-kept hedge is a joy in itself. The problem with hedges is, of course,

a) These old rough brick tiles still make excellent, natural-looking paths in gardens.

b) Patios provide a place to sit and enjoy the garden. Here very modern materials have been used.

c) A flagstone path. Flagstone is the most popular surface for paths.

d) Steps need to be carefully made or they can be dangerous, especially for the very young and the elderly.

that they have to be maintained, but with modern power-driven clippers this is very little trouble. Hedges should always be slightly narrower at the top than at the bottom, and the plants should be planted alternately 10 to 15 inches apart.

Privet is probably the most ubiquitous of of hedging plants. It is cheap, easily raised from cuttings, and relatively fast-growing. It withstands clipping well, does not suffer from winds, and will grow in practically any soil and situation. Its disadvantages are that it is apt to lose its leaves in winter, needs clipping at least three times a year, preferably four times, and that it has greedy roots that rob plants growing close to it.

Common privet is a dull green, but golden privet is cheerfully bright. The two can be intermixed, either planted alternately or planted two of golden privet to one of green privet, and hedges of this type are probably more colorful than hedges made of only one type of privet. Beech makes a more permanent hedge and is usually recommended where a taller hedge is required. It will make a good hedge up to as much as 8 or 10 feet. It thrives in all soils and stands clipping well, normally needing clipping only twice a year. It is valued for the freshness of the green of the new leaves as they appear in spring and for the russet coloring of its leaves in fall. These are retained through the winter. Apart from the green-leaved form, there is a purple-leaved form and the well-known copper beech, with leaves of a rather lighter color than those of the purple beech. Beech hedges may be composed either of all green-leaved plants or of these intermixed with the colored-leaf forms. Hedges made entirely of copper or purple beech tend to look rather heavy but are very striking when used for pleached hedges. Another plant suited to almost all soils is hornbeam, which is often confused with beech. Indeed, hornbeam is so much like beech that many so-called beech hedges are actually composed of hornbeam.

Evergreen hedges have the advantage of maintaining privacy throughout the winter months. They may be composed of either broad-leaved shrubs such as holly or of coniferous shrubs such as yew or cupressus. Of the broad-leaved evergreens there can be little doubt that English holly makes the most attractive hedge, particularly if it is allowed to grow tall — to about 12 feet. Such a hedge is practically impenetrable by winds or animals. The usual objection against using holly as a hedge is that the fallen leaves, with their persistent sharp spines, are liable to puncture tender fingers when weeding unsuspectingly in the garden. This is not a serious drawback: there are many forms that have only the terminal spine. The common holly itself has dark, shining green leaves, but there are forms with leaves variegat-

ed either gold or white, and these make more colorful hedges. It is not advisable to mix the green and the variegated forms, since they have very different rates of growth.

Cherry laurel, although often used, is really only suitable for gardens of the largest size. To look good it needs room to grow and should be at least 8 feet tall. Its main problem, apart from the space it requires, is that is needs to be trimmed by hand, each shoot being cut individually. If it is simply cut with shears or with a power-driven tool, the leaves that have been cut in half will turn brown and spoil the appearance of the whole hedge. And it has greedy roots: nothing worthwhile will grow within 10 feet of a laurel hedge.

Yew makes a particularly attractive formal hedge. It is favored not because of the slowness of its growth, but because it makes a particularly neat hedge and will stand trimming well. Yew hedges have great longevity, and the same hedge will look just the same in 100 or 200 years as it does today. It is extremely hardy and will grow on all soils and makes an excellent hedge from 3 to 20 feet high. There are few other backgrounds that show off the colorfulness of a herbaceous border better than a well-clipped yew hedge. There are forms with golden leaves, and these look good either mixed with the green form or on their own. Yew is poisonous to many animals, and this should be borne in mind when planting a yew hedge or disposing of the clippings.

How to trim a hedge A well-made hedge should always be narrower at the top than at the bottom. The diagram shows stages in the training of a hedge from left to right. Most hedges need pruning at least twice a year to keep them in good shape.

The Rose Garden

The Rose Garden
a) Roses are perennial favorites of gardeners.

If you choose your roses wisely, they will be in flower from April to November. The flowers, from fully double to single, and all extremely beautiful, have a wide range of form and every subtle shading and combination of color except blue.

Do not believe those who say that modern roses have no perfume. Some do not, but many do. However, this has always been true. Probably the enormous popularity of floribundas since the last war has been the cause of the all-too-common generalization. Large numbers of these new roses were scentless or nearly so, but breeders are bringing the scent back fast in the latest varieties. There has always been a good proportion of perfumed Hybrid Teas (HTs).

The range of size and form of rose bushes is quite varied — from the 6-inch miniatures for rockeries or edging plants, through short, medium, and tall shrubs, to 40- and 50-foot climbers.

Roses can be used for permanent bedding, formal or informal, and climbers and ramblers can cover your house, grow up pillars, cover arches and pergolas and fences, or wander at random through trees. Standards or weeping standards give height to a rose bed or can form colorful focal points on their own as solitary specimens. HTs, floribundas, and shrub roses can be used as hedging plants — low hedges to line a path or divide off part of the garden; spreading, undisciplined hedges of medium height, using some of the hybrid musk roses like "Penelope" or "Vanity" or some of the rugosa rose, which will be one mass of bloom for several weeks; or hedges up to 4 feet or so, like a line of guardsmen with pink hats, if you use a variety like "Queen Elizabeth." The thorns of many will make them intruder-proof.

Many of the shrub roses mix well with other shrubs, and those with long, arching sprays, laden with blossom along their whole length ("Frühlingsgold," "Frühlingsmorgen," "Canary bird," "Nevada") give a new dimension to rose-growing.

Inevitably, someone will say: "But shrub roses only flower once, don't they?" If that is your criterion, you should fork up your forsythias and dig up your buddleias for the same crime. But, in any case, this is not true of many shrub roses. There are many that are continuous or repeat flowering, and a great many of those that do flower only once have a bonus in the form of most decorative hips in the fall.

Some roses can be used for ground cover. The

A delightfully simple front garden using tree roses and bedding plants.

parent of many ramblers, *Rosa wichuraiana,* and some of its hybrids, such as "Max Graf," will grow prostrate along the ground, rooting as they go. Their shiny, dark leaves smother weeds, and their single white flowers (pink for "Max Graf") appear in summer and are borne over a long period.

Roses are still remarkably inexpensive. They cost less than most other shrubs and, unless you get a dud, they live for 15, 20, or more years. They do not really require a great deal of care, although they will certainly perform better with regular but not particularly arduous attention. How, then, to get the best out of them?

The most usual (and very effective) way of using HTs and floribundas is as permanent bedding plants. For some reason these two kinds of roses do not mix very well with other border plants. This is especially true of HTs, and it is best to have them in beds of their own. The size and shape of these beds will probably depend on the size and shape of your garden, but, if possible, try to surround them with grass, which makes the best framework, or with paved paths, which also are quite effective.

Island beds in a lawn are most attractive, but you will have to cut and edge the grass around them. If you are young enough, you will probably think it is worthwhile, but even then remember that straight-sided beds are easier to care for than round beds.

It will save a good deal of work if you have at least your main rose beds backing onto walls or hedges around the lawn, and here it is possible and much more attractive to have the front of the bed coming out in a wide, sweeping curve. This will break up the rectangular outline of so many gardens, and the mower will take such a curve with ease.

Hedges, especially those made up of privet, suck the fertility out of the soil like a vacuum cleaner. Plant your roses at least 18 inches from the hedge. Near walls, particularly the walls of a house with overhanging eaves, the soil is likely to be very dry. Roses need plenty of water (but good drainage), so do not plant them too close.

Very large or very small beds can be successful with a mixed planting of only one or two of each variety. Medium-sized beds can look spotty except during the main flush of flowers. If you want different varieties in an average-sized bed, group four or more of each variety together, but when you are choosing them, bear in mind their relative heights as well as their colors.

A round bed can be very attractive with cultivars planted in concentric circles and rising toward the center, by staging the heights. Or you can group different cultivars like the spokes of a wheel, widening from one bush near the center to three, four, or five at the circumference, depending on the size of the bed. A standard or half-standard makes a centerpiece to top it off, and it is probably best to choose a contrasting cultivar for this.

Color-blending is important. Strong colors may clash or kill each other; whites, creams, and pale pinks make good dividers. An unusual and striking bed can be made by starting at one end with white and shading to cream, apricot, pale pink, pink, light red, scarlet, orange, and finally yellow. Mauve roses can look washed-out if not placed carefully, but they go well with yellows and whites.

All this applies equally to HTs and to floribundas, although it is probably best not to mix the two, as their habit of flowering is so different. An edging of low-growing floribundas for a bed of HTs can, however, look well and will probably give color to the bed during the rest period of the HTs in July and August. Miniature roses, too, can form an attractive edging, and they start to flower very early, before most HTs. Give them plenty of room, though, or their bigger neighbors may grow forward and shade them.

On the subject of edging, another useful pointer is that gray-leaved plants always look well with roses and help to set them off. Try dwarf lavender or pinks around a bed or a clump of *Senecio laxifolius* at one end of a bigger bed to give contrast.

Shrub roses can be grown in a mixed group on their own (making sure that the taller ones are at the back) or interspersed with other shrubs, provided that they can get plenty of sun. The more lax growers will welcome the chance to strap-hang onto stronger branches growing through them. All the bigger ones make wonderful solo specimen shrubs, perhaps on a lawn, but once again do not forget that you will have to mow around them. The 7-foot, arching growths of cultivars like "Frühlingsgold" and "Nevada" will, like a hypochondriac, catch anything. They can be mixed with other shrubs, but leave at least a 3-foot circle of clear earth around each one for mulching and so that the roots of the other shrubs and the roses do not rob each other.

Climbers can be used in several ways. One of the commonest is on the walls of a house, but do not have only roses there, particularly if they are once-flowering. Grow them through something else — soft-blue ceanothus with yellow roses, for instance; chaenomeles, which will flower before the roses; or a climber like one of the many clematis, up through them. If you choose the right varieties, you can have bloom on your wall right through until fall.

Almost any climber or rambler of reasonable vigor will look wonderful wandering up at random through old trees, provided their habit of growth is not too stiff. If it is, they are apt to send out shoots at rather awkward and ungainly angles, and what is really wanted is pliable canes that will weep down with the weight of their flowers. Two wonderful roses for this, if you have a really big strong tree, are *Rosa longiscuspis* and *Rosa filipes* "Kifts gate." Another is "Wedding Day." All three have really huge clusters of small, sweet-smelling white flowers that will hang down from the branches like a vast lace shawl. But they are not for very small gardens. Try "Purity," "Sanders White," or the almost-blue "Veilchenblau" for them. If you want pink, "Chaplin's Pink Climber" is showy and has a long flowering season.

You may want to exhibit some of your roses. If so, choose varieties of HTs with large blooms that have high, firm, pointed centers, have reflexing outer petals, and that keep their shape well and do not open too quickly. They should be shown in the half- to three-quarter open stage, as a fully open rose will never win a prize. Since almost all roses will open much more quickly in a hot show tent, it takes a good judge of timing to achieve this, and Keats was surely in the marquee, staging his blooms, when he scribbled on the back of his show schedule: *As though the rose should shut, and be a bud again.*

Some good cultivars for showing and that are also good garden roses are "Rose Gaujard," "Pink Favorite," "My Choice," "Stella," "Fragrant Cloud," "Perfecta," "Grandpa Dickson," "Mischief," "Silver Lining," and "Peace," although most of them, if not all, will need the removal of all but the main bud on a stem if they are to achieve their best size. Floribunda trusses for showing should have the maximum number of unfaded and undamaged blooms out at one time. Almost any variety will do, provided the trusses are good ones for that particular variety.

Exhibiting is good fun and can make you a lot of friends.

Planting Roses

Roses will live longer and do better if the ground they are to grow in is well-prepared beforehand.

For your rose bed, choose a spot that gets plenty of sun, is well-drained, is not overhung by trees, and is not exposed to strong winds. Almost any type of soil will grow roses, but some will be rather better than others. Since you are hardly likely to move simply to get the best soil, the following suggestions will at least help you make the best of the soil you have.

In September, well before the roses arrive, the bed should be well dug over to about twice the depth of the blade of your shovel. Plenty of manure, if you can get it, or well-rotted compost should be dug into the soil. You and the bed now have about two months to recover and settle down before the roses come.

The roses will probably arrive in late October or November and should be planted as soon as possible.

Two of the most popular roses raised in this century, "Elizabeth of Glamis" and "Fragrant Cloud."

a) One of the best soft-yellow roses, "Golden Pride."

(b) *'Blanche Malleria',* one of the finest pure white HT roses.

If, however, it is frosty or raining and the ground is waterlogged, wait for a fine, frost-free day. If left in their packing and put in a cool, frost-free place, the roses will come to no harm for a few days. If the delay has to be longer than this, unpack them and check for damage or inferior plants, which should be sent back to the nursery for replacement. Soak them in a bucket of water for about an hour, and then heel them in. This means burying the roots at least 6 inches deep in a trench in a spare piece of ground; left like this, they will be quite happy for weeks, if need be. If you ordered your new roses late and they do not arrive until after Christmas, there is no need to worry. They can safely be planted any time the soil can be easily worked.

Planting day arrives, and you dig a hole for your first rose. This should be about 18 inches in diameter — large enough to allow the roots to be spread out. The bed has already been manured, but if you make the hole about 18 inches deep you will have room to put an extra shovelful of manure or compost at the bottom of it. Mix it with the soil there, tread it down, and cover it with about 3 inches of soil to prevent the roots from coming in direct contact with it until it is properly broken down, or it may burn them.

Mix a bucketful of soil and fine-grade peat and add three or four handfuls of bonemeal or powdered rose fertilizer to it. This is your planting mixture.

Bring your roses to the bed, wrapped in wet packing material to keep the roots moist. Take out the first of them and shorten any very thick or long roots by about one-third to encourage the fine, fibrous feeding roots to grow from them. Put the rose in the hole, with the roots spread out.

If you are lucky, the budding union — the thickened portion at the top of the root from which the canes are sprouting — will be just above soil level. You can check this by putting a bamboo cane or a hoe handle across the hole. If it is too low, add some more soil to the bottom of the hole. If it is too high, remove some, but do not expose any manure you may have put there.

I have often read that the soil at the bottom of the hole should be mounded up in the middle, the rose placed centrally on this, and the roots spread out evenly all down the sides of the mound. If you get roses you can do this with, you are lucky. I never have. As often as not they all point in one direction and are as reluctant to change direction permanently as spring steel. So spread them out as well as you can and, holding the rose in position with one hand, pull in some soil from the surrounding bed to cover them, interspersing it with handfuls of planting mixture. When there is enough in the hole to hold the rose steady on its own, tread it down gently but firmly, fill up the hole with more earth and planting mixture, and tread again. Finally, you can build up the earth slightly above ground level to allow for any settling that may take place.

That is it. Repeat for the other roses, spacing them about 18 to 36 inches apart, and finally give each one of them at least two gallons of water.

Planting Container-Grown Roses

Water these well about one hour before planting and then follow the procedure as outlined above, trying to keep the earth from the container as intact as possible, so that the roots are not disturbed.

Planting Standard Roses

Again the same general instructions apply, but drive a stake into the middle of the hole before planting. It should be left at a height where it will just reach up into the head of the standard to give it some support. Standards particularly should not be planted too deeply. Many are budded onto rugosa rose stock, and this will sucker freely at the best of times, but more so if it is planted deeply. It should be possible to see the soil mark just above the roots, showing the level at which it was planted at the nursery. Follow this.

(c) The HT rose 'Piccadily', remarkably good under most conditions.

d) A well-made rose garden contains a mixture of roses and needs a good background.

Secure with plastic ties, one about a foot from the ground and one just under the head.

Planting Climbing Roses

You will presumably plant these where they will have something to climb up or over, but find out from your nursery how big the rose will eventually be, and make sure your support is big and strong enough. If they are for the wall of your house and you have planted them correctly, well out from it where the soil is moist, you can still slant the long canes (which should not be shortened) in toward the wall and fan the roots out away from it. With many climbers you must be prepared to wait a year or two before they really become established.

If you wish to fill a gap in a bed where perhaps a rose has died, dig a hole at least 2 feet wide and 1 foot deep — more if there is room — remove the soil, and replace it with soil from another part of the garden. The old soil will be perfectly all right for growing other things.

Routine Care

Immediately after pruning (the joys of which I deal with a little later on), or at any rate in February or March if you are an early gardener, it is a good idea to spray the dormant roses with a rose fungicide to destroy or at least discourage overwintering disease spores. At the same time sprinkle a handful of a complete fertilizer around (not on) each plant and lightly hoe it in.

In April or May when the soil has begun to warm up, mulch the beds 2 to 3 inches deep with some organic matter. This will keep the moisture in and smother weeds. Trim off any wood that may have been damaged by frost since you pruned.

You now have a breathing space, but when the first flush of flowers begins to fade and drop in June or July, remove them promptly to encourage the production of new ones. Do not snap them off. Cut them with

pruning shears just above the first healthy, fully-grown leaf below the old flower. That is where a new bud will be lurking, and you should keep this up all summer if you want a continuous display.

A second handful of fertilizer per plant, also in July, will help bring on the second flush of bloom, but do not apply this later than the end of the month or new wood will be encouraged too late to ripen properly. In late autumn cut back the taller-growing roses by about one-third to prevent them from being rocked loose in the soil and possibly damaged from winter winds.

Throughout the summer and autumn watch for suckers. These are growths coming from the root stock, and they should be removed or they will weaken your plant. They will look very different from the rest of the plant. They are likely to be light green and may have seven leaflets, but not always. To be sure they are suckers, and until you have learned to recognize them immediately, trace them to their source by scraping away some of the earth where they join the plant. If they start below the budding union they are suckers and should be removed. Pulling away is the best way of ensuring that there are no sucker buds left behind. Cutting them at ground level is like pruning a rose and will only encourage more vigorous growth.

That is all there is to routine care, apart from keeping the beds clear of weeds, which is not peculiar to roses, and spraying against pests and diseases.

Pests and Diseases

Choose cultivars of rose that are known to be healthy; buy good strong plants and cultivate them well; their resistance will be that much greater. Spray as necessary.

The only diseases the average grower has to worry about are blackspot, mildew, and, sometimes, stem canker. Nobody knows how to cure any of them, but you can control them if you tackle them in time.
BLACKSPOT Round black spots on the leaves, generally seen first on the lower leaves in summer. They

A bed of the
floribunda rose
'Circus'.
Like most floribunda
roses,
this looks
best massed.

will spread, and the leaves will turn yellow and eventually drop off. If neglected over several years, this lack of leaves will weaken and eventually kill the rose. Pick off and burn any infected leaves — one of those delightfully simple things to say, like: "Be sure to pick up all the confetti afterwards."

MILDEW A whitish, powdery covering which, when bad, can cover and distort the leaves, new shoots, and buds so that they do not flower properly. It will not kill, but it looks horrible. It can appear as early as May but is not usually bad before July.

STEM CANKER Caused by a fungus that invades stems through wounds, causing a girdling of the stem by killing the tissues. It often appears as brown or purplish-brown areas on older stems.

Fortunately, there are good general rose fungicides on the market that deal with all diseases and insects. How often you spray depends on your locality, the weather, and the severity of the disease. It can be as often as once every 10 days, it can be no more than two or three times a year, or it could be not at all. In other words, each grower must find his own minimum, but when and if you do spray, wet the whole plant. The undersides of the leaves are just as important as the tops. Do not spray in the hot sun, or the leaves may scorch.

INSECTS The worst insects you are likely to be troubled with are greenfly or aphids. These and most of the lesser pests can be controlled for weeks on end by spraying with a systemic insecticide. This enters the sap of the plant and cannot be washed off by rain. Spray when attacks start. Some systemics can be mixed with the fungicides, which saves a separate spraying. If both are made by the same manufacturer it is quite easy to check this, and it will probably say so on the bottle or packet, but do be quite sure they will mix or you may be left with no leaves. Use one of the plastic pressure sprayers; they are a joy.

Pruning Roses

Most roses naturally send up new shoots each year, ideally from the base or near it, and the old shoots gradually die back. You can see this happening with wild roses in the hedges.

Roses will grow and even flower without pruning, but they will soon become leggy and deteriorate, may become diseased, and the flowers will get smaller. New shoots will be sent up, but many of these will come from the older, neglected ones, which are likely to pass disease to them and will produce few good, strong shoots.

Pruning is really only helping a rose to grow in its natural way, and, if you remember this, a lot of the apparent mysteries of pruning will vanish. You want masses of large, healthy flowers and leaves. What gives them? Strong new growth. The rose will supply it if you help.

PRUNING HYBRID TEAS Take a good sharp pair of pruning shears, look over your rose bush, and begin. Cut away, right to its base, every single weak, twiggy growth. If it is weak and twiggy, it will remain so and will not produce anything worthwhile in the future. Anything much thinner than a pencil comes into this class.

Now look for disease on any of the remaining main growths. They should be green and firm, with no traces of mildew, dieback, or other disease. If they look unhealthy, cut them out to the next healthy bud below the diseased portion. If the center of the stem you have cut is brown, this is a sign of dieback spreading downward, so cut again, moving down, bud by bud, until you reach a healthy, white wood. If there are canes crossing and perhaps rubbing against each other in the center of the bush, cut these back too, removing them completely if need be, as you should aim to open up the center of the bush to let in air.

After you have removed all the obviously undesirable elements, cut back the remainder of the canes so that they are 10 and 15 inches long, but do not go so far as using a ruler. If the bush is lopsided, you may also want to remove more from one side than the other to try to correct the balance.

Cuts should be made diagonally about ¼ inch above a healthy bud at about the same angle as the bud itself and sloping away from it. The bud should preferably face outward, so that the center of the bush you have just cleared will not become congested again, but do not worry too much about this. Sometimes you will not even be able to find a bud, but make your cut

Pruning of roses The top picture shows good and bad pruning cuts. *A* is too close to the bud; *B* is too far away from the bud; *C* is even worse; and *D* is a correct cut. The two pictures below show the pruning of bush and standard roses.

where you want it, anyway. There may well be a dormant bud hiding somewhere near, and, in any case, even if you have a bud to cut to, growth may come more vigorously from the next one down. You can and should cut off any useless stubs in the spring when you can see what is happening.

You can prune at any time during the dormant period, from about the middle of November to the middle or end of March, provided it is not frosty when you do it. In the north it is better to wait until March or even April if it is a cold spring, as the harder frosts there may cause damage. Prune roses that are planted after Thanksgiving at the time of planting, and do it more drastically than for those planted in the fall. Cut them to 3 or 4 inches, which will encourage them to produce new roots before starting on the top growth.

That is really all there is to it. It is easy if you remember why you are doing it. You may paint the ends of each cut with a protective paint to keep out diseases.

One final word. A few of the more vigorous HTs do better with less-severe pruning. "Peace" is one, and you can leave the canes 18 or more inches long. Some of the more sprawling growers, such as "Josephine Bruce" and "Percy Thrower," benefit from being pruned to an inward (or upward) facing bud. This encourages them to grow upward rather than outward.

PRUNING FLORIBUNDAS Most of what has already been said applies equally to floribundas, but as the idea with these roses is to produce masses of bloom rather than achieve quality in the individual flowers, the final stage of pruning can be less severe. Cut to the first good bud below an old flowering truss.

PRUNING STANDARD ROSES Prune as for HTs or floribundas, according to which kind your standard is grown from. However, as standards do not throw new shoots too readily from the head, pruning should be rather more severe to encourage them to do so. Try particularly to get a balanced head, as standards are generally seen from all sides.

PRUNING RAMBLER ROSES These in most cases send up whippy canes many feet long each year, coming from the base or from old wood fairly near to it. These will bear next year's flowers. After they are finished flowering, cut out all the old wood, either right to the ground or to the point from which a vigorous new shoot has sprung. The new canes should then be tied where you want them to grow, and, as all ramblers have an octopus in their ancestry, eyes in the back of your head and strong, thorn-proof gloves are recommended.

Some of the larger-flowered ramblers make the whole thing rather confusing, as they flower on both the old and the new wood. The very popular "Albertine," "Albéric Barbier," and "Paul's Scarlet Climber" are examples of this, and with them only old and obviously deteriorating wood need be removed and the side shoots trimmed back.

PRUNING CLIMBING ROSES These can often be left entirely alone unless they are actually coming in the windows. At most, the side shoots from the main growths should be cut back by about half in early autumn. Remove deadwood.

PRUNING SHRUB ROSES In general these require little if any pruning, the removal of deadwood or tangled growth, and the general shaping and control of the bushes being the deciding factor. Those that are, in fact, large floribundas should be treated as other roses of the same kind.

SELECTED ROSES

Here are a few suggested roses for your garden, from the many that are on the market. It is wise to check with other gardeners in your vicinity who are growing roses to find out which kinds do best. Check with garden club members or your local rose society. In selecting new cultivars, consider the All-American Selections. These have been evaluated in over 20 trial gardens throughout the United States for at least two years, and the selection of the winners is based on the observations and evaluations of the judges.

HYBRID TEA — GRANDIFLORA

The hybrid tea roses are the large, classically formed flowers, generally with pointed buds, on strong stems, and often with fragrance. They may be referred to as "monthly" roses since they flower throughout the growing season, although most abundantly in May or June and again in the fall. The grandiflora roses are similar but often with larger flowers on very strong stems and a vigorous plant. Flowers are in small clusters as in the floribundas.

White — Near White

Blanche Mallerin	Matterhorn
Garden Party	Pascali
John F. Kennedy	White Knight

Medium to Deep Yellow

Eclipse	King's Ransom
Golden Girl	Summer Sunshine

Yellow Blend

American Heritage	Lady Elgin
Champagne	Peace

Orange Blend — Orange Red

Allegro	Mojave
Comanche	Montezuma
Command Performance	Polynesian Sunset
Fragrant Cloud	Sunburst
	Tropicana

Light to Medium Pink

Bewitched	Pink Favorite
Camelot	Pink Peace
Laura	Queen Elizabeth

Deep Pink

Charlotte Armstrong	Portrait

Pink Blend

Aquarius	First Prize
Chicago Peace	Helen Traubel
Confidence	Swarthmore
	Tiffany

Medium Red

Christian Dior	Pharaoh
	Mirandy

Dark Red

Chrysler Imperial	Mister Lincoln
Crimson Glory	Oklahoma
	Scarlet Knight

Red Blend

    Granada   President Herbert Hoover

Lavender — Mauve

    Lady X   Sterling Silver

FLORIBUNDA

Vigorous plants, relatively low growing, flowers in a cluster. Especially useful where a mass of flowers is desired. The polyantha types are of smaller flowers in a somewhat tighter cluster.

White — Near White

Iceberg	Saratoga
Ivory Fashion	White Bouquet

Yellow — Yellow Blend

Circus	Goldilocks
Circus Parade	Little Darling
Golden Slippers	Redgold
Zambra	

Pink — Pink Blend

American Junior Miss	Fashion
Betsy McCall	Gene Boerner
Betty Prior	Mrs. R. M. Finch
Cecil Brunner	Seventeen
Elizabeth of Glamis	Vogue

Red — Red Blend

Europeana	Masquerade
Fire King	Permanant Wave
Floradora	Red Pinocchio
Frensham	Rumba
Ginger	Sarabande
Spartan	

Lavender — Mauve

Angel Face	Lavender Girl

CLIMBING ROSES

Two types of climbing roses are recognized. The large-flowering types typically have large flowers, sometimes in small clusters and resembling the hybrid tea roses. Some of these are climbing sports of familiar cultivars. The rambler roses are those with small flowers in dense clusters with more supple stems than the climbing, large-flowered types. These large-flowered types may have a scattering of flowers later in the season and are not limited to just one flower display in late spring or early summer as is characteristic of the ramblers.

White — Near White

Silver Moon	White Dawn

Yellow

Climbing Peace	Golden Showers
Lemon Pillar	

Pink

American Piller	Dr. J. H. Nicholas
Climbing Coral Dawn	Dr. W. Van Fleet
Climbing Queen Elizabeth	New Dawn
Dorothy Perkins	Rhonda

Red

Blaze	Don Juan
Climbing Chrysler Imperial	Excelsa
Climbing Crimson Glory	Gladiator
Climbing McGredy	Paul's Scarlet
Climbing Masquerade	Pillar of Fire

Lavender

Climbing Sterling Silver

Rose "Fragrant Cloud" has large double flowers and a strong scent.

SHRUB ROSES

Roses in this group represent those kinds that are more typically shrubs, some growing 3 to 4 feet and larger ones 8 to 10 feet. They are used in general plantings as other shrubs, although the smaller ones may be used with other roses. Many develop attractive, dark-green foliage and prominent red seedpods in the fall. This group includes the species roses and hybrids of these in many forms, as well as kinds that may be referred to as "old fashioned roses," such as the moss rose, cabbage rose, and the damask rose.

White — Near White

Bishop Darlington — Hy. Musk, cream to flesh-pink

Frau Karl Druschki — Hy. Perpetual, white, strong grower

Schneezwerg — Rugosa, semidouble, slight scent

Sea Foam — double flowers, white to cream color

Yellow

Agnes — Hy. Rugosa, light yellow, early spring, fragrant

Harison's Yellow — double yellow, very hardy, fragrant

Pink

Belinda — Musk, rose-pink, flowers in large clusters

Conrad F. Meyer — Hy. Rugosa, silvery-pink flowers, tall

Crested Moss — soft-pink, fragrant

Flamingo — Rugosa, pink to rose-pink, single

Fru Dagmar Hastrup — Rugosa, silvery-pink, single flowers

George Arends — Hy. Perpetual, rose pink, fragrant, spring

Jacques Cartier — Damask, light pink

Mrs. John Laing — Hy. Perpetual, pink, fragrant

Paul Neyron — Hy. Perpetual, large pink flowers, spring

Rosa Mundi — Gallica, striped pink and white

The Fairy — Shell-pink flowers in clusters, small foliage

Salet — Moss, rose-pink

Red

Grootendorst Supreme — Hy. Rugosa, clusters of flowers, red

Hansa — Hy. Rugosa, double reddish-violet, clove-rose scent

Henry Nevard — Hy. Perpetual, red, fragrant

Moyesii — Flowers raspberry red

Rose A Parfum de L'Hay — Hy. Rugosa, large red flowers, fragrant

Rose de Rescht — Damask, fuchsia red, heavy fragrance

Rugosa Rubra — rosy-crimson to magenta-purple, single

Therese Bugnet — Damask, rosy-crimson to magenta-purple, fragrant

Herbaceous Beds and Borders

In most temperate-climate gardens the herbaceous border is the main source of color from May to October. Certainly there is no other form of border from which so much color can be obtained over so long a period, and with so little trouble.

Herbaceous plants are those that do not form any persistent woody stem; these include annuals, biennials, and perennials. In fact, the true herbaceous border is made up almost entirely of perennial plants. Because of this all the plants in the border need virtually the same treatment, and the whole border can be dealt with as a single operation.

In spite of the tremendous variety of plants available, it is almost impossible to keep a herbaceous border in full flower throughout the year. To maintain the continuity of flower, spring bulbs are often planted in the front of the border, and annual or perennial bedding plants are used as stopgaps or to create special effects. In addition, a number of bulbous plants, such as *Crinum,* agapanthus, lilies (particularly the Madonna Lily, *Lilium candidum*), and tuberous-rooted plants such as *Alstroemeria*, are often used to extend the range of flower color and form. Exotic, half-hardy plants like dahlias and pelargoniums are also used to extend the season and brilliance of the border.

It is not sheer size that makes herbaceous borders effective. Their real charm comes from three main factors: first, the way the colors of the flowers are chosen to blend, clash, or contrast; second, the variety of flower-shapes and forms; third, the contrasts in foliage. Finally, to look its best, a good herbaceous border needs a background: the ideal is probably a well-kept evergreen hedge, but any hedge that is neat is effective. Fences and walls serve almost as well.

Planning

Effective beds and borders are planned — they do not just evolve. The first essential is to decide where the beds and borders are to be placed. The decision is usually a quite logical one: there must be room for it, and a sunny site is essential, since few herbaceous plants will do well in a shaded site. Traditionally, herbaceous borders are long and straight, but this is neither essential nor desirable. If the border has to go, as it often does, down the long, straight side of a garden, it is better to make slight variations in the edges. If it can be taken in a broad sweep around the corner of a garden, this will give greater depth. If it is to be made in front of a hedge, leave room between the hedge and the back of the border so that there is a pathway to walk on when trimming the hedge.

The next step is to mark the border with small stakes or bricks and then stand back and study the shape within the markers. If there is room, the border should be 8 to 12 feet wide; it should not be less than 5 feet wide. After marking the shape of the border, leave it for a week or two. Watch that plot of ground to assess the hours of sunshine each part receives, and plan accordingly.

Make a scale of the border on graph paper and work out the plants that are to go in it. If you have favorite plants, you may need to change the shape or size of the border to accommodate them all. To do this, draw up a list of all the plants you want to include in the border. Work out which are tallest-growing, which are middle-sized for the center, and which are small enough to go right at the front. Then pencil in the various planting sites with different colored crayons and label the plots.

The hallmark of a good herbaceous border is the way in which the colors are combined and contrasted. This is largely a matter of taste, observation, and experience, but there are a few general rules. Do not repeat clever and effective color groupings too often or too regularly. The brighter shades need to be spread across the border, and the most brilliant colors, such as scarlet and purple, need to be separated from each other by paler-colored-flowers or silver-foliaged plants. No one color should be allowed to dominate the border to the exclusion of others. Do not expect to get this part of the plan right the first time — it is better to make many plans than to lift and replant because you did not get the plan right before you started.

Preparation

Ground preparation is best done in late summer, so that the ground has time to settle again before planting. Because perennials stay in the ground, once the border has been planted no major cultural operations can be undertaken. Thorough preparation is essential, which means deep digging, preferably thorough double trenching. No amount of manuring and fertilizing after planting will ever make up for half-hearted initial digging. Add plenty of organic manure, as well as phosphate and lime. In sandy soils, add leaf mold or peat; on heavy soils, add some sand or ashes to make the soil lighter in texture. It need only be redone every 10 years, small sections at a time, and the effort is well worthwhile.

Planting

This can be carried out at any time from September until April, and plants from different nurseries, arriving at different times, can be planted as they arrive and according to plan. Label or number every plant according to the plan. Generally, the earlier plants are put in, the better they will perform the following year, since early planting gives roots time to settle in before frosts induce complete dormancy. There are a few plants, such as lupins, scabious, and pyrethrums that are better planted in spring, but they are exceptions. Put plants in the ground and work the soil in well between the roots. Plant to exactly the same depth as they were growing before. No planting should be done during freezing weather. Store plants received during cold spells in a protected location with almost-dry peat heaped over their roots, and plant as soon as the weather improves. Planting should also not be done when the ground is waterlogged. Plants should be well watered-in. A day or two later, break up the crust, fork out foot marks, and scatter on a topdressing of well-rotted organic matter or peat.

Maintenance

During the first growing season it is most important the border never dries out. Tall-growing plants will need staking, and many floppy plants, such as peonies, look better if given a support of stakes and a wire hoop; these should be placed in the ground as soon as the shoots begin to come through. Inspect plants periodically for attacks of insects and diseases. Hoe between the plants to keep weeds under control, but since hoeing encourages the soil to become dry, watering is particularly important. In autumn, cut off all dead growth to ground level, remove any weeds, and apply a mulch of well-rotted manure or compost to the whole bed.

Herbaceous borders need a general overhaul every three to five years. Plants such as peonies and delphiniums, which resent root disturbance, should be left alone, while plants like Michaelmas daisies, which are inclined to become invasive, should be lifted, cut back to size, and replanted. If you have found some color or foliage combinations less effective than they might be, make adjustments by moving the tolerant plants.

Finally, always keep an eye open for improved forms of the plants you already have — more startling plants and more striking color combinations.

Annual Beds

Basically the same principles apply to beds as to borders, but as they are mainly annuals or bedding plants, double digging is not essential, and planning mistakes can easily be rectified. In general the main idea of using annuals or bedding plants is to obtain a mass of color, but the best bedding schemes are usually those in which temporary plants and permanent plants are combined, or in which plants of contrasting colors are combined in bold blocks. Round, square, or rectangular beds lend themselves best to bedding schemes. In regularly-shaped beds, confine yourself to two types of plants, using the taller-growing ones in the middle, and the smaller-growing ones in a broad border around the edge of them. Where bedding schemes are to be carried out around some permanent feature, that feature should be really outstanding.

Perennials

Perennials are plants that die back to the ground every winter and shoot again in the spring. Each year they grow wider and produce a greater and greater quantity of bloom. Their main uses are in herbaceous and mixed borders.

There are two main methods of propagating perennials, by division and by seed. Seed, not feasible for hybrids and varieties that will not come true to type, should be gathered as soon as ripe and sown outdoors in spring or fall under protection or in frames. In some cases the seeds need the gentle warmth of a greenhouse. Most seeds need shade to germinate and should be covered with brown paper just until they appear above ground. Division is achieved by lifting the plants, inserting two forks back to back, and gently teasing the plants apart. Occasionally, perennials can be increased by cuttings, but this is the exception.

Biennials

Biennials are plants that take two years to complete their cycle of growth. During their first year they usually build up a rosette of leaves and a strong root system; they rest over the winter, then flower, set seed, and die. Like annuals, their main garden use is for bedding or for filling gaps in the border.

Biennials are usually sown the year before they are wanted in flower, but this presents the problem of where to grow them until they are put in their flowering positions. In small gardens it is usually better to buy biennials the year they are needed. In larger gardens, keep a place for propagating plants; sow seed outdoors in shallow furrows; cover large seed to three or four times its own thickness, small seed only shallowly. First work the soil to a fine tilth and enrich with superphosphate (2 ounces per square yard) and some fine peat to prevent drying out in hot weather. After germination the seedlings should either be thinned out to 6 to 9 inches apart or transplanted to nursery beds and planted 6 to 9 inches apart in rows 15 inches apart. Keep them well weeded and watered until fall, and then transplant them to their flowering positions.

Annuals

Annuals are plants that complete their life cycle in just one season. Though short-lived, most annuals produce an unrivaled wealth of bloom. Their main use is in bedding schemes; for filling gaps in the shrub or herbaceous border; or for window boxes, tubs, and

Herbaceous borders are the great achievement of the Anglo-American gardening tradition. The well-designed herbaceous border is packed with plants so that the earth does not show through and weeds have little chance of growing. The problem is to find effective color combinations, but once they have been found they should not be repeated too frequently. Pale colors, including white, show up from a great distance, whereas deeper colors, such as purple, are most effective when they are seen at close range. Once planted, a herbaceous border should be left alone and about a third of it lifted and replanted at three-year intervals, dividing the clumps as necessary.

other containers. Most come from sunny parts of the world and need to be grown in open positions in full sun. For best results, plant them in soil that has been well-prepared beforehand and enriched with compost, well-rotted manure, and superphosphate (2 ounces per square yard).

Annuals are subdivided into those that are hardy (hardy annuals) and those that are tender (half-hardy annuals). Their garden uses are the same, and, while both are raised from seed, the seed needs to be sown at different times and under different conditions.

Hardy annuals may be sown either in spring or in fall, preferably where they are to flower. The seed should be sown broadcast or in shallow furrows and only lightly covered. Seedlings will need thinning twice, first when they are about an inch high, and again when they reach half their ultimate height. The ideal distance between annuals is half their ultimate height. It is always safer to sow in spring; fall sowing is a gamble that means a longer flowering season if plants are not winter-killed. Plants should be about 3 inches high before frost sets in. August and September are the best months for sowing.

Half-hardy annuals are sensitive to frost and must therefore be sown outdoors after the frosts are over, usually in May or June, or they must be raised in a greenhouse or frame in boxes, the seed being sown in February or March and hardened off and planted in May or June. Raising them in a greenhouse ensures a longer flowering season.

Steps leading up to lawn, a grass path winding mysteriously through trees, combine to give a sense of distance to this garden in spite of the fence stopping the view at the end of the garden.

Border and Bedding Plants The flowering seasons and ultimate heights of all these plants are only approximate. Flowering time varies from year to year, depending on the weather. The size of plants also varies greatly. The ultimate heights given are those of the flower stalks.

Achillea/Yarrow, Milfoil

Hardy perennials. Prefer a sunny position; easily propagated by seed or division. Basal tufts of attractive, stout, leathery leaves, and flowers borne on stout stems. *A. filipendulina*, 4 feet, flat heads 5 inches across of long-lasting, daisy-like flowers. *A. millifolium*, 18 to 36 inches, white, pink, or red flowers: best-named forms are "Cerise Queen," 2 feet, cerise; "Fire King," 2 feet, deep glowing red.

Aconitum/Monk's Hood

Attractive, sun-loving, late-summer-flowering perennials. Propagate by seed sown in a cold frame in spring or by division. Plants usually grown are hybrids. Best are × "Bressingham Spire," 2½ to 3 feet, sturdy plant with tall spikes of violet-blue helmeted flowers; "Spark's Variety," 3 to 4 feet, branching spike of very deep-blue flowers. Both July/August.

Adonis/Pheasant's Eye

Pretty, showy annuals and perennials. **Annual Species** *A. aestivalis*, 1 foot, crimson flowers, June. *A. annua*, 1 foot, brilliant scarlet flowers, May to September. **Perennial Species** *A. amurensis*, 1 to 1½ feet, large yellow flowers, February to April; also a double form. *A. vernalis*, 1 to 1½ feet, yellow flowers, March to May.

Ageratum /Flossflower

Half-hardy annuals, useful for edging. Propagate by soft cuttings rooted in gentle heat or by seed. *A. houstonianum*, annual, 1½ feet: best varieties are "Blue Ball," deep-blue flowers; "Fairy Pink," rose flowers; "Imperial Dwarf," blue or white flowers.

Alstroemeria/
Peruvian Lily

Attractive South American plants; brilliant, lily-like flowers. Suitable for warm border or the foot of a south wall. Provide excellent, long-lasting cut flowers. Brittle roots resent disturbance, so buy pot-grown plants.

Transplant without disturbing the ball of soil, and plant 6 to 8 inches deep. Come easily from seed sown in pots. Do not transplant for at least 2 years. *A. aurantiaca*, showy, rich, orange flowers, June to August, 3 to 4 feet. "Dover Orange," selected form, orange-red flowers; and "Lutea," selected form, yellow flowers. "Ligtu Hybrids," shades of buff, cream, pink, and salmon. In the north, lift in the fall and store over winter in a frost-free area.

Althaea/Hollyhock

Tallest of perennial border plants, up to 6 or 12 feet. *A. rosea*, single or double, white, cream, yellow, pink, and red, often with a darker center to the flower. Easily grown in any good soil in sunny position, needs firm staking. Old plants tend to suffer from rust and should be dug up and burned. Raise plants from seed sown in the open in April or May and transplanted to their permanent positions in fall. Self-sown seedlings often appear and are worth keeping.

Anchusa/Alkanet or Bugloss

Striking border plants with fine blue flowers. Will grow in most soils in full sun, but prefer sandy soil. The main species are: *A. officinalis*, 15 inches, a many-stemmed clump, brilliant gentian-blue flowers, May to July; cut flower stems to ground level after flowering, will produce a second crop in September. *A. azurea*, 2 to 5 feet, depending on variety: "Little John," 2 feet, deep-blue flowers; "Loddon Royalist," 3 feet, very large flowers, bright gentian blue; "Morning Glory," 5 feet, huge flowers, deep, rich blue. Increase by division or by rooting stem-cuttings from near ground level in autumn.

Anemone/Windflower

Some colorful border plants; others listed under Rock-Garden Plants or Bulbs. Border species do best in deep, moist, rich soils and resent root disturbance. *A. japonica*, the original "Japanese Anemone," 2½ feet, semi-double rose-carmine flowers, August to October; "Splendens," 2½ feet, very large single flowers, deep-pink outside, paler inside. *A. × hybrida*, usually known as "Japanese Anemones." Some of the best are: "Honorine Jobert," 5 feet, white, August to October; "Loreli," 3 feet, delicate rose-pink; "September Charm," 3½ to 4

Alstroemeria aurantiaca and 'Ligtu Hybrids' combine to create a patch of brilliant color in keeping with the paving used on this patio.

92

feet, single pale pink with a lilac flush
on the back of the petals. Increase by
seed, root cuttings, or division.

Antirrhinum/
Snapdragon

Nearly-hardy biennials. *A. majus,*
likes a sunny position in well-drained
soil. Range through small, spreading
dwarf antirrhinums, up to 15 inches;
intermediate antirrhinums up to 30
inches; and tall antirrhinums up to 48
inches. Wide range of colors. All
flower May to October; usually propagated from seed sown in February or
March in the greenhouse and hardened
off and then planted out in May or early
June. Can also be grown from cuttings
taken in September and rooted in a cold
frame. Remove the tip of the stem when
4 to 6 inches to induce branching.

Aquilegia/Columbine

Highly ornamental, hardy perennials
for borders. Tend to be short-lived on
heavy or wet soils. Propagate by seed
sown in spring; seedlings flower the
following year. Or divide established
plants in spring. All garden forms derived from *A. longissima,* 2 feet,
long-spurred flowers, July to October; pinks, reds, yellows, blues,
or bicolor. Best forms include
"Clematiflora Hybrida," 2 to 3 feet,
large spurless clematis-shaped
flowers, blues and pinks; "Crimson
Star," 2 feet, long-spurred flowers,
crimson and white, May to June;
"McKana Hybrids," 2½ to 3 feet,
exceptionally large flowers up to 4
inches across, spurs 3 to 4 inches
long, wide range of colors; "Mrs
Scott-Elliot's Strain," 3 feet, art
shades.

Aster/Michaelmas Daisy

Not to be confused with "Asters,"
which are properly *Callistephus* and
are listed there. True asters, or
Michaelmas daisies, are among the
most colorful and useful of all perennial herbaceous plants, providing a
wealth of color from late summer to
the end of fall. Extremely hardy and
easy to grow. Form dense clumps that
need to be broken up every third or
fourth year. Most plants are hybrids or
selected strains, the tallest up to 6
feet, the medium varieties to 3 feet,
and the smallest 6 to 9 inches. Colors

An ambitious bedding scheme using almost entirely tender plants
against a background of shrubs. Color combinations can be
changed from year to year.

range through whites, pinks, deep
rose, to mauves and deep purples.
There are two groups, (1) those de-
rived from *A. novi-belgii,* with downy
foliage; and (2) those derived from *A.
novi-angliae,* with smooth leaves.
Among the best are: **Dwarf kinds**
"Victor," 9 inches, light blue;
"Snow Cushion," 10 inches, white;
"Pink Lace," 15 inches, double pink;
"Audrey," 15 inches, large pale
blue. **Medium** "Sonia," 2 feet,
clear pink; "Blue King," 2½ feet,
bright blue; "Apple Blossom," 3 feet,
cream overlaid pink; "Crimson
Brocade," 3 feet, double bright red;
"Lye End Beauty," 4 feet, pale plum;
"September Glow," 5 feet, rich ruby.
Tall "White Lady," 6 feet, pure white;
"The Cardinal," 5 feet, rose-red;
"Harrington's Red," 5 feet, clear pink;
"My Smokey," 6 feet, deep mulberry.

Begonia

Half-hardy plants often used for bedding. Some are grown for their flowers, produced in a continual succession all summer, others for the beautiful markings of their lopsided leaves.
Usually divided into two groups:
tuberous-rooted begonias, dealt with
under bulbs; and fibrous-rooted begonias, which include *B. acutifolia,*
white flowers in spring; *B. angularis,*
white veined leaves; *B. coccinea,*

scarlet flowers in winter; *B. foliosa,*
white and pink flowers, summer; *B.
glaucophylla,* pendulous habit, pink
flowers, winter; *B. haageana,* pink,
summer until fall; *B. hydrocotylifolia,*
pink, summer, *B. incarnata,* rose,
winter; *B. manicata,* pink, winter;
B. scharffiana, white, winter; *B.
semperflorens,* perpetual-flowering
pink. Also numerous hybrids. Those
with beautiful leaves are mainly hybrids from *B. rex* or *B. masoniana.*
Plants are usually grown from seed
sown in January in a temperature of
about 16°C. Sow the fine seed on
compost surface; do *not* cover. Will
germinate in a few days. Grow
shrubby perennial forms from cuttings taken in autumn. Most species
can be raised from leaf-cuttings.
Choose moist, sandy soil, partial
shade.

Bergenia

Extremely hardy perennials with big,
bold, round leaves; one of the
earliest-flowering hardy perennials.
In some the leathery, glossy leaves
turn purple in winter. Useful for the
front of borders or for growing among
shrubs. Will grow anywhere, including fairly deep shade. Propagate by
division at any time of the year.
Best-known species include *B. cordifolia,* pink flowers in very early

spring, 1 foot; *B. crassifolia,* 1 foot, pink, early spring; *B. delavayi,* 9 inches, leaves turn almost purple in winter, need full exposure to sunlight to color well, flowers purplish-pink, spring; *B. ligulata,* 1 foot, white or pink flowers, January and February. Among the best hybrids: "Ballawley Hybrid," 1½ feet, crimson flowers, dark purplish leaves in winter; "Delbees," 1 foot, rosy flowers, March/April, leaves turn red in winter.

Buphthalmum/Yellow Oxeye

Showy hardy perennials, rather coarse foliage, large daisy-like flowers. Best in a moist soil in a sunny place. Propagate by division. *B. salicifolium,* narrow leaves and bright yellow flowers, 2 feet, summer; *B. speciosum,* 5 feet, deep-yellow flowers, June to August.

Calendula/Pot Marigold

Popular, easily grown hardy annuals. All strains of *C. officinalis.* The modern hybrids and strains grow 12 to 24 inches, have single, semi-double, double, or quilled flowers in shades of cream, yellow, orange, and scarlet. Bloom continuously throughout summer and well into fall. Will grow in any ordinary garden soil, if not too rich; prefer a sunny location. Easily raised from seed sown outdoors in early spring. Thin plants to 9 inches apart. Best in areas with cool summer temperature. Useful in cool greenhouse in winter.

Callistephus /Aster or China Aster

Colorful half-hardy annuals with daisy-flowers in blues, pinks, mauves, purples, and white. All are strains of *C. chinenesis,* which has single purple flowers. Modern hybrids have single, semi-double, or double flowers up to 5 inches across and a wider color range. Easy to grow in any good garden soil, 6 to 30 inches, according to strain. Do best on a well-manured soil with a high lime content, and in sun. Propagate by seed sown in a cold frame in April and prick out when 2 to 3 inches high, or by seed sown in March in the greenhouse. Plant out seedlings 8 to 10 inches apart, according to vigor. More flowers are produced if the tip of the main stem is pinched out when seedlings are transplanted. Flower in July and August. Excellent as cut flowers.

Campanula/Bellflower

A large genus of annuals, biennials, and perennials, including many colorful garden plants, often with long flowering seasons. Excellent in borders. *C. carpatica,* 9 inches, blue, July and August, ideal for the front of a border; plant in the fall before the leaves die down; *never* move when dormant. *C. lactiflora,* undoubtedly the finest of the bellflowers, 4 to 5 feet, producing in July/August large trusses of lavender-blue flowers on branched stems; likes good, moist soil. The best varieties are "Loddon Anna," pale pink; and "Pritchard's Variety," deep blue. *C. latifolia,* 2½ feet, blue, June to August, one of the easiest species to grow, always puts up a good show and tolerates some shade; var. *alba,* a white form, also good. *C. persicifolia,* 2½ to 3 feet, lavender flowers in June and July, spreads by stolons. Many excellent named forms with flowers from white through pale blues to deeper blues. Best species for shaded part of the garden is *C. rotundifolia,* the harebell of England, the bluebell of Scotland, 3 to 6 inches, delicate species very thin, wiry stems, each with a single, nodding bellflower in July and August; easy and delightful on lime soils in full sun. All the above species are hardy **perennials** and enjoy a well-cultivated soil; most will tolerate some shade. Propagate by division or seed, which is dust-like and should be sown on the surface of a very fine compost and not covered, then be put in a frame in shade.

The Canterbury bell, *C. medium,* is a **biennial** species, with cup-and-saucer flowers in various shades of pink, blue, or white; 2 to 3 feet, mid-summer flowering. Propagate from seed sown in seedbeds or in the open and thinned to 6 inches apart, or in boxes and transplanted to a nursery bed when 4 inches high. Plant in flowering positions in autumn.

Carnation

Popular perennials. Divided into two types, "Borders" and "Perpetuals." Only border carnations can be grown outdoors, and are grouped by colors.

In this tiny garden brilliant use has been made of bedding plants, especially fancy-leaved pelargoniums and fuchsias.

In "Flakes" ground color is striped with another color; in "Bizarres" ground color is striped with 2 or 3 different colors or shades; "Selfs" have flowers of only one color; "Picotee" border carnations have the edges of the flowers a different shade or color from the rest of the flower. The term "Fancy" is used to cover any variations that do not come within the other categories. Outdoor cultivation is not difficult: the only essentials are a sunny location and light, well-drained soil. On heavy soils, plant in raised beds of specially prepared soil of equal parts of well-rotted manure or compost, good garden soil, and sharp sand. Prepare beds well in advance of planting. Plant in September or early October. Firm plants but do not plant too deeply; space 15 inches apart. Propagate by layering vigorous shoots in summer as soon as flowering is over. Fill a small hollow with coarse sand. Slit stem to be layered in an upward direction with a razor-sharp knife, strip off lower leaves and peg down layer at 45°. Water in dry periods. Rooting takes 5 to 6 weeks, then sever layers from parent plant and pot separately. If no cold frame or greenhouse is available, plunge pots in the soil until the plants are ready to plant out. Replace border carnations every 2 or 3 years. Never "top" border carnations by pinching, and disbud discerningly.

Cheiranthus/Wallflower

Very colorful, easily grown plants. A couple of gay perennial species are occasionally grown, but most are biennials. The **perennial** species are *C. cheiri,* 1 foot, flowers yellow, fragrant, May to June; the form "Harpur Crewe" has double yellow flowers. *C. semperflorens,* 1 foot, wine-purple shot with bronze, May to August. These will grow in almost any well-drained soil. Usual **biennials** are all forms of *C. cheiri.* Wide variety of strong colors, also mixed color forms, and varieties with double flowers; all are scented. Vary from 6 inches to over 2 feet. Sow seed outside in May for transplanting to their flowering positions in the fall. Desirable in a cool greenhouse because of fragrance.

Chrysanthemum

Group includes autumn chrysanthemums plus many other useful border plants, including the oxeye daisies

and the Shasta daisies. Annuals, all hardy plants, will grow in any fertile soil in a sunny position. Propagated from seed sown in April or May in the open where they are to flower, or from seed sown in February or March in a cold greenhouse or cold frame and planted out 6 inches apart in late April. Best of the **annual** species: *C. carinatum,* 2 feet, white and yellow daisy flowers, summer; var. *burridgeanum,* white flowers with a crimson ring; "*flore pleno hybridum,*" fringed double flowers in a variety of colors. *C. segetum,* the corn marigold, 18 inches, summer flowering, gay marigold-like flowers, contrasting bands of colors run around flowers in concentric circles — quite the gayest of the annual species. Best **perennial** species are *C. cinerariifolium,* 18 to 24 inches, flowers white, daisy-like, with a golden center. *C. coccineum* (pyrethrum), finely divided foliage and slender stalks, large daisy-like flowers in a variety of brilliant colors, May and June, 2½ feet. *C. leucanthemum,* the oxeye daisy, 2½ feet, flowers large, white with a golden center, July to September. *C. maximum,* the Shasta daisy, 1 to 3 feet, flowers large, single or double, white with a golden center, July to September. Many new varieties with frilled or shaggy petals. *C. rubellum,* 2 to 3 feet, flowers to 3 inches across, white, pink, red, purple, or yellow, August to October. *C. uliginiosum,* moon daisy, flowers white with a greenish-yellow center, 4 to 5 feet, August to October. All hardy perennials, easy to grow in any good garden soil, sunny positions. Increase by division of the roots in spring or autumn.

The popular autumn-flowering chrysanthemums are all hybrids and strains descended from *C. indicum* and *C. morifolium.* General cultivation is not difficult. Divided into three groups: (1) the early-flowering types, blooming before October, (2) the mid-season varieties, flowering from the beginning of October to mid-November, (3) late-flowering, from mid-November to the end of January. Chrysanthemums of the last class must be grown in the greenhouse. The early-flowering Chrysanthemums produce an abundance of blooms from August until mid-October, or later-flowering kinds may be selected in areas where frost does not occur until later. The modern varieties are

mainly double but have more or less shaggy heads and come in a wide range of colors, including whites, pinks, reds, yellows, magentas, oranges, burnt rusty-reds, and plums. Most effective in herbaceous border planted together in bold groups. Plant roots, or "stools," in early May in any good garden soil in a sunny position. Taller varieties will need staking; most varieties will produce sprays of flowers, but for particularly large flowers select a single bud on each stem and rub off all the other buds with the thumb. Many cultivars are not completely hardy and for those lift plants after frost and keep in a cool, airy place such as a cold frame. Slight frost will do them no harm. Cold, wet soil will kill them. Propagate by division of the roots immediately after lifting them in the autumn, or by cuttings taken in spring when the new season's growth is about 3 inches long. Insert in sandy soil around the edges of a pot. Will need greenhouse temperatures and plenty of light for rooting. Once rooted, in 4 to 6 weeks, move young plants to 5-inch-deep boxes, grow for another month, then harden off via cold frame. Cuttings may also be rooted in a hot bed or cold frame. Korean chrysanthemums are those developed from *C. koreanum* crossed with the florist types and are somewhat more winter-hardy. Large number of varieties, single or double flowers, very wide range of exceptionally brilliant colors. Bloom August to November, range in height from 18 inches to 3 feet. Forms of these may be started from seeds and selected plants then grown from cuttings rooted in the cold frame in spring, or by division of the roots.

Claytonia /Spring Beauty

Useful hardy perennials, will grow in any damp soil. Tolerate shade well. Plant in spring or fall, propagate by seed sown outdoors in October or March, or by offsets. *C. caroliniana,* 6 inches, pink flowers, May. *C. virginica,* 6 inches, white flowers, April. Foliage dies off by June. Native to northeastern United States.

Convalaria /Lily of the Valley

Beloved hardy perennials, heady scent. Only one species, *C. majalis,* 6

Chrysanthemum "Dallas." A large-flowered incurving chrysanthemum.

In this walled garden tender bedding and annuals have been used to fill gaps between perennials that have not yet established themselves.

inches, flowers in spring. Form *fortunei,* extra large flowers; *rosea,* light-pink flowers; "Fortin's Giant," has largest, extra-fragrant flowers. Also double form with longer-lasting flowers, and forms with variegated foliage. Do best in a good garden soil enriched with plenty of leaf mold; prefer shade, and plenty of moisture in the soil. Plant in fall; spread rapidly by underground stems. Benefit from a mulch of well-rotted manure, old compost, or leaf mold every spring. Propagate by dividing clumps in fall.

Coreopsis /Tickseed

Hardy perennials and annuals. Bright showy flowers, ideal for beds and borders. Thrive in sunny positions in any ordinary garden soil. Best **annual** species is *C. tinctoria,* 2 feet, yellow and crimson daisy-type flowers, summer: named cultivars include "Fire King," 9 inches, scarlet; "Dazzler," 10 inches, yellow and crimson; "Tiger Star," 12 inches, bronze and yellow; "Golden Blaze," 2 to 3 feet, burnt-yellow and maroon. Grow these from seed sown outdoors in March or April where they are to flower. Thin to 9 inches apart when 3 inches high. Best of the **perennials** are *C. grandiflora,* 2 to 3 feet, yellow flowers, summer; var. "Flore Pleno" has double yellow flowers. *C. pal-*

mata, 1½ to 3 feet, orange-yellow flowers early to late summer. *C. pubescens,* 2 feet, crimson and yellow flowers, summer. Propagate perennials by division of the roots in spring or autumn, by seed sown in spring outdoors, or by cuttings taken in spring. The last two species not commonly used as a garden plant.

Cortaderia/Pampas Grass

Fine, big-growing grasses, with bold foliage and huge feather-duster plumes. Suitable for the back of a border or isolated positions. Any sunny location, any well-drained soil. Species usually grown is *C. selloana* (also known as *C. argentea* or *Gynerium argenteum),* a clump of leaves up to 8 to 10 feet tall, flowers on stems 6 to 8 feet tall; var. *pumila,* dwarfer flower stems 4 to 5 feet; var. *rendatleri,* flowers 6 to 8 feet tall, pink plumes. All flower late summer and autumn. Propagate by seed sown in a sandy compost in spring, or by division of the clumps in spring.

Cosmos

Gaily-colored hardy annuals with daisy-type flowers and finely divided ferny foliage. All prolific in flower, excellent for cutting. Any well-drained soil, but prefer it light and

sandy; a sunny position. *C. atrosaguineus,* 1 to 3 feet, deep brownish-red flowers, summer to fall. *C. bipinnatus,* 3 to 5 feet, white, rose, or purple flowers, summer; many named forms in colors ranging through scarlet, rose, and pink, often with bicolored flowers. *C. sulphureus,* 3 to 4 feet, pale-yellow flowers, late summer; many named forms with deep-yellow or orange flowers. Increase from seed sown indoors in spring, prick out into boxes when 1½ inches high, harden off in a cold frame, and plant out in May or June, 1 foot apart.

Delphinium

Bold, very showy, almost indispensable border plants. Popular tall blue delphiniums are hybrid strains, derived from *D. elatum.* Buy the best and largest deep blue, the best and largest pale blue, and the best and largest mid-blue. Then extend the range by sowing seed outdoors in spring and transplanting seedlings to their permanent positions in the fall. Grow named clones from cuttings taken from the base of the shoots and rooted in a deep box half-filled with vermiculite or coarse sand and covered with a pane of glass; once rooted, plant cuttings and cover with a small cloche until established. Scatter a slug-killer around small plants.

The delphinium color range is now being extended not only through mauves, lavenders, violets, and purples but also through whites, creams, yellows, pinks, and reds. Recent Dutch hybrids include crimsons, oranges, tomato-reds, and salmons. Further hybridizing has been done using an African species, *D. leroyi,* with a freesia-like fragrance. A few are already available. All delphiniums do best in a rich, well-drained soil and a sunny position. Five to 10 feet tall, they need staking, and they flower during June and July. They are most suitable for gardens in areas with cool summers.

Belladonna delphiniums have a branched stem with several short spurs of flowers. Average height 2½ to 4 feet. Flowers single, semi-double, in shades of blue, June to August.

Other **perennial** species include *D. grandiflorum,* 1 foot, brilliant irridescent butterfly-blue flowers; and *D. nudicaule,* 1 foot, striking orange-scarlet flowers in June and July. Cultivation as for the blue-flowered hybrids. The **annual** Delphiniums, commonly called larkspur, are well worth growing. Hybrids include ''Giant Hyacinth-Flowered Larkspurs,'' ''Giant Imperial,'' ''Supreme,'' and ''Blue Spire,'' all in shades of blue, and others such as ''Dazzler'' in bright scarlet, ''Exquisite Pink,'' bright pink, and ''Miss California'' in salmon. Sow these in April in a sunny border where they are to flower, thin to 6 inches apart when 4 inches tall. In areas with mild winters sow seed outdoors in September. Young plants live over the winter and flower in June.

Dianthus/Pinks

Can roughly be described as small-flowered carnations. Genus also includes Sweet Williams. All useful as edgings but need a sunny site, well-drained, slightly acid to alkaline soil. Cold, damp winter soil, rather than frost, tends to kill them. The majority of garden pinks are ''Border Pinks,'' 6 to 9 inches tall, rosettes of silvery, lance-leaved foliage. Among best named forms are ''Betty Norton,'' large single rose-red with a crimson center; ''Dad's Favorite,'' double white with chocolate markings; ''Inchmery,'' double pale pink; ''Mrs. Sinkins,'' the common, fragrant double white form; and ''Rose of May,''

dwarf habit, double rose-pink. All flower June to August. ''Elizabethan Pinks'' are much more erect, have neat growth, greater hardiness. Among the best are ''Ashdown Forest,'' snow-white with a dark crimson center; ''St. Ives,'' very large semi-double flowers, creamy pink, ruby center; ''Sweetheart Abbey,'' very dark crimson with a white picotee edge (see Rock Gardens). *D. barbatus,* Sweet William, 6 inches to 1 foot, is a **perennial,** but usually grown as a biennial. Various colors, flowers in summer. Bed out in early spring, or raise from seed sown in the open garden in summer and transplanted to flowering positions in the fall. Propagate pinks by division or by cuttings obtained by taking hold of a shoot just below a leaf joint and pulling the section above the leaf joint away. Insert around the edge of a pot containing pure sand, protect with a cold frame until rooted; plant out.

Dicentra/Bleeding Heart

Dainty plants, fern-like leaves, pendent flowers in arching sprays. Will grow in any well-drained soil in sun or partial shade. Two perennial species for borders: *D. eximia,* 1½ feet, flowers white, pink, or reddish-purple, May and June; *D. spectabilis,* 1½ to 2 feet, flowers white or rose-crimson up to 1 inch long, heart-shaped, May/June. Propagate by seed sown outdoors in May or by division.

Dictamnus/Gas Plant or Burning Bush

Attractive, hardy perennial border plant. Gives off a highly volatile oil. On a hot, still day it is possible to ignite the oil by putting a lighted match close to the plant. This does the plant no harm. There is only one species generally grown, *D. albus;* to

Pampas grass, is striking both on account of its greyish leaves and the feathery plumes that are borne from autumn into winter.

3 feet, finely toothed leaves and fragrant white or purple flowers, in long spikes. Will grow in almost any soil; particularly useful in dry locations. Dislikes root disturbance. Propagate by division of the roots in early spring.

Digitalis/Foxglove

Easily grown, very colorful hardy biennials and perennials, excellent for borders. Thrive in sun, shade, almost any soil. The common foxglove *D. purpurea:* cultivated forms have larger flowers in deep magenta, pink, or white. Sutton's Excelsior Hybrids are best, with flowers held horizontally all around the stem. The colors include white, cream, primrose, pink, rose-pink, deep pink, and purple. Best treated as biennials, seed being sown in the open in April or May, transplanted to a shaded bed or border in July and transferred to their flowering positions in October.

Eremurus/Foxtail Lily

Among the most dramatic and striking of all hardy perennials. Produce a rosette of yucca-like leaves and tall stems packed for two-thirds of their length with colorful flowers. Need a warm, well-drained soil plus plenty of well-rotted manure, and shelter from strong winds. Plant brittle roots in early autumn at least 6 inches deep in a wide, flat-bottomed hole with roots spread out horizontally. Best species are *E. bungei,* 2 to 3 feet, bright golden-yellow, June. *E. elwesii,* 6 to 9 feet, white or pink on very strong stems, May and June; *E. robustus,* 4 to 6 feet, peach-colored flowers, June. The Shelford Hybrids have brilliantly colored flowers in shades of yellow, orange, pink, or white, 4 to 6 feet, June. Propagate by division of the roots or by seed sown in a cold frame: seedlings take 5 or 6 years to flower.

Ferns

Especially useful for growing in dense shade where little else will thrive, although some species will grow in full sun if soil is really damp. Best when grown with hostas, primulas, and the dwarf hardy cyclamen. The following is only a selection; anyone really interested in ferns should consult specialized books on the subject. **For**

A newly created garden. The main shape of the garden has been established and bedding plants are being used until the perennials among them become sufficiently established to make a show in their own right.

sunny situations *Pteretis struthiopteris,* 3 to 5 feet, ostrich fern. *Onoclea sensibilis,* to 36 inches, delicate light-green fronds turning yellow in autumn. *Osmunda regalis,* the royal fern, needs acid soil and a lot of moisture at the roots, 2 to 6 feet tall, depending on the moisture. Turns russet in autumn. Work plenty of peat or leaf mold into the soil. **For shaded situations** *Athyrium filix-femina,* the native Lady Fern, 3 feet, tufts of elegant light-green fronds. *Dryopteris filix-mas,* the Male Fern, 2 to 3 feet, luxuriant clumps of sturdy green fronds. *Polypodium vulgare,* the Common Polypody, 9 to 12 inches high, pinnate fronds. Best when planted in bold clumps and interspersed with hardy cyclamen and primulas. *Thelypteris dryopteris,* the Oak Fern, 6 to 9 inches, forms a carpet of delicate light-green fairy fronds. Ideal for carpeting under shrubs. Propagate by division in spring or autumn.

Gaillardia/Blanket Flower

Brilliantly colored hardy perennials, daisy-like flowers, thrive in any well-drained soil in sun. The plants

need support. Leaves oblong, toothed, flowers 4 inches across. Perennial forms all hybrids of *G. aristata.* Plants only last 4 or 5 years and then need replacing. This is best done by dividing the roots and planting in a new part of the border.

Geranium/Crane's Bill

A large genus with several species of useful and attractive border plants. For brilliant scarlet geraniums see *Pelargonium.* True geraniums thrive in most soils, but prefer well-drained sunny positions. Among the best for gardens are *G. endressii,* 1 foot, flowers rose-pink, summer to autumn, virtually ever-green; *G. grandiforum,* 12 to 18 inches, flowers blue with a reddish eye, July; *G. pratense,* lovely blue-flowered native plant, 12 to 24 inches high. Can be propagated by division or by seed sown outdoors.

Geum/Avens

Brightly colored hardy perennials flowering over a very long period. Grow well in almost any soil, sun or shade. Most garden varieties are forms of *G. chiloense.* Among the best are "Dolly North," 2½ feet, orange, June and July; "Fire Opal," 2 feet, scarlet, May to July; "Lady Stratheden," 2 feet, double buttercup yellow; "Prince of Orange," 18 inches, double orange-yellow flowers, May to July; and "Princess Juliana," 2 feet, bronzy-orange, June. Propagate by division.

Godetia

Popular hardy annuals, brightly colored poppy-like flowers, easily grown, any soil. Hybrids have been greatly improved in recent years. Among the best are "Firelight," crimson; "Orange Glory," deep salmon-orange; "Sybil Sherwood," pink, orange, and white. All grow 12 to 18 inches. Double flowered include "Cherry Red," "Rosy Queen," and "Ric Salmon," all with self-explaining names, all 2 to 2½ feet tall. Raised from seed sown in the open where they are to flower in April and thinned to 6 inches apart. Best in areas with cool summers. Excellent as a spring-flowering plant in the cool greenhouse.

Helianthus/Sunflower

Striking annual and perennial plants, large, brightly colored flowers. Grow anywhere in full sun, best in well-fertilized soil; perennial species need to be divided every 3 or 4 years and replanted, or size and quantity of flower begins to deteriorate. The common popular sunflower is an **annual**, *H. annuus,* up to 10 feet, summer to fall. There are now double forms in yellow, orange, and red. *H. debilis,* also annual, 1 to 3 feet, known as the miniature sunflower. Flowers yellow, orange, or pinkish-purple, July and August. Best of the **perennial** sunflowers are *H. decapetalus* "Loddon Gold," 5 feet, golden-yellow double flowers, August to October; *H. laetiflorus* "Miss Mellish," 6 feet, large bright-orange-yellow flowers, August and September; and *H. salicifolius,* 6 to 7 feet, a very striking plant for the back of the border, enormous inflorescences of lemon-yellow flowers, September and October. The perennial sunflowers mix especially well with Michaelmas daisies. Propagate by division in the spring.

Helleborus/Helebore

Genus contains both the Christmas roses and the Lenten roses. These hardy perennials flower in winter and thrive in shade. Best in a moist, well-drained soil rich in peat or leaf mold; resent root disturbance. The Christmas rose is *H. niger,* evergreen digitate leaves, long-lasting saucer-shaped flowers either pure white with yellow reproductive organs in the center, or white tinged pink. Flowers to 4 inches across, January/February, 1 foot. *H. orientalis,* the Lenten Rose. Usually evergreen, rather taller growing, 18 to 24 inches. Flowers, February to April, either cream, yellowish, pink, or purple; yellow and black forms are especially prized. Propagate by seed or by division as soon as flowering is over.

Hemerocallis/Day Lily

No border is complete without Day Lilies. Tufts of long strap-shaped leaves, flowers borne well above these on tall stems, each producing a long succession of flowers, each flower lasting only a day. Thriving in any good fertile soil, but prefer it fairly heavy, full sun. *H. minor,* dainty, dwarf species to 9 inches, medium flowers of clear yellow with a brown reverse. Hybrids excellent. All flower in June to September, depending on cultivar, grow 15 inches to 3½ feet. A selection of best modern strains is: "Alan," large cherry-red with a greenish-yellow throat; "Black Falcon," the nearest thing to black; "Cartwheels," really huge, wide-open flowers of a deep yellow; "Burning Daylight," beautiful rich orange; "Colonial Dame," apricot-rose, with a bright golden throat; "Display," garnet red; "Evelyn Claar" (2 feet), soft rose-pink; "Lavender Lyric," unusual lavender-pink; "Nashville," large creamy-yellow with an orange throat; "Nighthawk," ivory with a touch of acid lemon, huge flower; "Pink Prelude," a lovely dawn-pink with a paler midrib to each petal. Make excellent permanent plantings when

Day lilies (Hemerocallis). Hybrids are reliable border plants. Although each flower only opens for a single day, they produce a succession of flowers over many weeks.

combined with irises, hardy Agapanthus, red-hot pokers, and yuccas. Propagate by division.

Heuchera/Coral Bell or Alumroot

Beautiful and justly popular plants for the front of the border. Neat-growing rosettes of tidy evergreen leaves, slender stems topped with clouds of tiny flowers. Grow well in most soils, tolerate some shade. Flowers white, pink, or red, June to September on stalks 12 to 18 inches high. Best are the modern "Bressingham Hybrids," ranging from palest pink to deepest red. Propagate by division.

Hosta/Plantain Lily or Funkia

Handsome, hardy perennial border plants, form bold clumps of often variegated leaves and tall stems bearing pendent trumpet-shaped flowers. Indispensable in shaded borders, thrive in any soil not too dry in summer. *H. albormarginata,* narrow leaves edged with white and showy violet-mauve flowers, 18 inches, summer. *H. elata,* 3 to 4 feet, dense piles of sage-green leaves, flowers pale-bluish-mauve, June and July. *H. fortunei,* 2 to 3 feet, leaves green above, bluish beneath, flowers lilac-mauve or violet, June to August. Var. "Albo-picta," leaves bright yellow with a pale-green edge becoming pale green with a deep-green edge as the summer advances, flowers lilac, July/August. *H. lancifolia,* 12 to 18 inches, leaves shining deep green, pointed, flowers deep violet, August/September. *H. plantaginea,* does better in sun than shade; 2 to 2½ feet, leaves broad, yellowish-green, flowers huge white, trumpet-shaped, very fragrant, August/September, *H. tardiflora,* charming dwarf species, 12 inches, narrow dark-green leaves, flowers deep lilac, September and October; the last hosta to flower, and one of the most effective, particularly good when massed. Hostas form dense clumps in time. Divide in spring or fall. Some species come easily from seed, but the forms with variegated leaves can only be increased by division.

Iris

A huge family. The tall bearded irises grow 2 to 3 feet, occasionally to 4 feet, flower in May and June, wide range of colors. Dwarf bearded irises grow to 9 inches. Both types grow well in any well-drained soil and prefer a sunny position. Mix well with other herbaceous plants in the flower border. Plant creeping fleshy rootstock, half-covered with soil; it will then find its own level. Lift roots and divide every 3 years or so, and replant. Propagate by division. Colors range through light and dark blues, yellows, and creams, orange, amber, salmon, apricot, pink, and red, often with fascinating color combinations.

Other species are well worth growing. *I. kaempferi,* large flattish flowers up to 8 inches across in white, pink, red, purple, blue, or combinations. Many named forms, and many unnamed hybrids on the market. They reach 2 to 2½ feet, moist soil, grow well in bog conditions, June and July. *I. sibirica,* 1 foot, narrow lance-shaped leaves ¼ inch wide, flowers white, blue, purple, and intermediate shades. Damp soil, sun. *I. foetidissima,* the native Gladwyn iris, 2 feet, flowers lilac-blue, useful because it grows well in shade. Even more effective is "Variegata," with leaves striped creamy white.

Kniphofia/Red-Hot Poker or Torch Lily

Taller-growing kinds associate well with pampas grass, with hardy agapanthus and yuccas. Most species flower summer and fall. The stronger-growing kinds will tolerate fairly damp ground; smaller kinds prefer a well-drained soil. All flower best in sunny positions. *K. caulescens,* 4 feet, gray, yucca-like leaves and buff changing to red flowers, June. *K. galpinii,* dwarf, 18 inches, saffron-orange flowers, September and October. *K. macowanii,* 2 feet, dwarf, bright-green grass-like foliage, orange-scarlet flowers, summer. *K. nelsonii,* strong-growing dwarf, to 2 feet, flowers brightest-orange tinged scarlet, August and September. *K. northiae,* 4 feet, blue-gray leaves, huge racemes of red and yellow flowers. *K. uvaria,* the common red-hot poker, orange-scarlet and yellow flowers; very variable, some dwarf, others up to 5 feet.

Tall bearded irises are among the most varied and spectacular of border plants. The modern strains come in a vast range of colors. *Top,* Iris "Wabash"; *center,* "Fire dance"; *bottom,* Iris Staten Island."

"Stark's Hybrids," 3½ to 4½ feet, colors through yellow to bright red, excellent. Several named forms of this species and cultivars are most commonly available. Propagate by seed sown in a cold frame in spring or by division of the clumps in spring.

Linum/Flax

The best of this genus are easy-to-grow hardy perennials with richly-colored flowers. Light soil, full sun. *L. narbonense,* 18 to 24 inches, various shades of blue, May to July. *L. viscosum,* 18 inches, flowers white, blue, lilac, or lilac-rose, June to August. Propagate by seed sown in fall in a cold frame or by cuttings taken in July and rooted in a sandy compost.

Lunaria/Honesty

The common honesty is *L. annua,* 18 to 24 inches, white or lilac-purple flowers, then strange seed-heads which as they open peel off their outer covering to reveal a coin-like disk. An annual, but often behaves like a biennial. Any soil, part shade. Propagate by seed sown outdoors in May.

Lupinus/Lupin

Indispensable border plants, tall spikes packed all around with brightly colored flowers, individually like pea-flowers. Any good soil, sun or slight shade, flowers June and July, 2½ to 4 feet. The lupins usually grown are hybrids known as the Russell Lupins; they come in the widest possible range of colors and color combinations. Easily grown from seed, but seed collected from garden plants seldom produce true-breeding plants exactly like the parents. Propagate very good forms by cuttings taken from just above ground level in late March or April. Remove seed-heads unless seed is wanted.

Lychnis/Campion

Hardy perennials, brightly colored flowers, any ordinary soil, withstand dryish conditions. Among the best are *L. chalcedonia,* 2 to 3 feet, stiff, erect plant, brilliant scarlet flowers, June to August. Also pink and white forms. *L. coronaria,* 2½ feet, the whole plant covered with silvery hairs which give it a white, woolly look; flowers white, pink, or crimson borne on a branching stem, June to August. *L. flos-cuculi,* Ragged Robin, a well-known wild flower; garden forms much superior, with double flowers, well worth growing, 18 inches, June to August. *L. × haageana,* 1 foot, hybrids with white, orange, crimson, or scarlet flowers up to 2 inches across, June and July. *L. viscaria,* 1 foot, with sticky stems that often trap insects; flowers rosy-crimson on a branching stem, May to July. Single and double forms. Propagate by seed sown outdoors, or by division.

Mathiola/Stock

Showy annuals and biennials, colorful, deliciously scented. Any good garden soil in sun. *M. bicornis,* the night-scented stock, 1 foot, an **annual,** purplish flowers. *M. incana,* 18 inches, **biennial,** purple, summer, garden strains derived from this. Among the most notable strains are the Ten Week Stocks and the new Trysomic Seven Week Stocks, which are the earliest flowering of all; 12 to 15 inches. Raise these stock from seed sown in a greenhouse or frame in March and planted out in April or May. Night-scented stocks are sown outdoors in April where they are to flower. Stock are most satisfactory in areas with cool summers. Otherwise they grow vegetatively without blooming. Excellent as a greenhouse cut flower.

Mertensia/Bluebell

Low-growing hardy perennials, useful in shaded borders. Blue bell-shaped flowers in clusters. *M. ciliata,* 2 feet, blue-green leaves, blue flowers pink in the bud, May to July. *M. virginica,* Virginia cowslip, soft bluish-gray leaves and purplish-blue flowers in elegant sprays, May. Increase by seed sown in a cold frame as soon as ripe, or by division.

Mimulus/Monkey Flower

Very colorful hardy annuals and perennials, showy flowers. Do best in moist, cool, sunny places where they will often naturalize themselves. Among the best are *M. cardinalis,* the cardinal monkey-flower, 1 to 2 feet, perennial, bright scarlet flowers produced continuously through summer and well into fall, spreading habit. *M. cupreus,* perennial, 8 to 12 inches, flowers yellow to copper-red. *M. guttatus,* perennial, 12 to 18 inches, yellow flowers spotted red. *M. luteus,* 18 inches, perennial, yellow flowers. *M. moschatus,* 9 inches, yellow flowers sometimes spotted red; no scent. All summer-flowering. Increase by seed or division.

Myosotis/Forget-Me-Not

Familiar dainty blue-flowered bedding plants. Over 40 species, embracing annuals, biennials, and perennials. Any good garden soil in sun. Perennials not reliably hardy. The species usually grown are *M. alpestris,* 3 to 8 inches, azure blue with a yellow eye, June and July; *M. caespitosa,* 6 inches, perennial, sky-blue with a yellow eye; *M. scorpioides,* 6 to 12 inches, the common forget-me-not, perennial, blue with a yellow eye, May and June; *M. sylvatica,* 1 to 2 feet, blue with a yellow eye, many named forms ranging from deep-violet-blue through sky-blues and pale blues to pinks. Apart from *M. alpestris,* best treated as biennials. Raise from seed sown outdoors in April, May, or June and transplant in October 6 inches apart.

Nemesia

Among the most colorful and floriferous of all bedding plants. Plants usually grown in gardens are hybrids, treated as half-hardy annuals. Grow 6 to 12 inches, flower throughout the summer in all colors. Buy in packets of mixed seed. Blues can be obtained separately. Sow seed in well-drained soil in the greenhouse in March, harden in cold frame, plant out 4 inches apart in May. Best in areas with cool summers or as a winter-flowering pot plant.

Nemophila/Baby Blue-Eyes

Hardy annuals with attractive blue flowers with white centers, growing well in most soils in sunny positions. Two species usually grown are *N. maculata,* 6 to 12 inches, flowers white, veined, and blotched violet giving a pale-blue effect, summer; and *N. menziesii,* 6 inches, spreading habit, light blue with white centers, summer, var. "Alba" has white flowers with a black center. Easily raised from seed sown in the garden in March or April where the plants are to flower. Thin seedlings to 3 inches apart.

Nicotiana/Flowering Tobacco

Annual, perennial, and shrubby plants, usually with showy and strongly scented leaves and flowers. The species grown as garden plants are all annuals, do best in rich soil, full sun. *N. alata,* 2 feet, flowers white with a greenish back to the petals, exceptionally fragrant, summer; var. "Grandiflora," larger flowers, yellowish on the reverse. Named forms include "Daylight," 2½ feet, flowers pure white, staying open all day; "Dwarf White Bedder," 15 inches, pure white, flowers open all day; "Lime Green," 2½ feet, acid yellowish-green flowers. *N.x. sanderae,* 2 to 3 feet, flowers various shades of pink and carmine. *N. suaveolens,* 18 to 24 inches, flowers white, greenish reverse. *N. sylvestris,* 5 feet, long-tubed white flowers, exceptionally fragrant. Raise from seed sown indoors during March or April, harden off and plant 12 to 15 inches apart in May or June. Or seeds can be sown outdoors where plants are to flower in May. Self-sown seedlings often appear in late spring.

Paeonia/Peony

Among the largest-flowered, most colorful and useful of all hardy herbaceous perennials, indispensable in the border. Will thrive in any soil and almost any situation except really dense shade. Dislike being moved, will survive for 10 or 20 years, improving each year, 2 to 3 feet. All flower in May or June. There are a number of very beautiful species, but those usually grown are hybrids or selected forms mainly derived from *P. lactiflora,* large white flowers; "Madame Emile Debatene," double carmine, very large flower; "Madame Calot," pale pink, large flower, beautifully shaped; "Kelway's Brilliant," single glowing carmine; "Reine Hortense," deep-pink center, fading to white toward the edges of the petals; "Gleam of Light," one of the loveliest singles, deep-rose-pink petals, gorgeous yellow petaloid center; "Canarie," fragrant primrose passing to white; "Festiva Maxima," huge white flecked crimson; "Monsieur Martin Cahuzac," fragrant black-crimson, probably the darkest of all; "Sarah Bernhardt," apple-blossom pink, probably the most popular variety of all.

Species: *P. cambessedesi,* 12 to 18 inches, leaves green above and purple beneath, flowers deep rose-pink, 3 to 4 inches across, red filaments, best at the foot of a sunny wall. *P. emodi,* 2 to 5 feet, flowers single, purest white, 5 inches across, yellow stamens. *P. lactiflora,* 2 feet, parent of most of the garden forms, pure-white fragrant flowers. *P. mascula,* 2 to 3 feet, deep rose. *P. mlokosewitschii,* 2 feet, deep-yellow flowers. *P. officinalis,* 2 feet, the old cottage-garden peony with double flowers in white, pink, or crimson. *P. wittmanniana,* 2 feet, yellow. *P. veitchii,* 2 feet, deeply cut foliage, 3-inch wide flowers pale pink to red. Species and cultivars are propagated by division. Species are seldom available.

In any new garden the usual problem is to get plants to grow on very exposed sites. Here only low-growing subjects are used.

Oenothera/Evening Primrose

A large genus containing several useful border plants; other species suitable for the rock garden. In most species, flowers are yellow, but there are white, red, and pink forms. Biennials tend to open their flowers only at night, but many perennials flower during the day and are also fragrant. Many are monocarpic, i.e. they die once they have flowered. Grow best on light soils in sunny positions and are good in alkaline soils. Many species. The most useful include *O. biennis,* the true evening primrose, biennial, yellow flowers opening in the evening, 2 to 4 feet, summer; *O. caespitosa,* perennial, 9 to 12 inches, fragrant flowers white or pink, summer, flowers open during the day; *O. odorata,* perennial, 12 to 18 inches, flowers yellow turning to red, April to June. *O. speciosa,* 12 to 24 inches, perennial, fragrant white flowers turning pink, July and August. Increase by division or by seed sown outdoors in May or June where the plants are to flower.

Papaver/Poppy

Large family of colorful, easily grown, hardy annuals and perennials. Will grow in any garden soil, prefer sun. **Annual species:** *P. commutatum,* 18 inches, bright red, black blotch on each petal, summer. *P. glaucum* (the tulip poppy), 18 inches, deepest scarlet, summer. P. *rhoeas,* 1 to 2 feet, scarlet, black blotch on each petal, summer. From this species the Shirley Poppies, in a wide range of colors, have been derived. Many garden forms including doubles. Grow annuals from seed sown in April where they are to flower, and thin to 3 to 4 inches apart. The two **perennial** species most commonly grown and giving most color are *P. nudicaule,* the Iceland poppy, 1 foot, flowers white, yellow, or orange, summer; and *P. orientale,* the Oriental poppy, 2 to 3 feet, flowers orange-scarlet, 5 to 8 inches across, May and June. Named forms include "King George," most-vivid scarlet; "Marcus Perry," enormous flowers, orange-scarlet with a black blotch; "Perry's White," white with dark blotches; and "Salmon Glow," double pink flowers. Sow seed in spring in a cold frame or in summer in the open garden, or divide the roots in spring; or take root cuttings in winter. Seeds of named forms will not come true but are worth growing.

Pelargonium

Very large genus of perennial plants either grown in the greenhouse or used for summer bedding. The "Geraniums" belong to this genus. Other members grown for decorative leaves and flowers. Some 300 species have been named. Tremendous variety, many have scented leaves. Fall into four groups.

"Zonal" pelargoniums The familiar geranium, best known of the pelargoniums for bedding; also excellent pot plants. Flowers, single or double, deep crimson-purple, brilliant scarlet, pink, white, salmon. Leaves usually with a horseshoe of deeper green, but some variegated. Also dwarf forms. Hundreds of cultivars, including "Irene," scarlet red; "Dark Red Irene"; "Ricard," brick red; "Enchantress Fiat," salmon-pink; "Mme. Buchner," white. The carefree strain of geraniums are new kinds that are seed-propagated and available in a range of colors.

"Ivy-leaved" pelargoniums Forms of *P. peltatum,* a trailing species with brilliant flowers, mostly in shades of red, pink, or white. Some of the less-trailing types may be used for summer bedding. Choose from "Abel Carrière," purple; "Chas. Turner," rose-madder; "L'Elegant," white with purple markings; "Galilee," rose-pink; "Mme. Crousse," pale pink.

"Regal" or "Show" pelargoniums (see Greenhouses).

Scented-leaved pelargoniums Can be used for summer bedding, flowers insignificant.

Grow in most soils, easily raised from seed, or from cuttings about 3-inches long taken in spring or late summer and rooted. Lift plants before the first frosts, pot and use indoors or keep in a greenhouse. Plant out after danger of frost is past.

Petunia

Eternally popular summer bedding plants, wide-open trumpet-shaped flowers in a range of colors embracing whites, pinks, reds, purples, and bicolors, many with frilled petals. Present plants are hybrids derived from 2 out of the 40 species. Treated as half-hardy annuals. Sow the fine, dust-like seed in February or March indoors at a warm temperature. Harden off and plant out in May or June, 6 inches apart. Double forms may be propagated by cuttings taken in the fall and grown in a greenhouse.

Phlox

A large genus including hardy perennials and rock-garden plants. Only one **annual** species, *P. drummondii,* 1 foot, flowers in a wide range of colors. July until the first heavy frosts; easily raised from seed sown in

Peony 'Legion of Honour', one of a new generation of brilliantly colorful single peonies that are rapidly gaining in popularity. These single peonies need no staking and do not droop their heavy heads as do the old-fashioned garden types.

An old walled kitchen garden of Britain converted for use as flower garden. In such protected surroundings many tender and unusual plants can be grown to perfection. The paving further reflects and retains heat and helps to ripen the wood of tender plants.

frames or the greenhouse in March, hardened off and planted out in May 6 inches apart. Nip out leading shoot for bushy growth. **Perennials:** the border phlox, *P. paniculata* or *P.* ×. *decussata;* all flower July and August, about 3½ feet tall. "Aida," dark red with dark-purple eye; "Border Gem," deep violet; "Dorothy Hanbury Forbes," clear pink; "Fairy's Petticoat," soft mulberry with a darker eye; "Fanal," brilliant flame-red; "Karl Foerster," dark orange-red; "Mia Ruys," dwarf, pure white; "Milly van Hoboken," clear pink with a deep-red eye; "Olive Wells Durant," light rose-pink with a deep eye, an exceptionally large flower truss; "Otley Purple," large trusses, violet, dwarf; "September Snow," very late white with a rosy eye; "Widar," purple with a white eye. Propagate by taking a piece of the base of the stem with a couple of inches of root at any time during the growing season, plant it in a nursery bed or border and shade until established. Border phlox like rich soil and sun.

Platycodon/Chinese Bellflower

One species, *P. grandiflorus,* very beautiful, hardy perennial, 18 to 24 inches, wide-open 4-inch bell-shaped flowers on a tall spike, July to Sep-

tember. There are a number of named forms and all are good. Does best in fertile soil and full sun. Propagate by seed sown in March, by cuttings inserted in sandy soil in a cold frame in spring, or by division of the fleshy roots in spring once growth has started. First flowers the year after propagation.

Polygonum/Knotweed

Huge genus with over 300 plants, some ornamental hardy perennials. Will grow in any soil, in sun or shade, do best with plenty of moisture at the roots. *P. affine,* 1 foot, leaves deep green, becoming bronzy in winter, flowers red in dense spikes in August, September, and October. *P. amplexicaulis,* 2 to 3 feet, leaves heart-shaped, flowers bright crimson, purplish or white (the white form being fragrant), August to October. *P. cuspidatum,* 6 to 9 feet, leaves large, oval, carried on bamboo-like canes that curve outward. Many small creamy-white flowers in feathery sprays 4 to 5 inches long, July to October. The stems turn reddish-brown in winter, but cut them down in spring. Extremely vigorous and becomes a weed.

Primula

Family containing primrose, polyanthus, and many other beautiful plants. They need a moist, peaty soil and

shade during the summer. *P. vulgaris,* the common primrose, is essentially a woodland plant but can be grown successfully on the shaded side of deciduous shrubs. Also pink, white, and purple and double cultivated forms. Primula species have combined to produce the popular and colorful strains known as *Polyanthus.* Best grown in bold clumps or groups in a rich soil with some midday shade. Varieties include blue flowers and forms with individual flowers over 3 inches across. These all range in height from 6 to 12 inches. Can be propagated by seed sown in the open garden under a cover of glass in early spring and planted out in August 9 to 12 inches apart. Lift and divide every 2 or 3 years to maintain vigor. *P. denticulata,* the Drumstick Primula, purple or white flowers in a ball at the top of a slender stem. 1 foot, grow on the shaded side of deciduous shrubs or in clearings among shrubs or trees. Increase by seed or division.

Pulsatilla/Pasqueflower

Often listed as *Anemone pulsatilla.* Delightful spring-flowering, hardy perennials. Need a well-drained soil and a sunny position. *P. vulgaris,* 6 to 12 inches, lovely bell-shaped lavender-purple flowers covered with silky hairs, April. Form "Alba" is white, and seedlings of a red form are sometimes obtainable. Increase by seed sown in midsummer.

Island beds are a more satisfactory way of growing perennials than in a border against a hedge, where the hedge takes most of the nutrients from the soil and the plants have to lean forward to reach the light.

Rudbeckia/Coneflower

Attractive and showy hardy perennials with yellow daisy-type flowers. Good soil, likes sun. Excellent for cutting. *R. laciniata,* 2 to 7 feet, leaves deeply divided, flowers yellow, single or double, up to 3 inches across, August and September. *R. nitida,* 4 to 6 feet, flowers yellow with reflexed petals and a conspicuous green cone in the middle, July to October. *R. speciosa,* 2 feet, flowers yellow, up to 4 inches across, with a conspicuous purple-black cone, July to October. *R. hirta,* the Black-Eyed Susan and several hybrid forms collectively called Gloriosa Daisy. Flower the first year of seeds sown early.

Salvia

A large genus (over 700 species) containing many colorful and useful hardy annuals and perennials. Like a sunny place in well-drained soil. *S. azurea,* up to 5 feet, perennial, deep-blue flowers, August. *S. haematodes,* biennial, 36 inches, bluish-violet flowers, summer. *S. nutans,* perennial, 24 to 36 inches, violet flowers, June and July. *S. patens,* perennial, 18 to 24 inches, white, light-blue or deep-blue flowers, August and September. *S. splendens,* brilliant scarlet species often used for summer bedding, usually grown as an annual, 10 to 30 inches depending on kind. Increase by seed sown in February or March indoors, harden off, plant out in May or June. Increase perennial species by division.

Sidalcea

Hardy perennials; any soil, sun. Tall spikes of mallow-like flowers throughout summer. The species usually grown is *S. spicata,* 1 to 3 feet; several named forms in shades of pink and red. Increase by seed sown in April or by division in October or March.

Solidago/Goldenrod

Superior modern garden sorts derived from *S. canadensis,* to 6 feet, flower August and October, and *S. virgaurea,* 2 feet, flowers July to October. Best border varieties, which will thrive in a sunny position in any soil and are increased by division, include "Ballardii," 5 to 6 feet, golden yellow in branching sprays, September; "Golden Gate," 2 feet, lemon-yellow, compact growth; "Golden Wings," 5 feet, deep yellow in branching sprays, August and September; "Leda," a slightly orange-yellow in erect spikes, 3½ feet, July and August.

Sweet Pea/*Lathyrus odoratus*

Among the most charming, oldest, and colorful of all garden annuals. The modern "Spencer" varieties have the most elegant flowers of all sweet peas and come in a wide range of colors. The "Galaxy Hybrids" are an early-flowering strain, producing as many as 7 really large flowers on each spike. The "Knee-Hi" varieties grow to only 3 feet, need little support, and produce large flowers on a long, straight stem, which makes them one of the best sort for cutting. Even smaller are the "Bijou" types that grow to only 18 inches, producing quite large flowers on short stems.

Sow seed early outdoors. Seeds are hard-coated and should be nicked with a sharp knife, soaked in warm water, then sown. Seed may be sown

Foliage can contribute just as much color to the border as flowers. Here the grey-blue leaves of hostas make an excellent contrast to the more dainty flowers surounding them.

indoors in small pots and transplanted outdoors. After germination keep well ventilated. Water well during dry spells. Taller kinds need support of netting, trellis work, or strings. Remove fading flowers. Sweet peas are most satisfactory in areas of mild summers; also useful in the greenhouse in winter.

Tagetes/Marigold

They are among the most colorful of half-hardy annuals, thriving in any ordinary soil in a sunny position. *T. erecta,* so-called African marigold, 2 feet, flowers in shades of yellow or orange, 2 to 4 inches across, June to frost, named forms 9 inches to 4 feet, pale yellow to deep orange. *T. patula,* the "French" marigold, annual, 18 inches, flowers brownish-yellow, June on. Numerous named forms. *T. tenuifolia,* the Mexican marigold, 18 inches, yellow, summer. The form "Pumila" is particularly useful in small gardens as it grows to only 6 inches. Annual. Plants are raised from seed sown thinly indoors in March or in a cold greenhouse or frame in April. Plant out 12 to 15 inches apart (6 inches apart for the dwarf forms) after danger of frost is past. Need plenty of water in dry weather.

Tropaeolum/Nasturtium

Species usually grown is *T. majus,* large, trumpet-shaped flowers in reds, yellows, and oranges, of climbing or trailing habit, producing a succession of bloom throughout summer. Propagate by seed sown in the greenhouse or in a frame in March and plant out in May, or sow outdoors in flowering positions in May or June.

Verbascum/Mullein

Stately old-fashioned plants with attractive green or woolly-white leaves and tall spires of flowers. All hardy biennials or perennials; the perennials are best treated as biennials. Any soil, even dry, sun or part shade, particularly good in slightly alkaline soil. Species most commonly grown is *V. phoenicium,* from which most of the garden varieties have been derived; 2 to 3 feet, basal rosette of leaves and few leaves on the stem, arching sprays of violet, pink, or purple flowers, May to September. Increase by seed sown outdoors.

Vinca/Periwinkle

Popular trailing evergreen plants, useful ground cover under shrubs and trees or over sunny banks. Any soil. *V. major,* the larger of the two species, up to 2 feet, large bright-blue

A delightful garden
that combines the
elements of a raised
bed with stone
edging,
and shrubbery, the
shrubs at the top of
the mounded bed
giving height to the
whole scheme as
well as forming a
background to the
more colorful
plants in front.
*Photo
Frank Herrmann*

flowers produced continuously from May to October. Not winter-hardy in cold regions. Var. "Variegata," leaves blotched, margined creamy-white; particularly useful in dark, shaded areas. *V. minor* is a smaller-growing species, up to 6 inches, flowers bright blue, 1 inch across, continuously April to September. Varieties include "Alba," white flowers; "Atropurpurea," purple flowers. Winter-hardy in northern United States. Increase by detaching portions of the stem with roots on and planting where required.

Rock Gardens

Color in the garden is not just a matter of choosing flowers. Apart from foliage, berries, and the bark of trees, the color and texture of stone creates an atmosphere of its own. This applies particularly in the rock garden, where you can create a cool or cheerful effect by the use of stone in combination with plants. For instance, a rock garden made with yellow or red sandstone and screes covered with the bright-green leaves and gay flowers of the saxifrage family would be a warming sight on a sunny day in spring. Conversely, by setting a grayish sandstone in large slabs and interplanting it with dark-green conifers and evergreen shrubs, a distinctly somber scene would be created.

Limestones are often favored for rock gardens. Some are gray, others are yellow or brown, just as sandstone may be anything from yellow to red or green. Quite a reasonable color can be made by staining cement with a solution of iron sulfate, and if you make your own rocks, you will be able to decide the shape and size by making your own molds. Tufa, which weathers to a dark gray and is a soft, absorbent rock like pumice stone can be replaced by "hypertufa." Tufa is a good home for plants like the mossy saxifrages, but it is quite expensive. A substitute can be made by mixing two parts of peat with one each of sand and cement (all by bulk). The materials must be thoroughly mixed before water is added, although the peat should be moist. It is usually best to mix the water in until a thick cream cement is formed. It should be poured into specially prepared molds, made by digging large holes in the garden and lining them with large rocks or stones. When the "hypertufa" has dried, the other stones can be knocked out easily with a hammer or can be left. Pockets for plants can be cut with a chisel or formed when the mixture is poured into the molds. Cement colorants can be mixed in when making the "hypertufa."

Granite was used in the Victorian era for rock gardens, and although it is expensive, its crystalline qualities make it attractive. It may well become popular again with changing fashions in design. In former times rock gardens were conceived in the form of dells, with running water and ferny niches. In the early 1900s greater interest began to be shown in simulating the actual conditions of alpine regions to provide suitable conditions for the growth of alpine plants. Your choice will probably reflect your approach: that of an enthusiastic plantsman or that of a gardener seeking to add another feature to the garden to contrast with the flat lawn or to act as a focal point.

Much is made of the importance of obtaining rocks that fit in with local rock formations. Unless the local rock formations are visible and contiguous with your garden, this would hardly seem to matter. More important is the fact that if you obtain rock from some distance away the price per ton is likely to be three or four times higher. A ton of stone can be had for a few dollars, and a ton of sandstone would be enough for a small rock garden. Remember that the volume of a ton of rock will vary. The same volume of some limestones will be twice as heavy as sandstone.

Limestones and sandstones show varying degrees of stratification, which makes them easy to lay out if, in placing them, the lines of stratification follow nature. Generally, in designing rock gardens the rocks are laid as though they formed part of a natural outcrop, and this is a good system to follow. If you have a sloping garden, it is easy to set rocks in the slope to make a rock garden. The rocks should slope backward so that the rain falling on them runs back into the ground and not down the hill. If your garden is on a level, the easiest procedure is to dig out a hole to make both a mound for the rock garden and a site for a pool at the same time. It is also quite feasible to build a rock garden on the level with long, flat pieces of stone sloping slightly upward. If these are interspersed with an occasional tall conifer of the cypress family, fine horizontal and vertical effects can be obtained. The main reason for the slope in a rock garden is to achieve the extra drainage needed by many rock plants, and this can be obtained without either rocks or a slope by making a raised bed using railway ties or concrete slabs. If you have a garden sloping toward the south, you have the ideal site.

If, owing to the flatness of the area, you are worried

about the drainage, it is best to dig out the soil and put in a central base of rubble, broken brick, coarse gravel, and so on. If the soil is a heavy clay it will be necessary to mix fine gravel and sharp sand with it when returning it to the site. How you set the rocks will depend on their shape and the number available. A large number of flat stones will enable you to set one on top of the other with gaps and crevices for smaller stones and soil in the style of an outcrop. If you are dealing with a smaller number of block-shaped stones, it will be a simple matter to set them out like ramparts to form small compartmented terraces of soil. If you are including a pool in the design you may like to incorporate a water course with a submerged pump to pump water from a pool on a lower level to one on a higher level. Such a system will require an electrical supply to operate the pump and a water supply to keep up the level of water lost by evaporation.

If you are building terraces, you have the basic requirement for constructing a scree. A scree is simply a pile of broken rocks found at the foot of a steep cliff. It is ideal for certain alpine plants that require dry conditions where they meet the soil. Dig out about 1 to 2 feet of soil and at the bottom put in a layer of small rocks a few inches thick. Over this lay some fibrous material, such as sphagnum peat, to prevent the topsoil from penetrating the drainage area. Cover this with a top layer of crushed stone, gravel, peat, loam, and finely decomposed leaf-mold. The stone chips and gravel should form four-fifths of the total bulk.

If you are incorporating running water in your rock garden, you can also construct a moraine, which is simply a pile of stones at the foot of a glacier, on which many fine-flowering plants have been found to thrive. The moraine is similar to the scree except that the bottom of the excavated area and halfway up the sides are lined with puddling clay or cement to make an underground lake. An outlet is made at the lower end of this lake a few inches above the level of the bottom, and layers are laid down as above for a scree. Water is let in at the upper end of the slope. It is important not to try to grow acid-loving-plants in a moraine or scree made with limestone.

Soil for the rock garden is best made of four parts loam, two parts humus, and two parts sharp sand or fine gravel. The best loam for most garden purposes may be thought of as a fertile garden soil with both good drainage and moisture-retaining constituents (sand and clay). The humus may be provided by peat, compost, or leaf-mold.

The use of plenty of loose granite or limestone chips on the surface makes for an attractive appearance, keeps down weeds, and helps to retain moisture. Chips should be added to screes and wherever there are poor-soil-loving plants.

Here a York stone retaining wall has been used to blend the edge of a rock garden with the stone path that leads to the lawn. Low-growing plants are used at the front, taller growing subjects further back.
Photo
Frank Herrmann

Climbers and Wall Shrubs

Planting
It is not necessary to plant the rock garden at the same time it is constructed. This is usually inconvenient, and planting can best be done later. It is often recommended that rock gardens be constructed in the fall, so that spring-flowering plants will have time to settle-in and be ready for the following season.

Dry stone walls
Low retaining walls or walls for edging or for raised beds built of large stones or colored paving slabs can form a warm-looking feature of any garden. Four feet should be the maximum height of a wall of such loose construction, which is held together only by soil and the roots of the plants growing in it.

For extra height a retaining wall can be built with terrace beds forming wide steps. A foundation trench should be excavated to a depth of about 9 inches and filled with rubble well rammed down and topped with a layer of ashes or soil. In building retaining walls, the stones should be laid tilting slightly back, so that their weight rests partly against the ground behind. For raised beds 2 or 3 feet wide, the stones can be laid almost vertically, with a step of ½ or 1 inch between each layer. Sandstone looks good, but you can even use the rough-faced bricks made of stone composition for a low dry wall. Follow the pattern of bonding seen in brickwork, as this makes for greater strength, and for the "mortar" use a soil mixture of 3 parts fibrous loam, 1 part peat and 1 part sand. You will find it easy to incorporate any rock plants as you build the wall. Make sure there is plenty of soil behind the wall, and keep it moist. Leave gaps for the plants to expand and places for those you would like to add when they become obtainable. Most alpines will do well, but the following are obviously suitable: *Alyssum, Arabis, Aubrieta, Campanula, Dianthus, Genista, Gypsophila, Hypericum, Phlox subulata, Saxifraga aizoon,* Sedum, Sempervivum, and *Zauschneria californica* (Californian fuchsia).

Sunken gardens, paved areas, and paths
A sunken garden, paved area, or path is a feature often associated with rock gardens, and these are often the home of creeping plants between irregular-sized paving stones. A foundation of rubble is first rammed down and covered with sand. Paving stones, old bricks, or precast slabs may be used singly or in tasteful combinations and either mortared or left with gaps and cracks to accommodate the plants. Some suitable sandy compost should be inserted in places where plantings are made. Mint and thyme *(Mentha requienii* and *Thymus serpyllum)* yield a scent when crushed and are tolerant of this treatment. Creeping Jenny *(Lysimachia uummularia)* is rampant and hardy, and *Cotoneaster horizontalis* is typical of the low-growing shrubs which are excellent for larger paved areas. Many other rock plants will thrive under these conditions.

Alpine Lawns
Paving plants are often suited to alpine lawns, which are simply places where low-growing flowers or creeping plants form a carpet, which may adjoin the rock garden or even form part of it. Stepping stones or rocks may be interspersed through them, and the ground may be sloping or flat. Low-growing bulbs, such as *Crocus* or *Narcissus bulbocodium, Chionodoxa, Scilla,* and *Puschkinia,* will make colorful sights in spring, to be followed by other hardy dwarfs leading to the lovely fall crocus *Colchicum* and *Cyclamen neapolitanum,* with its marbled foliage and pink flowers. A few larger plants, up to a foot, and 1 or 2 dwarf shrubs may be included in larger lawns. Strictly speaking, an alpine lawn has no grass, and the bulbs and larger plants appear through a carpet of low-growing alpine plants.

Stone sinks
A miniature rock garden that needs little attention can be created in an old-fashioned glazed or stone sink. It can be set in a bank or raised bed, supported on stone pillars, or legs like a tub. The drain hole should be kept open with a piece of broken pot and a layer of broken pots placed in the bottom and covered with sphagnum peat to prevent overdrainage. Fill it up with compost and set rocks among dwarf conifers and low-growing alpine plants, or make it into a miniature "willow-pattern" garden or Japanese garden.

Ferns
Ferns do not generally grow so well under quite the same conditions as true alpines. They belong rather to the cool, shady, and rocky dell more favored in former times. However, a large number of hardy ferns will settle in a moist soil with plenty of leaf mold or peat and some sand. Ferns are certainly more popular than they were, and the evergreen kinds are particularly useful. A good one to start with might be the Ebony Spleenwort *(Asplenium platyneuron),* which grows to a foot, likes the shade, and might be good for an old wall. It is evergreen and has rich, light-green pointed fronds. *Dryopteris phegopteris,* the beech tern, is another handsome species. It is a native fern and grows 6 to 9 inches high and also likes a sheltered spot with partial shade. It is deciduous. The well-known Hart's Tongue Fern *(Phyllitis scolopendrium)* has shiny, bright-green fronds tapering off to a point in the variety "Crispum" or with a crest in the variety "Cristatum." They are evergreen and will grow up to a foot or more and withstand quite severe frosts, when they are most attractively outlined in white. Another attractive fern for the rock garden, *Polystichum acrostichoides* (Christmas Fern); grows from 1 to 2 feet high and is deciduous, with thickly divided fronds. All these ferns may be planted in spring.

Rock-garden plants
A select list, these plants may be augmented by most types of low-growing hardy bulbs and the table of alpine plants to be found under Greenhouses. Colorful dwarf conifers may be selected from *Cedrus, Chamaecyparis, Cryptomeria, Juniperus, Picea,* and *Thuja* genera, and among the shrubs you may select dwarf or low-growing forms of *Betula, Berberis, Cotoneaster, Daphne, Erica, Gaultheria, Pernettya, Rhododendron, Salix, Skimmia, Sorbus, Syringa, Teucrium,* and *Vaccinium.* In choosing, be careful that when the plant reaches full growth it does not take too much nourishment from the alpines or be-

come too big for the size of your rock garden. Most of the plants below will establish themselves as perennials.

Achillea/Milfoil, Yarrow

A. × "King Edward" (syn. *A.* × *lewisii)* is perhaps the best-known species and is a good ground cover. Flowers rich yellow, 4 to 5 inches, June to August. Other species are *A. ageratifolia,* leaves gray-white, flowers white, 4 to 6 inches, June to September; *A. tormentosa,* leaves gray, flowers yellow-gold, 9 inches, June to August.

Aethionema/Stone Cress

The hybrid "Warley Rose," with its bright rose-pink flowers, is the most popular. Not long-lasting, 9 inches, May to August, compact. *A. cordifolium,* flowers rose, leaves blue-gray, 6 to 9 inches, May to August. *A. iberideum,* flowers white, leaves gray, 6 inches, May to July. *A. pulchellum,* flowers rosy-pink, leaves gray, June to July.

Androsace/Rock Jasmine

The perennials are best, of which mixed species are sometimes obtainable in seed packets. *A. lanuginosa,* flowers pink, leaves trailing, 6 inches, is an easy one to try.

Armeria/Thrift

A sandy soil suits them. *A. maritima* (Sea Pink) provides some good varieties, such as "Vindictive," flowers red-pink, 6 inches, early summer. A good sandy loam and sunny position. *A. caespitosa,* flowers lilac-pink, 2 inches, June to July, is a good plant for a scree.

Aubrieta

Many beautiful varieties obtainable from specialized nurseries or from seed sown in spring or summer. More suitable for hanging down walls. Should be well cut back after flowering to get new growth. The flowers vary from dull to brilliant purple,

rose-red, and lilac and bloom in spring.

Campanula/Bellflower

Popular plants that will do well if given a well-drained position in sun or partial shade. *C. carpatica,* blue, violet, white, etc., 6 to 12 inches, summer, spreads easily. *C. fragilis,* blue, trailing foliage, summer. *C. cochlearifolia* (syn. *C. pusilla),* blue, etc., 6 inches, summer, good grower.

Cyclamen

A carpet of the hardy species under deciduous trees is a delight, and different species will give flowers from late summer until early spring. Start with small plants in August or earlier or with good fresh tubers planted an inch or more deep. *C. europaeum,* crimson, marbled foliage, 3 inches, August to September. *C. neapolitanum,* rose, marbled foliage, 3 to 6 inches, September to November. *C. orbiculatum coum,* carmine, deep spot, plain foliage, 3 inches, January to March. Best grown in areas of mild winters.

Dianthus

A few species of this big genus are suitable for the rock garden. They like sun. *D. alpinus,* rose, 3 inches, May to June. *D.* × *arvernensis,* pink, 6 inches, May to June, likes slightly acid to slightly alkaline soil. *D. deltoides,* dark crimson, white, etc., 6 to 8 inches, summer, known as the Maiden Pink. A number of hybrids are worth growing, including "Mars."

Cyclamen neapolitanum 'Album', a delightful little plant that will naturalize itself on the rick garden or in woodland. The commoner pink form is shown elsewhere in this book.

Dryas/Mountain Avens

A mat-forming plant with attractive leaves and white, strawberry-like flowers, *D. octopetala* grows 3 inches on sunny ledges.

Gentiana/Gentian

Beautiful bell-like or trumpet-like blue flowers are typical of the many species suitable. *G. acaulis,* rich blue, 3 inches, spring. *G. septemfida,* bright blue, 6 to 12 inches, July. *G. sinoornata,* blue, 3 inches, fall, dislikes lime. Best in areas of cool summers.

Geranium/Crane's Bill

The dwarf geraniums are easily grown in sunny, well-drained positions. *G. cinereum,* pink or white, 3 inches,

Polypodium vulgare 'Longicaudatum', one of the many striking forms of this fern suitable for a shady spot on the rock garden.

A rock garden edging a drive. Here local flint has been used. Though not an ideal stone for building a rockery, it is usually easiest and cheapest to create a rockery from local stone.

summer, var. "Subcaulescens," carmine, dark-centered, 6 inches, June to September.

Gypsophila

Propagate by heel cuttings in spring. *G. cerastioides,* white veined red, 3 inches, spring, dense mats for the paved garden. *G. dubia,* white pink stained, dark-green matted leaves, spring, for niches and walls. *G. repens,* white, trailing, summer, var. rose-pink.

Helianthemum/Sun Rose

There are a large number of varieties of the Common Sun Rose, *H. nummularium,* 6 to 12 inches, trailing, summer, of which "Jubilee" is double yellow and "Mrs. C. W. Earle" is double scarlet. Mixed colors may be obtained from seed. Good ground cover for dry, sunny spots.

Iberis/Candytuft

Choose the dwarf kinds for the rock garden. *I. sempervirens,* pure white, 6 inches, spring; "Little Gem" and "Snowflake" are named varieties that may grow slightly taller. Well-drained, sunny positions suit them. The foliage is evergreen.

Leontopodium alpinum/Edelweiss

The famous edelweiss is easily raised from seed sown in early spring and gives rosettes of white flowers in July to September, 6 inches.

Linaria/Toadflax

The purple, golden-tipped flowers of *L. alpina* are similar in form to a small-flowered snapdragon, 3 to 6 inches, June to September. Easily raised from seed.

Lithospermum/ Gromwell

L. diffusum, best grown from cuttings, needs an acid soil, but suitable to dry, sunny positions; blue, 6 inches, summer. "Heavenly Blue" and "Grace Ward" are good cultivars.

Maianthemum

M. bifolium (Twin-leaved Lily of the Valley), white, 6 to 9 inches, May to June, is excellent for carpeting shady places. Plant a piece of the creeping rhizome. Seldom available.

Gentiana septemfida, one of the easiest gentians to grow, and an ideal rock plant. It will often seed itself freely.

Meconopsis betonicifolia/Blue Himalayan Poppy

Not suitable to the small rock garden. Its translucent blue flowers with golden yellow centers reach 2 feet in May to June. They require little or no lime in the soil and moist, cool shade. A difficult plant to grow.

Oxalis

Beware of weeds formed by rampant varieties of this flower. *O. enneaphylla* has pale-pink or snow-white flowers, 2 inches, spring. A plant for partial shade.

Penstemon

Usually good plants for the scree or hot, dry conditions. *P. pinifolius,* bright orange-scarlet, spiny leaves, 9

inches, summer. *P. scouleri,* lavender, 9 to 12 inches, June to August. There some good modern hybrids, including "Six Hills," rose-lilac, 8 inches, June to August. Seeds are available, or cuttings may be taken from hybrids.

Phlox (See Alpine plants table under Greenhouses)

Also *P. amoena,* carmine-pink, 6 inches, spring. There are many named varieties of the dwarf species. All like sun but not too much wind.

Potentilla/Cinquefoil

Well-drained, gravelly soil in full sun is best. *P. aurea,* "Plena," golden yellow, 3 inches, spring. *P. nitida,* pink, 2 inches, summer, a good plant for the scree. *P. tonguei,* orange spotted crimson, 4 inches, spring. *P. verna* var. "Nana," yellow, 1 inch, spring. Propagate by seed or like strawberries, which some species resemble. These plants may overgrow and become weeds.

Primula/Primrose family

A wide variety of plants requiring differing conditions. Not easy but worth growing for their beauty. *P. hirsuta,* pink, etc., 3 inches, spring, partial shade, gritty loam, peat, and sand. *P. denticulata,* ruby, violet, etc., 12 inches, spring, deep, rich, moist loam with peat in partial shade. *P. rosea,* var. "Grandiflora," rose-carmine, 6 inches, spring, rich, moist loam in semi-shade. There are many fine hybrids of these and other species.

Pulsatilla

Formerly included under the anemones, which they resemble apart from their feathery seed-heads. The foliage is feathery, too. *P. vernalis,* white tinged violet-bronze, 6 inches, spring. *P. vulgaris* (Pasque Flower), violet, 12 inches, spring, likes lime. Propagate from seed.

Primula vulgaris 'Sibthorpii', a pink version of the common primrose. Happiest running through crevices on the rock garden.

Romonda

They like a shady, cool, moist crevice. *R. pyrenaica,* lavender, pink, or white, 4 inches, spring. *R. nathaliae,* lavender, pink, or white with orange center, 4 inches, spring.

Ranunculus

R. amplexicaulis, large white buttercup flowers, 8 inches, May to June. *R. gramineus,* golden-yellow 6 to 12 inches, May to June. These dwarf buttercups are easy to grow in moist soil. Propagate by division or possibly seed.

Saxifraga/Saxifrage, Rockfoil

Encrusted, with silvery-margined foliage. *S. aizoon,* a number of variations include *S.* "Baldensis," flowers white rising on 4-inch stems of 2-inch silver-rimmed gray rosettes, May to July; *S.* "Lutea," slightly taller with yellow flowers; *S.* "Rosea," flowers pink. Cushion of Kabschia (Himalayan) types: *S.* × *apiculata,* primrose-yellow, green cushions, 4 inches, early spring, suitable for crevice or moraine. Mossy types, forming cushions of mossy foliage: there are many hybrids all of which are excellent. "DuBarry," "Pearly King," and "Peter Pan" are crimson, white, and red, respectively; adaptable but like well-drained slopes. Other types for the rock garden include the Englerias with small silver rosettes and as in *S. grisebachii* "Wisley" have

thick outer petals (calyxes) to the flowers. There is also a miniature London Pride (*S. umbrosa* "Primuloides"), which reaches 4 inches with deep-pink flowers in June.

Sedum

Useful plants for hot, dry, bare places — often known as the Stonecrop — they are easily propagated by division. *S. spurium* "Schorbusser Blut" has attractive carmine flowers from summer to fall and pleasant, rather warm-looking, coppery-red and green foliage, 6 inches.

Sempervivum

Useful succulents for hot, arid places. There are many species and varieties, all typified by compact rosettes of leaves, often pointed with tips of red. Some, like *S. arachnoideum,* the cobweb houseleek, have fine webs of hair joining the tips of the leaves. Propagate by division.

Thymus

A number of species of this fragrant herb will thrive in hot, sunny places. They form mats of delicate leaves, and small flowers are prolific in summer. "Silver Queen" has variegated foliage.

Veronica/Speedwell

V. prostrata, blue, 6 inches, summer, trailing, there are several varieties in varying shades.

Shrub and Tree Gardens

Shrubs and decorative trees give a garden permanence, but they also do a great deal more. They add a new dimension: they give it height and a sense of space. They help to bind the garden together, giving it a sense of unity, harmony, and flow.

When selecting trees and shrubs for the garden, scale is probably the most important consideration. The great forest trees look superb in the rolling parkland of ancestral mansions, but in a modern housing development, no matter how well that development has been designed, those same trees may seem too large and out of place. One reason for this is that in order to appreciate the full beauty of any tree it is necessary to be able to see all of it.

The same principles apply in smaller gardens. If you plant trees or shrubs that will ultimately grow too big, they will never show their full beauty, because there will not be sufficient distance in which to view the whole tree. Over-large trees will be disfigured by the removal of major limbs and will become nothing but a nuisance.

Any shrub or tree planted in the garden brings about melodramatic changes in its immediate environment. First, it casts a shadow, and this will affect the types of plants that can be grown on the shaded side. Second, it will dry out the soil to some extent, and this too will affect the type of plants that can be grown close to it. While both of these factors can be a disadvantage if the tree or shrub is wrongly placed, they can be exploited if the tree is rightly placed. The shade of a small tree can be a joy on a patio or can be exploited to grow shade-loving plants such as rhododendrons. The

dryness, too, can be used to advantage. Most spring-flowering bulbs like a good soaking in winter, which they will get if planted under a deciduous tree, and like to be very dry during the summer while dormant, which they will also get if planted under a tree. For example, a silver birch about 30 feet high will have some 200,000 leaves, and these, in the process of transpiring, will evaporate some 15 gallons of water a day. In hot weather they will evaporate as much as 60 gallons a day. The leaf canopy itself further prevents some of the rain from actually reaching the ground, making it even drier. The degree of dryness under trees should not be underestimated.

There are other equally practical problems in positioning a tree or shrub. If it is planted too close to a fence or road it will technically be trespassing on someone else's property, and they may, if they feel so inclined, lop it back to keep it strictly on your side of the fence. That can totally destroy the essential symmetry of the tree.

In a 2-acre garden there is room to plant one tree for beauty of bark, one for spring blossom, another for variegated summer foliage, another for fall color and yet another for winter berries. In a sixth-of-an-acre plot the ideal plant would be a single tree that combined all these effects. There is no tree that actually combines all these seasons of beauty, but there are many, such as flowering cherries and hawthorns, that have two or three periods of glory each year.

There is no garden that is too small for at least one tree. *Prunus* "Ama-no-gawa," the Lombardy-poplar cherry, forms a tall, narrow spire, smothered in

Shrubs and trees give a garden depth, distance, and new vistas.

Shrubs produce more color for less work than any other plants.

spring with pale-pink blossoms, and it is narrow enough for the most confined garden. Some forms of the Japanese cut-leaf maple, *Acer palmatum* ''Dissectum,'' can be grown either as mushroom-shaped shrubs or as small standards with a stem 4 feet high and a head extending about the same height above it. Remember that the shape, color, and form of trees is as important a part of their decorative quality as their flowers, leaves, or fruits.

Buying

The first essential when buying any tree or shrub is to know what you want. That does not necessarily mean the genus and species, but you should know the amount of space the plant can occupy when it is mature, whether you want an evergreen or deciduous plant, spring- or summer-flowering, or whether you want it for fall color. Given that much information, any good nurseryman can advise you on species and varieties suitable for your soil and for a garden your size.

Many people buy from catalogs and do not see the plant until it arrives. This is a convenient way of purchasing plants, but on the whole it is better to go to the nursery and select the plant you want. This has been made much easier by the advent of garden centers, where you can see the plant you want in leaf and growth, pay for it, and take it home with you, without having to wait until the winter planting season.

Most people are tempted to buy whichever plant in the lot looks most vigorous. This is not necessarily the best plant to buy. In general it is better to select a plant of moderate vigor, with firm wood and of good shape, than to choose one that is excessively vigorous. However, avoid plants that look weak or sickly, have made poor growth, or have poor leaf color.

If you buy by mail through a catalog, it is important to examine the plant on arrival. If you think there has been a mistake, phone the nursery at once. Next look at the roots of the plant. If it has a few long, straggly roots, and particularly if those have been damaged, it is bad stock; it will not get a good start. Send it back, politely requesting the refund of your money, including the shipping cost.

Planting

The planting of a tree or shrub is the most important single cultural operation that will ever be carried out on that plant. If it is done well, the plant should thrive; if it is done badly, you will have only yourself to blame if the plant does not do well. No amount of after-care will ever make up for bad planting.

Deciduous trees and shrubs should be planted when they are dormant, i.e. leafless, usually between the months of October and April. Container-grown plants can, of course, be planted at any time of the year, but the ground still needs the same preparation, and they need even more after-care. Evergreen shrubs and trees are usually planted in the spring, but many hardy evergreens can be planted with success in the fall. Plants that are difficult to transplant usually are dug with a ball of soil or have been grown in a container; the ball of soil should be disturbed as little as possible when planting.

Prepare the ground by making a hole 3 feet across and 18 inches deep. The sides should be vertical and the bottom flat. Break up the bottom soil with a fork; then mix in a layer of soil and organic matter a foot deep. Examine the roots of the shrub to be planted, and prune away any damaged ones. Planting a tree is a job for two people — one to hold the tree, the other to fill in the soil. Lay a lath across the hole, level with the normal soil level, and then hold the tree or shrub in position so that when the soil is replaced it will come to precisely the same level as the soil in which the plant originally grew. Planting too deep may cause the collar to rot. Spread the roots out across the bottom of the hole, and then fill in the soil 6 inches at a time, treading each layer firmly. A tree will need to be staked firmly. The stake should be put in after the first layer of soil has been firmed and should be driven with a mallet or sledgehammer right down into the subsoil.

After-care

After planting, soak the ground thoroughly. Then put a mulch of well-rooted manure, leaf mold, or wood or bark chips around the tree or shrub. This will help prevent the soil from drying out. In frosty weather the young plant may lift out of the ground; if so, tread it back in firmly. For the first summer keep the ground around the plant mulched and clear of weeds. Once it is established, plant bulbs or ground-cover plants around it.

The golden Japanese maple *Acer japonicum* 'Aureum', one of the most effective of all yellow-leaved, slow-growing small trees.

Trees and shrubs usually do little more than re-establish their root systems their first year after planting. The second year they grow vigorously. The third year they continue growth and, depending on the kind, may begin to flower and fruit.

Pruning

This is essential to the success of many flowering shrubs but not usually so necessary with trees. The primary object of pruning is to secure vigorous, healthy flowering or fruiting shoots; the second is to keep the plants in shape. Pruning trees prevents branches from becoming crowded in the center and removes any deadwood.

There are three methods of pruning shrubs: (1) Shrubs that flower on wood of the current season's growth should be pruned to older wood in February or March. (2) Those that flower on the previous year's growth should have the shoots that have flowered in the current year cut out as soon as they have finished flowering. (3) Those that flower on old wood generally need little or no pruning.

Pruning inevitably damages the tissues of the plant. The sharper the instrument, the less damage there is. Blunt pruning shears crush the wood instead of cutting it. Any cut that leaves a wound exceeding half an inch in diameter leaves old wood exposed, and this is a potential place of fungus infections. Such cuts should always be painted over with an asphaltum tree paint and the paint reapplied annually until new bark has grown over the wound.

Propagation

There are more different methods used for increasing trees and shrubs than there are for any other class of plants. These include seed, division, layering, cuttings (mature or semi-hard), budding, grafting, and inarching.

In general, shade trees are grown from seed, but the maturation process may take 10 to 20 years before they are of landscape size. Seed is, however, a practicable way of growing many shrubs. Shrubs can also be increased from cuttings of two types: soft or summer cuttings, which should be taken in August or September and rooted in a frame or under a bell jar; and winter or hardwood cuttings, which can be taken after leaf-fall and placed in the ground outdoors. They root the following spring and may be moved to permanent positions the same fall. Layers in general should be allowed to remain attached to the parent plant for 2 years and then severed. After they have been severed, they should be allowed to grow for another year before being moved to their new positions.

As with all other garden plants, hybrids or forms with variegated leaves or other special peculiarities will not come true from seed and must be propagated vegetatively.

Selected Trees and Shrubs

Abutilon/Flowering Maple

Handsome, fast-growing shrubs; excellent for a sunny south wall. *A. megapotamicum,* deciduous, 8 to 10 feet, red and yellow bell-shaped flowers. *A. vitifolium,* deciduous, 10 to 20 feet, very fast growing, large mallow-type flowers 3 inches across, purple, mauve, or white, July to October. Usually a short-lived shrub. Increase by seed or cuttings taken in August. Useful outdoors in frost-free climates. Some species are grown as house plants.

Acer/Maple

Mostly deciduous, maples have attractive leaves and bark, often brilliant fall coloring. Will grow in any soil with peat or leaf mold mixed in. *A. ginnala,* to 20 feet, vivid fall color. *A. griseum,* the Paperbark Maple, 20 to 25 feet, has a richly colored trunk and main branches that shed their bark, revealing, beneath the rich brown old bark, the bright orange new bark; exceptionally good fall color. *A. hersii,* the Snakebark Maple, 20 feet, green and white striped bark on the stem and main branches, good fall color. *A. negundo variegatum,* 20 feet; delicate leaves marked with light green and white. "Japanese" maples: all are shrubby forms of *A. palmatum. A. p.* "Dissectum," finely divided leaves of a soft green. *A. p.* "Dissectum Atropurpureum,"* leaves finely divided, bronzy crimson. *A. p.* "Dissectum Flavescens," leaves soft green in spring, becoming deeper green in summer. All give fiery fall color. They make mushroom-shaped bushes up to 3 to 4 feet but can be trained into a pillar up to 10 feet tall and about 3 feet wide. Protect from biting north and east winter winds and give some light shade during the heat of the day. No pruning, increase by layering or grafting.

Andromeda/Bog Rosemary

A. polifolia is an 18-inch evergreen shrub with clusters of pinkish-white flowers from May to July. No pruning. Increase by removing runners or by division.

Araucaria/Monkey Puzzle

Araucavia araucana, sometimes listed as *A. imbricata,* exotic evergreen conifer. The needles are broad, flattened, and triangular, held all around the twigs. The female trees produce handsome red fruiting cones which explode when ripe, throwing the seeds a great distance. Thrives in any moist, well-drained soil. Not suited to exposed positions, withstand only slight cold. Slow-growing, ultimately 50 feet tall. Prune only to remove deadwood. Propagate by seed sown in greenhouse or cold frame.

Arbutus/Strawberry Trees

Exceptionally decorative evergreen shrubs or small trees. A. unedo, the Killarney Strawberry Tree: lily of the valley-type flowers, white or pink, produced in small bunches in November, together with the preceding year's fruits, which are like orange and red lichees. Small, neat, dark-green leaves. In time will make a small tree. Best in frost-free areas. Hybrid *A.* × *hybrida* (syn. *A.* × *andrachnoides*) has peeling, cinnamon bark and larger, smoother leaves and larger flowers, but less spectacular fruit. *A. menziesii,* the Modrona: large, polished, deep-green leaves, large panicles of white flowers in early summer, cinnamon-red peeling bark on trunk and main branches. Native to California north to British Columbia. Propagate by seed sown in a cold frame or greenhouse; plant out without disturbing the roots; put plants in permanent positions when very young. No pruning.

Arundinaria/Bamboo

They create a sub-tropical effect. They like a deep, moist soil, shelter from cold winds. Slow to establish themselves. The dead canes can be cut out and used in the garden. Sometimes listed under *Bambusa* or *Phyllostachys. A. anceps,* to 10 feet, graceful growth, very hardy, thicket-forming. *A. fastuosa,* tallest and most exotic, reaches 20 feet, needs space around it; hardy and very handsome. *A. fortunei,* "Variegata," pretty, 3 feet, small, narrow, pointed leaves striped white, rapidly forms a dense clump; thrives in sun or slight shade. *A. japonica,* to 10 feet, easiest to grow, handsome large leaves; not in-

vasive. *A. nitida,* to 10 feet, very handsome, remarkably graceful habit; dark stems and light-green leaves; does well in sun or shade. Prune only to remove dead canes; propagate by offsets.

Azaleas

Azaleas belong to the genus *Rhododendron.* Among the most brilliantly colorful of all shrubs; no other group offers such a wealth of bloom in such a variety of colors. Acid soil plus large quantities of peat or leaf mold, some shade during the heat of the day. Most garden azaleas are hybrids, but one species, *R. luteum,* is worth growing for its deep-yellow flowers, perfume, and fall coloring.

Deciduous azaleas reach 5 to 8 feet and the same width.

Deciduous

CALENDULACEA Large trusses of yellow, orange, or scarlet flowers. Native of Smokey Mountains.
KNAPHILL-EXBURY AZALEAS Finest brilliant fall foliage, full hardy. Thrive in moderate sun or shade. Many have delicious fragrance.
EVERGREEN AZALEAS Mostly small plants, 3 to 4 feet high, small, neat, dark-green leaves, flowering prolifically, May and June. Mostly hybrids or forms of the Kurume azaleas. Hardy, but prefer shade. The Glenn Dale Hybrids, hardy to 20°F, enormous blooms. Satsuki Azaleas, the finest evergreen azaleas; mostly very hardy, large flowers, pale colors striped, margined, blotched, or flushed with shades of rose, violet, pink, purple, or red; many have frilled petals. No pruning needed. Propagated by layers or cuttings. Deciduous kinds can also be grown from seed but will not come true; all seedlings are worth planting out. Seeds from mixed color forms of the Exbury-Knaphill group, and mixed unflowered seedlings are excellent and an economic way of acquiring a large color range.

Berberis/Barberry

Evergreen and deciduous shrubs, small dainty leaves, prickly stems, valued for neat growth, usually golden flowers and pink, red, or black berries. Any soil, not waterlogged, sun or shade. **Deciduous** *B. aggregata,* 5 feet or less, dense habit, yellow flowers, huge quantities of red

Many shrubs cover the ground and keep weeds down.
Shown here are
a) decidious azaleas,
b) rhododendrons
c) evergreen azaleas

berries in fall, fiery fall coloring. *B. chitria,* 8 feet, large leaves, yellow flowers, pendulous clusters of red berries, each ½ inch long. *B. koreana,* 6 feet, yellow flowers, fall foliage dark red, fruit bright red. *B. thunbergii,* 4 feet, best of the deciduous barberries, very free-flowering, unsurpassed for the brilliance of its fall foliage and its wealth of scarlet berries; compact, tidy growth. "Atropurpurea," slightly taller growing, reddish-purple leaves. "Atropurpurea Nana," dwarf, compact. None need pruning. **Evergreen** *B. darwinii,* 6 feet, flowers richest orange-yellow, blue, berries in autumn; hardy along Pacific Coast. *B. stenophylla,* 6 feet, leaves narrow-lanceolate, dark-green above, pale beneath, flowers golden-yellow in clusters, fruit black. *B. pruinosa,* 6 feet, sea-green leaves, soft-yellow flowers; berries blue-black with white bloom. *B. verruculosa,* 4 feet, neat, compact habit, small glossy green leaves white beneath, yellow flowers, good berries. Prune evergreen barberries in April. Propagate by seeds, hybrids, and named forms by cuttings, layers, or by division.

Betula/Birch

Beautiful, hardy deciduous trees. Grown for their white or yellow bark, the delicate tracery of their twigs, their small, neat leaves, and often yellow fall color. Sun or shade, good or poor soil. *B. ermanii,* 30 feet, creamy-white trunk, yellow branches, very distinct. *B. papyrifera,* (the Paperbark Birch), 35 feet, shining white trunk, good yellow fall leaves. *B. pendula* (Silver Birch), silvery-white bark, yellow fall leaves. *B. p.* "Tristis," slender, pendulous branches: *B. p.* "Youngii," Weeping Silver Birch, 15 to 20 feet, similar to weeping willow. *B. p.* "Fastigiata," narrowly columnar tree, like a Lombardy poplar, good for the smallest gardens: *B. p.* "Purpurea," purple-leaf birch, slow-growing to about 20 feet. Prune away lower branches only.

Buddleia/Butterfly Bush

Fast-growing summer-flowering shrubs. Any soil, preferably a sunny position. *B. davidii,* has long spikes of purple flowers in July and August. Prune really hard almost to the ground

line each spring. "Black Knight" has the deepest purple flowers. "Charming" is the best pink-flowered cultivar; "White Cloud" the best white, "Nanhoensis," a dwarf form, mauve flowers. *B. globosa* (Orange-ball tree), striking tall shrub, orange ball-shaped flower clusters. Useful in mild climates. Propagate from August cuttings out-doors or in a frame.

Calluna

A heather (see also Erica). Must have an acid soil, does best on poor soils enriched with peat, best in full sun. Flowers August and September. Many named forms, single or double flowers, white, pink, purple. Give a light clipping with the shears in spring. Propagate by layers, division, or half-ripe cuttings.

Camellia

Among the most beautiful of evergreens; flowers 2 to 8 inches across, white, pink, or reds, often striped or splashed; single, semi-double, or double. Most common is *C. japonica,* glossy, deep-green leaves, 4 to 15 feet, slow-growing, flowers during winter months in southern states, and late-flowering cultivars in more northern areas flower March and April. Over 1,000 named varieties. *C. × williamsii,* tough hybrids, small, matt leaves, usu-

ally many single or semi-double flowers. *C. × williamsii* "Donation," large, semi-double beautifully formed flowers, brilliant mid-pink. All need acid soil, with plenty of leaf mold or peat in the soil, a mulch with decayed leaves in early spring every year, and a position in light shade; excellent against a west or north wall. No pruning; increase by grafting, cuttings, or layering, or by seeds sown in gentle heat as soon as ripe; may take five months to germinate. Seed used only for production of understocks or in breeding.

Caryopteris/Bluebeard

Small shrubs, gray-green leaves, spires of deep lavender-blue or violet flowers, August to October. *C. × * "Heavenly Blue," 2 to 4 feet. Prune in spring. Grow in full sun. Increase by cuttings.

Ceanothus/ California Lilac

Deciduous and evergreen shrubs, blue flowers. Well-drained soil, sunny location. Useful in Pacific Coast states. Not winter-hardy in northern states. Grow **deciduous** varieties, including "Gloire de Versailles," light powder-blue; "Indigo"; and "Gloire de Plantières," deep blue. These flower summer and fall, on wood of the current year's growth; prune hard

Camellia japonica 'Grand Slam', one of the most striking of the newer American varieties. Camellias need an acid soil and some shelter from sun.

annually in April. **Evergreen,** neat, shining green leaves, mostly powder-blue flowers in May and June. All do best on a sunny wall. Prune only to keep in shape. "A. T. Johnson," free-flowering, deep blue, May and again in autumn. "Cascade," pendulous habit, bright-blue flowers. *C. thyrsiflorus,* strong-growing, up to 15 feet, hardiest evergreen, pale blue, May. *C. veitchianus,* the most popular species, 10 feet, bright-blue flowers, June. Root cuttings in pure sand in August; pot up as soon as possible. Plant out when young.

Ceratostigma/ Plumbago

Late-flowering, low-growing shrubs, deep-blue flowers. *C. plumbaginoides,* 12 inches, tops kill to ground in winter, also used as a ground cover; and *C. willmottianum,* 2 to 4 feet. Flower September to November, leaves turn red in fall. Well-drained soil in a warm corner. Cut to the ground in spring. Increase by division.

Cistus/Rockrose

Useful, decorative small evergreen shrubs. Aromatic foliage, large, single flowers. Hardy in the south, and in mild climates. Good on limestone soils. Full sun and well-drained soil, does well in dry positions, June to July flowering, flowers 3 or 4 inches across, white or shades of pink, usually a dark blotch at the base of the petal. Pink: "Silver Pink," one of

Ceanothus species, are among the bluest of all blue-flowered shrubs, suitable for Pacific coast.

best, up to 2 feet, gets leggy with age; *C. skanbergii,* 3 feet, pale pink; *C. crispus,* 2 feet, rosy-mauve; var. "Sunset," carmine-crimson; *C. purpureus,* 4 to 6 feet, brilliant reddish-purple. White: *C. ladaniferus,* 5 feet, extra large flowers, maroon blotch on each; *C. cyprius,* 6 feet, white with deep-red blotches; *C. corbariensis,* 3 feet, white with yellow markings. Easily increased by cuttings or layers. Plant out when young. Cuttings flower in their first year. No pruning.

Cornus/Dogwood

Two distinct groups of hardy deciduous trees and shrubs. One grown for brilliant winter color of the bark on the twigs, the other for flowers. **Flowering Dogwoods** *C. mas,* Cornelian Cherry, shrub or small, spreading tree to 15 feet, masses of small, rich-yellow flowers in February; any soil, sun or shade, best on a poor soil; red, cherry-like fruits in fall, rich tints; in other flowering species the flowers are technically bracts. *C. florida,* shrub or small tree, white flowers of 4 bracts, var. "Rubra," rich-pink bracts, 10 to 20 feet. *C. kousa,* abundant creamy-white long-lasting bracts. *C. k. chinensis,* larger bracts. *C. C. nuttalli,* to 20 feet, the finest of all, creamy-white bracts beautifully shaped, long-lasting, needs a sheltered position; useful primarily in West Coast areas. The "flowering" dogwoods do best in soil enriched with leaf mold or peat. No pruning. **Colored Bark** *C. alba* "Spaethii," one of the most useful variegated shrubs, oval leaves brightly marked with yellow. *C. alba sibirica* "Variegata," similar, leaves are variegated white. Both with brilliant red twigs throughout winter. *C. stolonifera* with red twigs and *C. stolonifera flaviramea,* yellow twigs, will grow to 10 feet without hard pruning. Any soils, including poor and waterlogged ones. Take outdoor cuttings in November.

Corylus/Hazel

C. avellana "Contorta," Harry Lauder's Walking Stick, or Corkscrew Hazel: strangely twisted twigs, branches, and stems; best in spring when laden with catkins, 6 to 12 feet. No pruning. *C. maxima* "Atropurpurea," large leaves, rich, deep purple. Prune hard in spring. In-

crease by layers or suckers. Any soil, sun or shade.

Cotoneaster

Large family, shrubs and trees, moderate-size leaves, brilliant berries. Any soil not waterlogged. Sun or partial shade. Best planted when small. Tree-like types good on lawns, some shrubby ones make good hedges, others excellent ground cover. **Tree-like:** *C. × cornubia,* evergreen, 20 feet, heavy crops of large, bright-scarlet berries weigh the branches down. *C. bullata,* deciduous, 15 feet, arching branches, clusters of cherry-like fruits. *C. frigida,* 20 to 25 feet, evergreen, rapid initial growth, regular, heavy crops of brilliant orange-red berries; var. "Hybrida Pendula," a weeping form. Both excellent on limestone soils. *C. simonsii,* semi-evergreen, 10 feet, upright narrow habit; grows almost anywhere. **Shrubby kinds:** *C. horizontalis,* branches arranged herringbone fashion, excellent covering for north or east wall; good ground cover when allowed to spread. Fall foliage brilliant orange and scarlet; bright-red "Variegata," attractively variegated form. *C. dammeri,* evergreen, grows along the ground, excellent ground cover, large red fruits in abundance in fall. Prune only to shape; increase by seeds sown outdoors as soon as ripe, preferably stratified, or by layers.

Crataegus/Hawthorn

Small deciduous trees or shrubs. Neat, rugged appearance. Good in flower and fruit, ideal for smaller gardens, 20 feet, any soil. *C. oxycantha,* the best species. *C. o.* "Coccinea Plena," double, crimson flowers. *C. o.* "Gireoudi," leaves mottled pink and white, flowers white. *C. o.* "Plena," double white flowers. *C. o.* "Rosea Flore Pleno," double rose-pink flowers. All bear red berries in fall. Some good fall tints. *C. monogyna,* var. "Aurea," yellow berries; var. "Pendula," white flowers, graceful weeping habit; var. "Pendula Rosea," weeping pink; var. "Stricta," Lombardy Poplar habit, white flowers, ideal for smallest gardens; "Tortuosa," twisted corkscrew branches and twigs, flowers white, fascinating specimen tree. No pruning. Increase by grafting on stocks of the type.

Cytisus/Broom

Quick-growing shrubs, bright pea-shaped flowers, short-lived, ideal for filling gaps. Any soil, full sun, best in poor soils. Plant when very young; difficult to move. *C. albus,* the Spanish White Broom. *C. nigricans,* 4 feet, bright yellow, August. *C. praecox,* 4 feet, compact habit, masses of primrose flowers, early spring, no pruning. *C. scoparius,* its hybrids and named forms, 4 to 8 feet, varying shades of crimson, yellow, white, cream, ruby, and bicolors. Prune all except *C. praecox* hard, back to old wood, in April. Increase from seed or August cuttings.

Daphne

Choice small-growing deciduous or evergreen shrubs, deliciously scented, capricious. Any good soil, sun. *D.* × *burkwoodii,* 3 feet, pale mauve-pink, very fragrant, deciduous, May/June. *D. Cneorum,* evergreen, 1 to 2 feet, slow spreading, dainty growth, clusters of rosy-pink flowers, strongly scented; needs leafmold mixed in the soil; layer branches as they spread. *D. mezereum,* 3 to 4 feet, deciduous, flowers February to April on bare branches, flowers pale mauve to deepest violet-purple, very fragrant, any soil, sun or shade; propagate from the round red berries produced in fall, protect berries from birds. Never prune.

Embothrium/Chilean Fire Bush

A small, spectacular tree hardy in California. Some forms tender, but *E. coccineum lanceolatum* "Norquinco Valley Form" generally hardy: semi-evergreen, lance-shaped leaves, brilliant orange-scarlet flowers in great profusion May/June. Plant from pots when very young in any reasonably moist, humus-rich, lime-free soil, preferably in the shelter of other trees; rapid growth to 6 feet, when flowering starts and growth slows, final height 15 to 20 feet. Prune young growths to make bushy. Avoid disturbing the roots. Increase by seed sown outdoors.

Erica/Heathers

Lime-free soil, full sun. Excellent, weed-proof ground cover. **Tree**

Heaths *E. arborea,* white flowers. *E. australis,* pink flowers. Upright habit, prolific flowers, May/June; prune straggly shoots. **Low-growing** *E. carnea* 9 to 12 inches, deep pink, December to April; will grow on chalk. Many other forms. *E. vagans,* 2 feet, spreading habit, lime-hating, pink flowers. July to October. Give light clip with shears after flowering; increase by layers (often naturally occurring) or by August cuttings in a cold frame or propagating case.

Eucryphia

Ornamental evergreen and deciduous shrubs or small trees. Flower in late summer. Lime-free soil, well-drained but moist, sheltered from cold winter winds in coastal areas of California. All have white flowers, 2 inches across, slightly fragrant. *E. glutinosa* (also known as *E. pinnatifolia*), 8 to 15 feet, slow-growing, flowers freely July and August, brilliant fall foliage. *E.* × *nymanensis,* evergreen, 15 feet or more, tall, spire-shaped plant covered in white flowers in August and September; very variable. No routine pruning; increase by seeds or layers.

Euonymus/Spindle

Hardy shrubs, easy, any soil, sun or shade. Deciduous forms have brilliantly colored fruits, bright fall colors; evergreens often with variegated leaves. **Deciduous** *E. europaeus,* 10 feet, brilliant reddish-pink seed cases reveal bright orange seeds, last well into winter; var. "Purpureus," purple leaves. *E. alatus,* 12 to 15 feet, bright fall colors, white flowers early summer, heavy crop of bright-red berries. **Evergreen** *E. radicans* "Variegatus," small-leaved creeping or climbing plant, leaves variegated white; good ground cover, useful for growing on walls. Any soil, sun or shade. No regular pruning. Increase from seeds, August cuttings, or layers.

Fagus/Beech

Noble trees of the largest dimensions, suitable for parks.

× Fatshedera

× *Fatshedera lizei,* cross between the *Hedera helix* and *Fatsia japonica.*

Handsome evergreen, polished, bright-green palmate leaves; excellent in shade. Any soil. No pruning. Increase by cuttings or layering. Useful in mild climates.

Fatsia

Fatsia japonica. One of the largest-leaved evergreens. Any soil, sun or shade. Leaves palmate, 8 inches across, leathery, stems thick, 8 to 10 feet. Flowers white, October/November, followed by black berries. Excellent shrub for subtropical effect on a patio; a good indoor plant. Increase by August cuttings in gentle warmth.

Forsythia/Golden Bell

Showiest of spring-flowering shrubs. Any soil, sun or some shade. All flower February to April. *F.* × *intermedia;* 8 to 10 feet, vigorous, upright; best forms are "Lynwood," large rich-yellow flowers produced freely all along the branches; "Primulina," flowers pale yellow; "Spectabilis," large flowers, rich yellow, very free; "Vitellina," deepest yellow form. *F. suspensa,* rambling shrub up to 10 feet, best as a standard allowed to weep or trained over a shed, old tree stump, or up a trellis; flowers mid-yellow. Prune back to within 1 or 2 buds of old wood immediately after flowering. Increase by August cuttings or layers.

Fraxinus/Ash

The common ash, *F. excelsior,* is too large-growing. "Pendula" is a beautiful weeping tree with a mushroom head. Any soil. Sun.

Fuchsia

Graceful shrubs, brightly colored flowers, mid summer to first frosts. Any soil, sun or shade. *F. magellanica,* typical fuchsia coloring: "Alba," flowers white; "Riccartonii," common hardy type, peeling reddish bark. Hardy in mild climates; protect tops over winter in colder areas. *F. hybrida,* florists Fuchsia, many cultivars, used for summer-flowering plants or in a cool greenhouse; hardy in mild areas of Pacific Coast.

Genista/Broom

Tough shrubs, many brilliant-yellow pea-type flowers, May to July. Any soil, full sun; useful on poor, dry soils. *G. aethnensis,* the Mount Etna Broom, small tree, 8 to 12 feet. *G. anglica,* dwarf, spiny native, 2 feet. *G. hispanica,* Spanish Broom, 2 feet, hummock-forming, ideal on dry sunny bank. *G. horrida,* dwarf, rigid spiny shrub, grayish hue, flowers July to September. *G. lydia,* floriferous dwarf, slender green branches. *G. tinctoria,* Dyers Greenweed, late-flowering, to 2 feet; var. "Plena," double brilliant-yellow flowers. No pruning. Satisfactory in mild climates.

Ginkgo/Maidenhair Tree

G. biloba, the only species, a "living fossil," is a curious deciduous conifer with leaves like those of the maidenhair fern but larger and turning clear yellow before falling. The fossil record shows that this tree has hardly changed in 150,000,000 years. Any good soil, sun. Slow-growing, ultimately 60 feet or more. Choose a male plant as the fruit on the female plant has a disagreeable odor.

Hamamelis/Witch Hazel

Beautiful, choice winter-flowering shrubs. Naked branches covered with clusters of usually fragrant flowers made up of strap-shaped petals. All give good fall color; leaves hazel-like. Any good soil, sun or light shade. *H. mollis,* 10 feet, cowslip-scented bright-yellow flowers, December to March. *H. japonica,* 10 feet, pale yellow, scented, December to March. All slow-growing; prune only to shape. Increase from seed, layers (which should not be severed for 4 years), or grafting selected types onto stocks of *H. virginiana.*

Helianthemum/Rockrose or Sunrose

Low-growing evergreen, sun-loving; summer-flowering plants, brightly colored saucer-shaped flowers ideal for covering dry, sunny banks, 6 to 9 inches. Any soil. Clip lightly with shears to keep low and neat. July and August cuttings root easily.

Hibiscus/Rose of Sharon

Showy deciduous shrubs, flowering after most other shrubs are over, 7 to 9 feet, July to October. Any good, drained soil and full sun; in the north, best against a sunny wall. *H. syriacus,* large, bell-shaped flowers: "Blue Bird," the best single blue; "Duc de Brabant," double red; "Hamambo," extra-large, wide-open blush flowers with deep maroon blotch; "Monstrosus," single white; "Violaceus Plenus," double wine-purple; "Woodbridge," extra-large flowers, rich rose-pink with maroon blotches. Single varieties more effective than double. Prune only to shape in early spring; increase by layering or from cuttings in a cold frame.

Hydrangea

Indispensable, summer-flowering shrubs. Any good soil, sun or some shade, best in shelter. Most usual *H. macrophylla* (*H. hortensis*). This species satisfactory in mild climates, flower buds hardy to 20°F. There are numerous named forms, flowers in white, pinks, reds, purples, and blues. Sometimes flowers of different colors on same bush; 3 to 6 feet. Many pinks blue naturally on acid soils, but others stay pink on all soils. The blues need

Modern fuchsias have larger flowers and are hardier than the older species and greenhouse varieties. Though usually killed to ground level in winter, in mild districts they will form small shrubs.

Hydrangeas are probably the most showy of all summer flowering shrubs. The showy, sterile flowers start to color in June and take until about September. There are named forms in pink, blue, lavendar and white.

acid soil to continue to produce blue flowers. Flower June to August, leave dry heads on plant through winter to protect young buds. Prune only to remove weak shoots. *H. paniculata,* large creamy-white flowers in a cone-shaped head, gradually fade to pink. Increase by layering or by half-ripe cuttings.

Hypericum/
Saint-John's-Wort

Evergreen summer-flowering shrubs, large yellow flowers. Any soil, sun or shade. *H. calycinum,* 1 foot, spreading, dense growth, 3-inch golden flowers, June to September. *H. hookerianum,* 4 feet, 2-inch-deep golden flowers, August to frost. *H. × moserianum,* 18 inches, golden flowers, late summer. *H. patulum,* "Hidcote," to 6 feet, largest flowers of all, golden-yellow, July to October. *H.* "Rowallane Hybrid," finest of all, 8 feet, needs mild climate or good against a sunny wall. No pruning; division or August cuttings.

Ilex-Holly

Extremely hardy, mainly evergreen trees and shrubs. Brilliant winter berries on females. Many have beautifully variegated leaves. *I. aquifolium,* English Holly, slow-growing to 80 feet; most named forms slower growing and smaller. Choose from "Argenteo-marginata," leaves margined silver; "Argenteo-marginata Pendula," Perry's Weeping Silver Holly, very graceful, leaves edged silver; both female and free-fruiting. "Aureo-marginata," leaves edged yellow, male; "Flavescens," leaves canary-yellow shaded old gold, male; "Polycarpa," the best green-leaved holly for the garden, hermaphrodite, extra free-berrying; "Silver Queen," broad leaves with creamy-white margin. *I. crenata,* Japanese Holly, many cultivars, small foliage, fruit black. *I. opaca,* American Holly, to 50 feet, many cultivars, fruit red, held through winter. *I. macrocarpa,* deciduous holly, huge black cherry-like berries. Any soil, sun or shade. Cut out green-leaved stems as soon as they appear on variegated forms. Increase by layers or cuttings.

Acer japonicum dissectum has the fieriest autumn color of any hardy shrub. This applies to forms with purple or black leaves, as well as the green-leaved form.

Laburnum/Golden Chain Tree

A popular small tree. Deciduous, not more than 20 feet, dropping clusters of brilliant yellow flowers in May and June. Any well-drained soil, sun. Seeds poisonous when green. *L. anagyroides,* common laburnum. *L. vossi,* longer flower clusters. Increase from seed; no pruning.

Laurus/Sweet Bay—Laurel

Laurus nobilis. Evergreen trees, naturally spire-shaped, 20 feet, any well-drained soil, full sun, dislikes bleak, drafty locations, excellent in mild coastal districts. Flowers greenish, insignificant. Stands clipping. "Angustifolia," hardier than type. Increase by September cuttings in a cold frame. Also grown as a shrub in greenhouses in the north.

Lavandula/Lavender

Popular gray-leaved aromatic low shrubs, spikes of blue or purple flowers. Any well-drained soil, sun. Plant either singly or in groups in borders, or use low hedges or edging. Cut flowers for drying before fully open;

prune lightly to shape in April. *L. spica,* Old English Lavender: "Grappenhall Variety," the strongest growing, to 3 feet; "Nana Munstead Dwarf," very compact, deep lavender; "Rosea," pale lilac-pink flowers; "Twickle Purple," bright purple, tidy habit, *vera,* very dwarf, less silvery than most, very fragrant. *L. stoechas,* French lavender, 1 foot, dark-purple flowers, light-green leaves. Increase by September cuttings, sandy soil outdoors.

Ligustrum/Privet

Easily grown shrubs for general purposes and hedges. All kinds grow in sun or partial shade, any well-drained soil. Propagate by cuttings. *L. amurense,* semi-evergreen, olive-green foliage, to 10 feet. *L. obtusifolium regelianum,* Regel privet, deciduous, hardiest of cultivated privets. *L. ovalifolium,* California privet, deciduous to semi-evergreen, widely planted for hedges, to 12 feet. *L. lucidum,* Glossy privet, hardy to 20°F, white flowers in June; cv. "Suwannee River," dwarf spreading form.

Magnolia

The most beautiful of all woody plants, very large, usually cup-shaped flowers, generally on bare branches in spring. Over 50 species to choose from, forest trees to small shrubs. Well-drained soil, rich in humus; shelter from strong winds. Plant in holes 18 inches deep and 3 feet across, break up bottom soil, fill with equal parts good garden earth, leaf mold or peat and a little sand. Stake securely when young. Most common, *M. × soulangeana,* very large cup-shaped pink flowers on bare branches, March/April. Named forms include "Alba," pure-white flowers; "Lennei," extra-large flowers, vigorous growth; "Rustica Rubra," the best pure-pink form, shrubby, flowers when young, to 15 feet, slow-growing, can be trained to a small tree. *M. stellata,* Star Magnolia, purest-white star-shaped flowers on bare branches in March/April, very slow-growing to 5 feet, suitable for the smallest gardens. "Rosea," pale pink; "Rubra," deep pink. *M. grandiflora,* Bull Bay or Southern Magnolia, huge white flowers in summer, large, glossy evergreen leaves, fragrant flowers up to 10 inches across. "Goliath" has even larger flowers. *M. denuda*, the Yulan or Lilytree, erect, fragrant white bell-shaped flowers, April to May; magnificent once established. *M. kobus,* a small pyramidal tree with starry white flowers, March and April, slow to start flowering, superb once it does. No pruning except to thin twigs or branches that rub each other. Increase species by seed sown as soon as ripe, layers or grafting. Half-ripe cuttings in gentle bottom warmth sometimes strike, but are difficult. Transplant only in small sizes with a ball of soil or as container-grown plants.

Mahonia

Evergreen flowering shrubs, pinnate leaves, clusters of showy yellow flowers usually in winter. Any soil, even poor ones, sun or shade; some thrive in dense shade. *M. aquifolium,* 3 to 4 feet, glossy leaves, yellow flowers January to March, grows in complete shade, flowers better with some sun, leaves color during cold weather. *M. bealei,* 10 to 12 feet, large leathery compound leaves, semi-shade. No pruning; layers or seed.

Malus/Flowering Crab

Popular, early-flowering, small trees suitable for smaller gardens, masses of blossom April/May. Any good soil, sun. Named forms include "Chilko," large purplish leaves, crimson flowers, purple fruits; "Profusion," green leaves, deep-crimson flowers, orange-red fruits; "Wisley Crab," large wine-red flowers and very large red fruits. All 12 to 15 feet. Prune to keep the center of the tree open. Trees usually grafted.

Morus/Mulberry

M. alba, white Mulberry, a round-headed deciduous tree, 30 feet, any deep, warm soil. *M. nigra,* the common Mulberry, gnarled, rugged tree, 20 to 30 feet, large downy leaves, slow-growing, fruits like loganberries. No pruning. Seedlings often come where not wanted.

Paeonia/Tree Peony

Paeonia suffruticosa. A most spectacular shrub, 4 to 6 feet, similar spread, huge flowers, often 12 to 18 inches across, like enormous crumpled poppies, white, palest pink, deeper pink, carmine, crimson, scarlet, mauve, maroon, purple, or black, often streaked, splashed, or edged with a contrasting color. Single forms have jewel-like flower centers, dusty golden anthers surrounding a ruby-red heart. Also semi-double and double forms. There are over 5,000 named forms. Good on slightly acid to alkaline soil. Plants are grafted. Plant with graft-joint 3 inches below soil surface. Plant moutans shaded from early-morning sunshine. Any soil, sun or light shade. Keep bushy by pruning. Growths semi-woody, dying back about one-third of their length each autumn. Cut back to sound wood of the same season's

Mahonia lomariifolia, a striking evergreen with spiny leaves producing its flowers in earliest February and March.

Malus, the flowering crab, spectacular both in flower and fruit.

growth every autumn, as close to a bud as possible. Propagate by seed of single varieties sown outdoors, stratified. *P. × lemonei,* very similar to the above, needing the same treatment, but with predominantly yellow flowers. "Alice Harding," huge deep-yellow flowers; "Souvenir de Maxim Cornu," bright golden-yellow, edged carmine with orange shading, huge double flowers, fragrant.

Pieris/Lily of the Valley Bush

Beautiful, evergreen shrubs, acid soil, some shade. Lily-of-the-valley flowers in spring. Best is *P. formosa forrestii,* 6 to 10 feet, slow-growing, flowers April/May, young leaves brilliant scarlet. *P. japonica,* slow-growing to about 5 feet, occasionally more, new leaves copper. No pruning. Increase by cuttings, layers, or seed.

Populus/Poplar

Strong-growing deciduous trees only suited to the largest gardens.

Potentilla/Shrubby Cinquefoil

Low-growing, very tough deciduous shrubs, large, usually white or yellow flowers over a long summer period. Any soil, sun or a little shade. Numerous varieties. Prune lightly in March. Increase by layering or by fall cuttings in a cold frame.

Prunus

Huge family including the flowering cherries, almonds, peaches, and the laurels used for hedging. Any soil, preferably sun.

Flowering Cherries All flower April/May. No other trees produce such wealth of blossom. A small selection of the best are "Accolade," semi-double, soft pink; "Amanogawa," erect growth, suitable for even the smallest gardens, masses of

pale-pink fragrant flowers; "Kwanzan," large double deep-pink flowers; "Pink Perfection," new, even better; "Shimidsu Sakura" ("Okumiyako"), double flowers, pink in the bud, opening pure white. "Kiku Shidare Zakura" ("Cheal's Weeping Cherry"), deep double pink flowers on weeping branches that reach to the ground. *P. subhirtella,* winter-flowering cherry, small pinkish-white flowers in mild spells. November to March, 20 feet. Various colors and forms.

Ornamental Plums *P. cerasifolia* "Atropurpurea" (syn. *pissardii*), known as the Purple-Leaved Plum. Popular. Masses of small white flowers in April, plum-colored leaves. Two much-improved forms are "Nigra," much darker-colored foliage, pink flowers, neater habit; "Hessei," shrubby form, attractive, variegated crimson foliage.

Almonds and Peaches The common almond is *P. amygdalus*: var. "Alba" has white flowers; "Roseoplena" has double flowers; "Macrocarpa" is equally good in flower but produces the best nuts for eating. *P. persica,* flowering peach, small fruits; "Clara Meyer," a very rich, deep pink; "Russell's Red" is almost red; "Iceberg," pure white. Treat all for peach leaf curl regularly with a fungicide in mid-February and again in early March. *P. triloba* is a popular dwarf almond often grown as a short standard: "Multiplex" bears bright-pink rosette-like flowers all along its branches in March and

April. *P. tenella,* beautiful small shrub to 4 feet, suckers slowly; the best form is "Fire Hill," with very bright pink wide-open flowers in April, comes from Siberia, very hardy.

No pruning. Named sorts are usually bud-grafted. Species can be raised from seeds.

Pyracantha/Firethorn

Quick-growing, semi-evergreens, clusters of off-white hawthorn-like flowers in June, huge crops of brilliantly colored berries in fall and winter. Any soil, sun or light shade. Excellent trained against the north or east walls of houses. Prune close to the wall. Allow to assume natural shape in open. *P. atalantioides,* large oval leaves, berries crimson: var. "Aurea," rich-yellow berries. *P. coccinea,* brilliant scarlet berries. *P. crenulata,* red berries; "Flava," bright-yellow berries. Increase from seeds or late-summer cuttings.

Quercus/Oak

The native oaks are large for some gardens. Often used as specimens or as street trees.

Rhododendron

One of the most spectacular evergreen flowering shrubs, huge trusses of brightly colored flowers in every imaginable shade. Acid soil, best in light shade. Planted with peat and leaf mold in the soil. Mulch annually in the spring with peat or leaf mold. More than 500 species and 1,000 hybrids, ranging from mat-forming dwarfs with 2-inch leaves to forest trees with 3-foot leaves. A selection of plants gives bloom from April through spring and early summer. Enthusiasts should consult specialist books. Those listed here grow to about 8 feet and are reasonably hardy. Winter and very early spring-flowering: "Nobleanum," in crimson, pink, or white forms; "Lee's Scarlet," rich pink, earliest of all, flowering in late November; "Jacksonii," pink with a deeper stripe; "Praecox," a small-leaved dainty species with brilliant lilac-purple flowers. Mid-season hybrids: "Blue-Diamond," brilliant purple-blue, small-leaved, neat habit; "Elizabeth," beehive-shaped bush to 5 feet, covered with brilliant large scarlet flowers; "Susan," the best of the large-leaved "blues"; "May Day," fine bright scarlet, midseason, spreading wider than tall, 6 feet; "Fabia," June-flowering, orange-salmon or apricot; "Hawk," the best hardy-yellow, late-flowering; "Vesuvius," very hardy late brilliant red; "Lady Chamberlain," lovely long dropping lapageria-type bells in shades of orange; "Vanessa," large pastel-pink flowers, late; "Dr. Stocker," the best white. *Rh. serotinum,* white. No pruning. Remove dead heads after flowering; take the seed head between thumb and fingers, twist and pull. Increase by layering or cuttings.

Rhus/Sumac

This genus has now been divided into two: plants with round leaves are now properly *Cotinus,* those with pinnate leaves in *Rhus. R. cotinus* (now *C. coggygria*), round green leaves, fine feathery inflorescences smother the bush in June, followed by brilliant fall colors, 8 to 10 feet; the purple-leaf form, listed either as "Atropurpurea" or "Foliis Atropupureus" far superior; "Notcutt's Form" is the darkest of all. Increase by August cuttings or layers. *R. glabra,* Smooth Sumac, 5 feet, leaves pinnate, 18 inches long, brilliantly colored fall foliage. *R. typhina,* Stag's Horn Sumac, to 15 feet, leaves pinnate, 2 feet or more long, turning brilliant yellow, orange, and scarlet in fall, stems furry. Best on poor soils. No

pruning. Increase from suckers. Sap of *R. glabra* and *R. typhina* can cause severe irritation on some skins.

Ribes/Flowering Currant

Pretty, early spring-flowering deciduous shrubs. Any soil, sun or light shade. *R. alpinum,* 5 feet, dense growth, suitable for hedges, scarlet fruit. *R. sanguineum,* 7 to 8 feet, pale-pink to deep rosy-red flowers in drooping clusters followed by black fruits: "Pulborough Scarlet," the

brightest red form. No routine pruning. Increase from late summer cuttings.

Robinia/Locust or False Acacia

Attractive deciduous trees, pinnate leaves, clusters of pink or white wisteria-type flowers. Any soil, wood brittle, protect from wind. *R. hispida,* rose flowers. *R. kelseyi,* bright rose. Both flower May/June and grow

The smoke bush, *Cotinus coggygia,* produces feather heads of flowers in summer. In autumn the leaves turn brilliant scarlet.

6 to 10 feet as shrubs or can be trained into small standards. Prune hard on poor soils. Increase by seed or suckers.

Rosmarinus/Rosemary

R. officinalis, popular evergreen shrub, aromatic leaves and blue flowers, 4 feet. Well-drained soil, sun or a little shade. Shorten long growths, *never* back to old wood. Increase by half-ripe cuttings in July. Suitable for mild climates. In the north use in a cool greenhouse.

Salix/Willow

Weeping Willow, *S. alla* "Tristus," 60 feet, totally unsuited to smaller gardens. Smallest of the weeping willows are *S. caprea pendula,* 8 to 12 feet. Any wet soil, sun. No pruning. Twigs placed in water at any time in the growing season root rapidly. Hardwood cuttings (including large branches) outdoors when dormant.

Sambucus/Elderberry

S. canadensis, to 10 feet, rank growing for poor soils, usually too vigorous for small gardens.

Sophora/Japanese Pagoda Tree

S. japonica, 50 feet, flowers yellowish-white, in panicles, in June to July, foliage dark green, withstands city conditions.

Sorbus/Mountain Ash

Deciduous small trees, decorative in leaf, flower, and fruit. Any soil, sun or shade. Flowers are white in June, berries usually red in fall. *S. americana,* to 40 feet, flowers white, fruit bright red. *S. aucuparia,* leaves green, pinnate, fruits orange-red, best in north; var. "Fastigiata," narrow Lombardy poplar habit, suitable for small gardens: var. "Pendula" is a stiffly weeping form; "Xanthocarpa" has yellow fruits. No pruning. Increase by seed stratified.

Spartium/Spanish Broom

Green twigs, bright-yellow pea-shaped flowers, June to August, 9 to 10 feet. Any soil, sun. Tends to legginess; keep tidy and bushy by cutting back almost to old wood in April. Increase by seed. Best in southern United States and west coast.

Spiraea

Dainty deciduous summer-flowering shrubs. Any soil, sun or light shade. *S. bullata,* 18 to 24 inches, rosy-pink, July. *S. japonica,* var. "Anthony Waterer," deep pink, 3 to 4 feet, July/August. *S. × vanhouttei,* white, 4 to 6 feet. Prune only to thin overcrowded twigs, remove dead flower heads; increase by layering, seed, or late summer cuttings.

Symphoricarpus/ Snowberry

Deciduous plants, smooth round leaves, branches laden with white marble-size berries from October well into winter. Any soil, sun or shade, to 10 feet. Spreads rapidly by suckers. No pruning. Increase by suckers.

Syringa/Lilac

Among most popular shrubs, pyramids of very showy, fragrant flowers in summer. Any rich soil, sun or light shade, will grow on alkaline soil. Tend to dry out the soil around them. Remove dead heads once flowering is over, cut out weak or straggly growth. When buying, ask for plants on their own roots. Plants grown are generally named forms and hybrids mainly derived from *S. vulgaris.* Among the best are: **Singles** "Clarke's Giant," very large lilac-blue flowers in pyramids up to 12 inches long; "Lavanensis," pale pink; "Madame Fransisque Morel," violet-pink, very large panicles, tall, erect growth; "Marechal Foch," massive panicles and large individual flowers, deep-carmine in the bud, opening bright carmine-rose and fading to mauve; "Marie Legraye," one of the best pure whites; "Primrose," thick pyramids of primrose-yellow flowers; "Purple Heart," early-flowering deep pure purple with individual flowers as much as 1½ inches across; "Souvenir de Louis Spath," a popular dark-red variety; "Vestale," a superb white variety.
Doubles "Charles Joly," dark red, an old and popular variety; "Madame Antoine Buchner," tall, late-flowering, extra-large panicles, soft carmine-rose; "Madame Lemoine," very large, white, very popular; "President Grevy," massive panicles

Lilacs are justifiably among the most popular of shrubs.

of lilac-blue. Of the species *S. persica,* the Persian lilac is a delightful miniature edition of the more popular lilacs, growing to 5 feet. All may be increased by cuttings or layers. Seed of named sorts will usually produce good seedlings, though not identical with the parent.

Tamarix/Tamarisk

Hardy shrubs, easiest culture, will withstand salt gales, perfectly hardy inland. Unique feathery foliage and feathery plumes of pink flowers in late summer. Any soil, sun. *T. anglica* is the commonest kind, 5 to 7 feet. *T. pentandra* is smaller-growing, to 4 feet. *T. parviflora* is similar to the latter. Prune hard in April. Increase by sticking almost any piece of twig or branch firmly in the ground in early winter.

Ulmus/Elm

Too large for any but really large gardens.

Viburnum

Important deciduous and evergreen shrubs, indifferent to soil or situation; avoid extremely dry or waterlogged soils. **Evergreen** *V. burkwoodii,* 5 to 6 feet, fragrant pink-budded white flowers, January to April. *V. davidii,* 2 feet, valuable in smaller gardens, lovely turquoise-blue berries borne throughout winter; plant male and females to obtain berries. *V. henryi,* 10 feet, white flowers in June, brilliant red winter berries, later turn black. *V. rhytidophyllum,* up to 15 feet, very striking large, deeply veined, felted leaves, huge clusters of white or pink flowers in May/June and brilliant red berries in winter; will fruit singly, but more prolific if several planted. *V. tinus,* known as laurustinus, 8 feet, pink and white flowers, early spring. **Deciduous** *V. × bodnantense,* vigorous hybrid and the best of the winter-flowering deciduous group, very fragrant rose-flushed flowers over a long period. *V. carlesii,* one of most Beautiful viburnums of all spring-flowering shrubs, 5 feet, very sweetly scented, daphne-like flowers, pink in the bud, opening pure white in a round cluster in April and May. *V. fragrans,* the best-known of the deciduous winter-flowering groups, ultimately 12 feet, flowers on bare wood in mild spells, flowers blush-pink, very fragrant. *V. opulus,* the native Guelder Rose, conspicuous in flower, fruit, and fall color, flowers white, hydrangea-like, May/June, berries red, translucent, persisting well into winter: "Compactum" is a dwarf, very free-flowering and free-berrying form; "Sterile," known as the snowball tree, ball-shaped clusters of flowers, a very spectacular shrub. *V. tomentosum* "Sterile," 8 feet, the Japanese snowball bush, very large ball-shaped clusters of pure-white flowers, a fine flowering shrub. No pruning. Seed, layers, or cuttings taken in August and given gentle bottom heat.

Yucca

Striking evergreen shrubs with narrow, pointed sword-like leaves and spectacular tall spikes of inverted, creamy-white cup-shaped flowers. Invaluable for creating a tropical effect on a patio. Any well-drained soil, full sun. Grow on raised beds in damper gardens. Species with rigid spine-tipped leaves can be dangerous. *Y. filamentosa,* stemless species spreading by offsets, leaf margins fringed with white threads, leaves not rigid; flowers on stems 3 to 6 feet high produced when young; the best species for general cultivation; the form "Variegata," with leaves striped cream and white is more beautiful but more tender. Y. flaccida is very similar. No pruning. Increase from seeds, or offsets potted in pure sand until rooted.

Rhododendrons need acid soil and some shade.

Clematis montana "Rubens," one of the most popular of climbers.

The walls of any house provide a sheltered environment for tender shrubs and climbers.

Climbers and Wall Shrubs

For the keen gardener the walls of a house are a bonus, an added dimension to be exploited by a wealth of plants that could be grown nowhere else in the garden. There are climbing plants that, if carefully selected, can provide color throughout the growing season, but without those walls they would be missing from the garden altogether.

There is also another bonus that the keen gardener appreciates. Brick and stone facing the sun collect the sun's warmth and return it to the atmosphere during the cool of the night, and any inhabited dwelling gives off an appreciable amount of heat. Thus, plants that would be too tender to survive in the open garden can be grown against the walls of a house. The warmth reflected from the brickwork helps to ripen wood, and the extra warmth in winter can make all the difference between the death by frost of a tender plant and its survival. Thus, plants such as the pomegranate, *Punica granatum;* the New Zealand cherry trees, *Hoheria* species; and the Australian bottle-brushes, *Callistemon* species, may thrive against the south or west wall of a house while they would not stand a chance exposed to the elements in the open garden. These could otherwise be grown only in the greenhouse. For this reason it is worth reserving the south wall and specially sheltered corners for particularly tender and less-hardy plants.

Wall shrubs and climbing plants need the same basic treatment as shrubs planted in the open garden. The ground should be well-prepared before planting, and the planting hole should be dug to an adequate depth and an adequate width. Unless the plant will thrive in a poor soil, remove all builder's rubble and replace it with good garden soil. When planting a climber or wall shrub, make sure that the stem is at least 18 inches from the wall. The eaves cast a rain shadow, and little rain will fall on the soil 6 inches to 1 foot away from the brickwork. Furthermore, the stem that may be planted as a slender twig no more than an eighth of an inch in diameter may in time grow into a heavy trunk.

Most shrubs grown against walls can be allowed to assume their natural shapes, but some need to be kept fairly flat against the wall. Stretch strong wires between masonry nails and tie the plant back to these wires. Put the wires in position before the shrub reaches the stage at which it needs tying to the wires.

Plants climb by one of two means: either they cling to any wall or other flat surface by means of aerial roots with sucker pads, or they themselves or their tendrils twine around supports such as twigs or trellises. Ivy is a typical self-supporting climber, using aerial roots; wisteria is a typical stem-twiner; and clematis is a typical tendril-climber.

Many different types of support can be used for twining plants. A trellis of thin wooden strips painted green or stained with a wood preservative is one possibility. Another is a plastic-coated wire mesh; chicken wire may also be used. For some plants it is sufficient to stretch wires between masonry nails, with the wires spaced 8 to 12 inches apart. The important thing is that the support is not placed flat against the wall.

Against a stucco finish or a white-painted wall, fix a trellis or other support to a large wooden frame and then attach the frame to the wall by means of large hinges at the bottom, securing the top with simple bolts or latches. When repainting, it is only necessary to unlatch the frame and move it away from the wall on its hinges, plant and all. Since the hinges will probably be used only once every four years or so, it is important to keep them well covered in a thick layer of grease to prevent them from rusting solid.

Aristolochia/Birthworts

Very vigorous deciduous twining plants of the easiest culture, producing in summer fascinating flowers shaped like a Dutch pipe. *A. durior,* the Dutchman's Pipe, large leaves and curious yellowish-green and purple-brown "Dutch pipe" flowers. Very vigorous, up to 30 feet. *A. tomentosa* has slightly smaller, felted leaves. No pruning; increase by layers.

Callistemon/Bottle Brushes

Spectacular Australian shrubs with brightly colored flowers. Need a sunny south wall and a well-drained soil. Hardy in the south. More generally grown as shrubs and need training to vine patten. *C. linearis,* 6 to 8 feet, brilliant crimson flowers, August. *C. pithyoides,* 5 feet, yellow flowers, June to August. *C. rigidus,* 5 to 6 feet, brilliant large scarlet flowers on arching branches. *C. salignus,* 3 to 4 feet, slow-growing compact habit, creamy-yellow flowers, July and August. Prune out weak shoots after flowering. Propagate by seeds or hardwood cuttings.

Campsis/Trumpet Vine

Often wrongly listed as *Tecoma* or *Bignonia* which are related but different plants. The true *Campsis* are spectacular hardy, vigorous climbers, with deciduous leaves like those of ash, and brilliantly colored trumpet-shaped flowers. Any soil, south wall. *C. × grandiflora,* flowers deep orange and red, late summer, 20 feet; needs a trellis or wires for support. *C. radicans,* self-clinging with aerial roots, flowers scarlet and orange, freely produced, August and September. *C. × tagliabuana* "Madame Gallen," a hybrid between the two previous species, flowers salmon-red, very large, freely produced; best for general planting. Do not prune when young; once established prune hard back to the main stem in March. Increase by layers or suckers.

Clematis

Propably most popular of all climbing plants. Any soil, good on slightly alkaline types; most will thrive in sun or light shade. All mentioned here are hardy. Keep roots in shade and "heads" in sun; place a paving slab or

Clematis 'Barbara Jackman', one of the newer large-flowered hybrids.

large boulder over the roots, or grow some small shrub to cast shade. All climb by winding their leaf stems around support. Against a wall they need some form of trellis or can be allowed to climb naturally through shrubs or small trees. Plant young from pots and do not disturb the roots. Increase by layering, but peg the layer down into a pot, and place a stone over the point where the stem is to root. Clematis are divided into species and large-flowered hybrids. The species are, on the whole, easier to grow.

Species: *C. alpina,* 6 to 8 feet, a delightful, dainty blue flower and a central tuft of staminodes, best in a cool position. *C. armandii,* a strong-growing species with evergreen leaves and creamy-white 2-inch flowers produced abundantly in April; "Apple Blossom" is a form with pink flowers. *C. montana,* the most popular of the species, producing enormous quantities of white flowers on the bare wood in May; "Grandiflora," larger flowers; "Rubens," pink flowers; "Rubens Superba," deepest pink of all forms. *C. tangutica,* masses of deep-yellow lantern-shaped flowers in summer and fall, last flowers of the season mixed among feathery seed heads. *C. viticella,* flowers 1½ inches across, violet or red-purple, borne in huge quantities in summer and early fall; "Alba Luxurians," flowers white, tinted mauve; "Kermesina," flowers crimson; "Royal Velours," deep velvet purple. The only pruning is the removal of dead-wood in spring.

Large-flowered hybrids, flowers 6 inches or more across. Grouped by pruning required. *C. jackmanii* and *C. viticella* hybrids: varieties of these flower on young wood of the current season's growth; prune back hard every February, to within 9 inches of the ground. "Jackmanii," the most popular of all, huge deep-purple flowers over a long period; "Comtesse de Bouchard," soft rose-pink; "Gypsy Queen," rich, velvety violet-purple; "Madame Edouard Andre," bright red; "Mrs. Chlomondeley," semi-double light blue with a dark bar on the petals; "The President," very popular, deep plum-purple; "Duchess of Sutherland," petunia-red, darker bar; "Huldine," pearly-white with lilac-pink bar; "Lady Betty Balfour," deep velvety purple; "Ville de Lyon," bright carmine-red, darker at the edges.

C. lanuginosa, large flowers borne on old wood of the previous season's growth. Pruned lightly in February, merely thinning out weak or overcrowded growths. "Beauty of Worcester," blue-violet with showy white stamens, occasionally produces double flowers; "Blue Gem," sky-blue; "Crimson King," deep rose-red; "Daniel Deronda," deep violet-blue; "Henryi," large creamy-white; "King George V," flesh-pink with a bright-pink bar; "Lady Northcliffe," lavender-blue; "Marie Boisselot," pure white; "Prins Hendrik," extra-large sky blue; "W. E. Gladstone," extremely large lilac with a brighter bar.

C. patens, prune lightly as for the previous group: "Lasurstern," very large, blue-purple; "Nelly Moser," one of the most popular of all, pink with a darker bar.

Clianthus/Lobster Claw or Parrot's Bill

Clianthus puniceus. One of the most beautiful and striking of all climbing plants, ferny semi-evergreen pinnate leaves, large clusters of brilliant scarlet flowers, each like the claw of a lobster. "Alba" is a rare white form. Unfortunately tender; needs a sunny position in well-drained soil in the south or used in a greenhouse. No pruning, increase by layers.

Cobaea

Cobaa scandens. Annual climber with large cup-and-saucer-type Canterbury bell-like flowers; self-

clinging. Any soil, sun. Must be started under glass from seed each year.

Decumaria

Decumaria barbara. A self-clinging semi-evergreen climber closely related to the hydrangeas and producing corymbs of white flowers in June and July. Any soil, preferably in regions with mild winters. No pruning; increase by layers or mature cuttings.

Eriobotrya/Loquat

Eriobotrya japonica. Striking large-leaved evergreen shrub suitable for growing against a sunny wall. Grow outdoors in frost-free areas, otherwise require protection or as a greenhouse plant. Leaves large, up to 9 inches long, deeply corrugated. Flowers hawthorn-like, produced in winter. Ultimately 15 feet, but slow-growing. Any good garden soil; good on limestone soils. No pruning. Increase by seeds or August cuttings.

Clematis 'Mrs. Oud', a striking single with large, pure white flowers and a good center.

Callestemon citrinus, a bottlebrush from Australia. Strictly for mild climates or in a greenhouse.

Ficus/Fig

Ficus carica. Deciduous shrubs or small trees grown for their very large, handsome, lobed leaves; 10 to 15 feet, best against a sunny wall. Will withstand light frosts and temperatures to approximately 25°F; injured at lower temperatures. Any soil; prune only to shape; increase by cuttings 10 to 12 inches long placed outdoors in a sheltered position under a wall in winter.

Hedera/Ivy

The most diverse family of climbing plants. All ivys do well in city and town gardens, impervious to atmospheric pollution. All those mentioned here are hardy even in the bleakest gardens. Any soil, sun or shade; flowers insignificant. No pruning; increase by cuttings taken in September and rooted in a shaded border, or put cuttings in a jar of water until the roots appear, pot up when roots are about 2 inches long, keep very wet for another week. *H. canariensis,* the large-leaved ivy, less hardy than English Ivy; Variegata'' is usually grown, leaves dark green at the center, merging into silvery-gray and bordered with white. *H. helix,* the Common or English Ivy, innumerable named forms, often with variegated leaves. The following is a small selection: "Aureovariegata," leaves irregularly suffused gold, branches occasionally revert to green and should be cut out; "Buttercup," leaves gold, the best golden ivy; "Marginata" (also listed as "Silver Queen" and "Argentea Elegans"), leaves broadly edged creamy white and suffused pink in winter; "Tricolor" (also known as "Elegantissima" or "Marginata Rubra"), leaves small, gray-green, bordered white and edged with pink in winter; "Golden Arrow," leaves bright-gold edged green.

Hydrangea

Climbing Hydrangeas are particularly useful for covering cold or shaded walls, but flower more profusely on a sunny wall; also excellent rambling up trees. Self-clinging, 30 feet. *H. petiolaris,* large flat corymbs of white flowers late summer and fall, deciduous; prune branches that grow away from the wall. *H. integerrima,* evergreen with neat small dark-green leaves; flowers iridescent light

Paeonia suffruticosa 'Jitsu Getsu Nishiki', one of over 5,000 named varieties of the tree peony. These woody peonies have the largest flowers of any hardy shrub, often over 18 inches across.

yellow-green; ideal for covering a low wall; prune out straggly growths. Increase by layer or fall cuttings.

Jasminum/Jasmine or Jessamine

Very popular. Any soil. *J. nudiflorum,* winter-flowering jasmine, bright-yellow flowers even during mild periods of winter; ideal on a north or east wall. Not a true climber, needs to be tied to a trellis or wires. Left to ramble unpruned it forms dense mass of twigs and its flower production declines; cut back hard to within 2 buds of the old wood as soon as flowering is over. Increase by layers, divisions, or August cuttings. *J. officinale,* the common white jasmine, elegant pinnate leaves, highly scented white flowers in continual succession from June to October. Not as winter-hardy as *J. nudiflorum.* Any soil, sun. It does not need any pruning, but remove crowded growths to keep tidy. Increase by layers or August cuttings.

Lonicera/Honeysuckle

Grown for their clusters of long, tubular flowers and for their scent. Natives of hedgerows, and natural climbers through shrubs, most are adaptable to training up a wall but need the support of a trellis or of wires. Most prefer some shade, any soil. *L.* × *americana,* a vigorous deciduous hybrid, flowers white passing to pale and then deep yellow, fragrant, June and July. *L.* × *brownii,* the "Scarlet Trumpet Honeysuckle," a semi-evergreen species of moderate vigor producing masses of scarlet trumpets early in the year and again in late summer. *L. japonica,* an evergreen species with very fragrant creamy-yellow, tinged pink, flower produced continuously on the growing shoots; has become a weed in areas where escaped from cultivation; planted as a ground cover in rough areas and banks; "Aureo-reticulata," leaves green with a network of yellow veins. *L. periclymenum,* flowering from June to September, very fragrant, yellow; "Belgica," the Early

Dutch Honeysuckle, flowers yellow flushed red-purple outside, May and June, and again in late summer; "Serotina," the Late Dutch Honeysuckle, flowers rich purple-red, July to October. *L. tragophylla,* flowers bright golden-yellow, scentless, 4 inches long, in large clusters, June and July; needs almost complete shade. No routine pruning. Increase by seed or layers.

Mutisia/Climbing Gazania

Beautiful evergreen tendril climbers; one of the few climbing plants producing daisy-type flowers. Like clematis, need their roots in shade and their heads in sun, full sun. Rich soil, mulch annually with organic matter. *M. clematis,* 15 feet, compound leaves and flowers rich red; tender, coastal areas only. *M. decurrens,* 15 feet, somewhat hardier, flowers brilliant-orange, 5 inches across. *M. ilicifolia,* 10 feet, the holly-leaved mutisia, flowers lilac or pink, borne continually throughout summer. The hardiest species. *M. oligodon,* similar to *M. ilicifolia* but more compact in growth, leaves small, tendril-tipped, flowers bright pink, 2½ inches across, borne continually from May until frost; exceptionally beautiful; needs a trellis. No routine pruning; plants look tidier if deadwood is cut out. Increase by seed or layers. Grown outdoors in frost-free areas or as a cool greenhouse plant.

Parthenocissus/ Virginia Creeper

Self-clinging deciduous climbers noted for brilliant fall coloring. Any soil, sun or shade. The true Virginia creeper is *P. quinquefolia;* the bright-green leaves turn orange and scarlet in fall. *P. thomsonii* has compound leaves and equally brilliant fall color. *P. himalayana,* similar to the true Virginia creeper but leaves larger, similarly brilliant fall coloring and a bonus of deep-blue ''grapes'' in summer. *P. tricuspidata* ''Veitchii,'' probably the most brilliant of all for fall coloring. Prune only to keep within bounds; increase from layers.

Hedera colchica 'Varietgata', a spectacular large-leaved variegated ivy. It needs some support to help it climb for mild climates.

Passiflora/Passion Flower

Vigorous climbers for sunny walls, producing a long succession of unique, fascinating, and beautiful flowers. Need a poor soil; in rich soil they overgrow and do not flower. *P. caerulea,* common Passion flower, flowers blue, 3 to 4 inches across; ''Constance Elliott,'' pure-white form; both hardy provided they are grown against a hot sunny wall. *P. edulis,* producing Passion Fruit, can only be grown outdoors in the milder frost-free parts of the country, and needs a sunny wall. No pruning. Increase by softwood cuttings or seed.

Pittosporum

Dainty evergreen shrubs, but may be trained on a support as a vine; grown mainly for their attractive habit and foliage. Mainly tender, well-suited to coastal areas, south-wall cultivation. *P. tenuifolium,* any well-drained soil, full sun. *P. crassifolium,* 15 feet, leathery leaves, chocolate-purple flowers, scented. *P. ralphii,* slightly hardier, 10 feet, long gray-green leaves, similar flowers. *P. tobira,* 10 feet, dark polished leathery rhododendron-like leaves and conspicuous clusters of fragrant creamy-white flowers, recommended for coastal gardens. *P. tenuifolium,* 8 to 12 feet, flowers chocolate-purple, inconspicuous except by their scent, dainty rippled light-green leaves; ''Golden King,'' golden leaves fading to soft yellow as the sunner advances; ''Tresederi,'' leaves amber crinkled, mottled gold. Plant when very young and do not transplant. No pruning. Seed or layers.

Solanum

Decorative wall shrubs for south or west walls in sheltered gardens. Any soil. *S. crispum,* the potato tree with rich purple-blue flowers with yellow centers produced in huge quantities throughout summer. A rambling shrub needing support rather than a true climber. No pruning. Good for home greenhouse.

Vitis/Vine

Deciduous ornamental tendril climbers useful for covering old buildings, garden sheds, concrete garages, and old tree stumps. Any soil, preferably sun. Prune back to 1 inch from the old wood in November. Increase by layers or hard cuttings. The grandest of all the species is *V. coignetiae,* huge leaves over 12 inches across making a fiery show of orange and crimson in fall. *V. vinifera,* the Grape Vine: it is from varieties of this that both the edible grapes and the wine-making grapes come. This European grape is grown commercially in California.

Wisteria

Among the most widely grown of climbing plants, having pinnate leaves and drooping racemes of blue, mauve, or white flowers. Need good soil and full sun to do their best. Excellent on slightly alkaline soils. The species usually grown is *W. sinensis,* with individually large mauve flowers carried in drooping racemes 8 to 12 inches long; ''Alba'' has pure-white flowers; ''Plena,'' double, long-lasting mauve flowers. *W. floribunda* ''Macrobotrys'' is the most spectacular of all, with racemes of lilac flowers 2 to 3 feet long; lovely grown over a pergola. Main flowering period May/June; most plants flower sporadically from then until fall.

Good pruning is essential for flowers. Will throw up new growths as much as 10 feet long in a year and can cover a wall 30 feet high and 50 yards long. Are amenable to training and may be kept to a predetermined size. Plant young, tie vigorous growths in to final positions to create the basic "skeleton" of the plant. Once it has reached roughly its allotted space, prune back all unwanted shoots and from there on prune annually and prune hard as soon after leaf-fall as possible. Cut all the current season's new growths back to within 3 inches of the previous season's wood; leave only long shoots needed to build up the shape of the plant.

Clematis macropetala, a species with flowers that are naturally double.

Water and Bog Gardens

Water adds a new dimension to any garden. Its ever-changing face reflects the open sky and the passing clouds. Its surface ripples gently in the wind or is troubled by the playing of a fountain, while beneath the surface, in the translucent depths, the red, gold, and orange gleams of goldfish flash as they move dreamily among the water-lily stems.

A water garden is such a distinct feature that its placement in the total garden plan requires considerable care. However, the needs of the pond itself do much to determine where it may and may not go. Both water plants and fish need plenty of light to flourish. Rotting leaves from nearby trees make it more desirable to locate the pond away from trees, because rotting vegetation is likely to poison the fish. The natural position for a pond is at the lowest level of the garden, so that the surface is always visible. Whether the pond is to be formal or informal, it is best to locate it as a focal point in the garden. What shelter the water garden needs can be provided by the planting of tall evergreen waterside plants on the north side. Marginal plants will provide some shade; fish, although they need the light, do not like direct sun all day.

Whether the pond is to be of a geometrical shape or irregular in outline depends on the general garden design. For formal ponds, an oval or hexagonal may be just as pleasing as square, rectangular, or round ponds, and a pool in the shape of a cross would have a functional advantage for those who wanted to breed different types of fish in different parts of the pool; it would allow the arms of the cross to be partitioned off. The profile of the pool in depth may include ledges for marginal plants.

Depending on the size of the garden, the water area should be as large as possible. Tubs or giant-sized plastic basins might be used to make miniature water gardens for specialized purposes, such as growing a particular plant, but for all practical purposes size is important. Most aquatic plants are rampant, and it is most unattractive to see a pond overcrowded with plants, with no open surface area to act as a background to the foliage and flowers and to give a clear view of the fish and reflections of the sky. Also, the water temperature will fluctuate more in a smaller pool. The same considerations apply to depth. A shallow pond will make it difficult for the fish to escape excessive heat in summer or intense cold in winter. Certain aquatic plants will not grow satisfactorily in shallow water. A considerable portion of the pond should be at least 18 inches deep, although if you are constructing ledges for marginal planting instead of supporting them on blocks in containers, parts of the pond may be half that depth.

The best time for constructing a plastic-or composition-lined pool is in the early spring, which will allow the plants to settle into the pool as they come into vigorous growth. However, for concrete ponds frost-free fall weather is best, so that the finished pond may be filled with water and left over winter. Fill and empty the pool several times over periods of several days so that any free lime from the cement, which would otherwise poison both plants and fish, is leached out. Then treat the concrete with a "curing" solution which will prevent additional lime from leaking into the pond. This would also expose leaks that would be difficult to discover once the pool was planted and stocked. However, plastic and composition liners are now so reliable and durable that, unless there is some very special reason, the work involved in the construction of a concrete pool is really not worthwhile.

The shapes of formal ponds can be marked out using the same methods as those described for laying out flower beds. An irregularly shaped pool can be created by using a length of garden hose to mark the shape. The hose can be laid in attractive curves. Pegs can then be used to stake out the design. When digging the hole, turf or soil around the perimeter of the future pool must be removed so that whatever form of edging is used will be level with the surrounding ground. Paving stones are generally laid so that the edges of the stone protrude slightly over the pool to hide its plastic banks. Gaps between the stones can be filled with creeping or low-growing rock plants. Use a spirit level and boards to make sure that all edges are level.

Laminated Reinforced Nylon PVC

The most expensive of these materials are strong enough to support water in a pool of almost any size, and it could be constructed by welding the edges together. Cheaper materials in this range would be quite suitable for a pool of any size up to 100 square feet. As these materials are more or less flexible, to calculate the amount of sheeting you need add twice the maximum depth of the pool to the maximum width and the maximum length. Thus, a pool of 9 feet by 6 feet by 18 inches would require a piece of plastic 12 feet by 9 feet. It is always assumed that irregularly shaped pools require a piece of plastic sheeting corresponding to their maximum length and maximum width calculated as above. Remove any protruding objects in the excavated hole; line with sand; stretch the material with a slight sag in the middle over the pool, using the edging stones to hold it in place; then gently allow the water to run in. Trim around the edges, allowing a sufficiently wide margin to be weighted down by the edging stones, but do not make any nicks which might lead to splits.

BUTYL   This is the most long-lasting and elastic, but also the most expensive, of the flexible materials. As it does not wrinkle, it is often used for unusually shaped pools. It has one fault — plants have been known to pierce it, and this danger increases the more it is stretched.

POLYETHYLENE   This is less long-lasting and is not generally recommended.

Preshaped Plastic Liners

These are predesigned pools and may be made of either flexible or rigid plastic. In either case the pool must be dug to the dimensions for which they are designed. The rigid ones are the most expensive, in some instances costing as much as four times the price of some of the more flexible liners. However, the small, rigid fiberglass or sophisticated plastic pools have a definite value in constructing intricate watercourses with waterfalls, and so on. In some instances they have lips which can be used to make systems leading from one miniature lake to another, or they may be made in sections that can be fitted together in all sorts of shapes and sizes (the joints must be sealed, however). It is possible to make rigid plastic liners in the excavated hole using polyester resins and hardeners. However, this really requires some previous experience in making laminates.

Fountains and Waterfalls

These are easily made using modern pumps designed for underwater or pondside operation. The earth taken out for making a pool is often piled up to make a rock garden in which the above-mentioned rigid liners may be incorporated to make a series of lakes. The same pump will send water through a three-quarter-inch or more diameter pipe to the top of the rock garden and emit a jet through a fountain either at the side or in the pool. One or both may be switched off either by physically turning off the fountain or the waterfall or by cutting off the supply of electricity that powers the motor. If the motor is submerged, the special cable to it can be conveniently located under the paving slabs or stones around the pool. For those who dislike high-voltage cables in the garden, there are systems involving transformers or low-powered batteries. Waterfalls should be constructed in such a way that they do not involve too much movement in the body of the pool, as not all plants like moving water, particularly waterlilies.

Stepping Stone

If the pool is large enough, stepping stones of natural stone or concrete are a pleasant feature. Common sense, however, must be used to ensure that they are safe to walk on and do not damage the plastic lining. Nothing looks better in water than stone statuary or ornamentation. The choice is wide, and many ornaments include fountains or flowing water.

Bog Garden

When constructing the pond, allow a slight overlap at one point leading to a bog garden. In an irregularly shaped pool, instead of trimming the plastic away, it could perhaps be allowed to continue into the bog garden. In any case, the plastic should run down to a level of about 18 inches below the surface and the resulting hollow filled with peaty soil, incorporating plenty of well-matured manure or compost, over a layer of stones topped by inverted turves. It does not matter if the bog garden leaks a little: in fact it should, provided there is a moist sump into which water from the pool can overflow. Bog plants like moisture but they do not want to be drowned.

Planting

Aquatic plants are best started in the pool in spring or early summer. They do not need anything but fertile loam. Compost, leafmold, manure, peat, and sand might adversely affect the water. Plastic containers with perforated sides rather like baskets are obtainable from most water-plant suppliers, and by stringing up the four corner holes, with two people, one on either side, suspending the container over the pool, it is possible to lower it at the deepest part of the water without accidents. The strings are then withdrawn. Or stout boards can be laid across the pool, this latter method being a way of retrieving containers from the pool as well. Plant firmly, ramming the soil around the roots to prevent it from being washed away, and cover the soil with a layer of clean gravel or pebbles. Be sure that you have the right depth of soil for the roots and the right depth of water for the plant.

Stocking

It is well to leave a newly planted pool for about three weeks before introducing fish. Once the plants are

Water adds a new interest to any garden, reflecting the changing moods of the seasons and the weather. They can be formal, as in the top picture (where the pond is actually part of a roof garden) or informal (below), according to the general design of the garden. Modern plastics have revolutionized the making of garden ponds.

established they will not be affected by fish feeding off them, but if the fish are introduced at the same time as the plants, the plants may not have time to settle down. Provided you follow this advice, do not worry about the appearance of the pool. You are aiming at a properly balanced pool, and once you have the pond stocked with the right types of plants and fish in the right quantities, problems such as algae and green water should disappear. It should never be necessary to change the water of a healthy pool.

When it comes to figuring out how many fish a pond will hold, there is a simple rule of thumb: allow 1 square foot of water for every 2 inches of fish. Thus a pool of 9 by 6 feet = (54 square feet) might accommodate 108 inches of fish: 27 fish, each 4 inches long. Obviously the fish will not only breed but will grow in length, and an 18-inch deep pool of these dimensions will hold at least three times that number of fish. However, it is best to start on the low side to avoid the dangers of overstocking.

Make your selection according to your own taste, but definitely avoid including catfish, perch, or pike and other predators.

When buying fish, do not put them directly into the pool from the container, as the violent temperature change could kill them. Lay the container in the water for an hour and then make the transition. Avoid overfeeding; hardly feed at all in cold weather. Do not smash ice on the pond with a hammer: the shock waves could kill the fish. Keep the water open by leaving a plastic ball floating on the surface; when the water freezes, lift off the ball and bail out enough water to leave an air-space between the ice and the water. Then replace the ball. Alternatively, use a thermostat heater worked from the mains, which will keep the pond at an even temperature without ice completely covering the pool. In the fall cover the pool with a wire frame to keep leaves from falling into it.

Goldfish is the name given to selected strains of fish of gold or similar color. Apart from the true red-gold "goldfish," many fancy-colored strains such as black, red, silver, or yellow have also been selected. Shubunkins are related to goldfish but have non-shiny scales and come in a very varied range of colors, including mottled combinations. Other types include *comets* (long tails), *nymphs* (round bodies), and *calicos* (fantails). Other fish which it is safe to introduce include golden and silver orfe, golden and silver rudd and tench.

Scavengers
Goldfish and other ornamental fish are not purely decorative: they contribute to the health of the pool by scavenging. However, it would not hurt to introduce a few water snails, about a couple of dozen for a new pool. A pool that has accumulated a fair amount of muck on the bottom is the ideal place for tench, which feed on scraps that fall to the bottom. Once introduced, the tench are never seen near the surface again.

The sound of water falling, as much as the sight of water, adds an extra dimension to the garden. The scheme shown here, using both natural materials, like the stone of the walls, and modern materials like concrete, suggests how well these elements can be combined.

Recommended Water Plants

Submerged oxygenating plants

A pool should be started with plenty of submerged oxygenating plants—the more, the better. They can always be weeded out with a rake if they become too prolific. They are generally supplied as cuttings and may be put into containers and planted anywhere on the bottom of the pool.

Anacharis canadensis (Elodea, American pondweed), dark-green mass, brittle stems; check uncontrolled development. *Ceratophyllum demersum* (Hornwort), dark-green bristle-like leaves; handle with care and plant in deepest part of pool. *Myriophyllum proserpinacoides* (water milfoil or parrot's-feather), delicate-looking leaves and stems, found in fresh-waters. *Ranunculus aqualitis* (water crowfoot), the foliage and white buttercup-shaped flowers reach the surface.

Waterlilies A wide range of brilliant hybrids are available, flowering June to September, varying considerably in vigor and therefore in the size of pools to which they are suited. Some are miniatures which will grow in a few inches of water, others need 4 or 5 feet of water in which to flourish. Planting depths in the water are given in this selection. Great care should also be taken when fixing the roots in their pots. The white fleshy roots will be old anchorage roots and should be cut off. The young feeding roots are black and fibrous. They should be kept and planted firmly in moist soil. Tuberous types should be inserted in the soil horizontally, with the crown just above the soil. Place plenty of gravel, pebbles, and even heavy stones over the soil to keep the lily from floating upward and to prevent fish from working over the soil and

An attractive series of linked ponds. The first pond uses polyethylene, but the smaller pond is of concrete.

causing the water to be muddy. Place the container on blocks high in the water, and gradually lower it by removing the blocks as the stems develop, until the water lily reaches its correct planting depth. Water lilies may be thinned out by removing unwanted clumps with a knife. Propagate from "eyes" taken from the roots in spring. RED "Attraction," deep red, large flowers edged white; plant 18 inches to 2 feet 6 inches or more deep. "Escarboucle," brilliant red flowers, large and prolific, very popular; plant 10 inches to 2 feet deep. "James Brydon," carmine flowers, purple leaves, becoming green; stands shade, plant 18 inches to 2 feet deep. "Froebelii," bright wine-red flowers in great numbers; plant in 3 to 18 inches deep. Laydekeri hybrids, red, purple, carmine, rose; plant 3 to 18 inches deep. PINK "Mme. Wilfron Gonnère," fine pink beautifully shaped flowers, many-petalled; plant 18 inches to 2 feet deep. "Marliacea Rosea," flowers attain full color after a year or so, very vigorous; plant in 18 inches to 2 feet of water. *Nymphaea odorata* "Rosea," fragrant rose-colored flowers, vigorous; plant 1 foot to 18 inches deep. *N. odorata* "Turicensis," fragrant rose flowers; plant 1 foot to 18 inches deep. "Laydekeri Lilacea," pink fragrant flowers, becoming deeper in color; plant in 3 to 18 inches of water. YELLOW "Marliacea Chromatella," bright-yellow flowers and mottled leaves; plant 18 inches to 2 feet deep. "Moorei," canary-yellow flowers with bright yellow stamens, leaves brown speckled; plant 18 inches to 2 feet deep. "Comanche," dark-gold to coppery flowers, long flowering period; plant 1 foot to 18 inches deep. *N. odorata* "Sulphurea," soft-yellow star-shaped flowers held well above the water; 3 inches to 18 inches deep. "Pygmaea, Helvola," a true miniature with delicate yellow flowers; plant in only 3 inches to 1 foot of water. WHITE "Gladstoniana," magnificent large white flowers, vigorous; plant in 18 inches to 3 feet of water or even more. "Gonnère" ("Crystall White"), double flowers erect; plant 18 inches to 2 feet. "Lactea," purest white flowers with yellow centers; plant 1 foot to 18 inches. *N. candida,* small white flowers with red stigma, not too vigorous; plant 3 to 18 inches. "Pygmaea Alba," the smallest white of all,

Cypress knees' on the swamp cypress *Taxodium distichum*. These 'knees' grow up off the largely submerged roots.

very delicate and needing winter protection; plant in no more than 3 to 9 inches of water.

Floating plants These require no containers and are placed on the surface of the pond. They sometimes sink at first but rise to the surface again. They are valuable because they reduce algae and provide vegetation for the fish to nibble. About 4 such kinds of plants would be sufficient for a pool 9 × 6 feet. *Azolla caroliniana* (fairy moss), green mazy fronds changing to red and brown at the end of summer, needs over-wintering in frost-free conditions but invasive in summer. *Lemna minor* (duckweed), winter-hardy, sinks in the fall but rises in spring. *Hydrocharis morsusranae* (frogbit), water-lily-like leaves, white flowers in July, the plant sinks in winter but comes to the surface again in spring. *Stratiotes aloides* (water soldier) spiky dark-green leaves, white flowers, also rests on bottom in winter.

Deep marginals Besides water lilies there are a number of other decorative plants that produce floating leaves and whose flowers appear above the sur-

face. They should be planted in containers in 6 to 18 inches of water. About 2 such plants are enough for a pool 9 × 6 feet. *Aponogeton distachyum* (water hawthorn), oblong dissected leaves, white fragrant flowers from spring on; plant in 15 to 18 inches of water. *Hottonia palustris* (water violet), sometimes placed among submerged oxygenators because the finely divided foliage remains below the surface of the pond, although the flowers of lilac or white may be held a foot above the surface in summer; it overwinters on the bottom in the mud; plant in 6 to 18 inches of water Nymphoides peltatum (syn. *Limnanthemum nymphoides, Villarsia nymphoides*) (water fringe), floating water-lily-like leaves, fringed yellow flowers in summer; plant 6 to 18 inches deep. *Orontium aquaticum* (golden club), broad bluish-green leaves, golden-yellow tipped flower spikes in spring; roots must be lodged deeply in soil so it cannot be grown at the edge of sloping sides; plant in 6 to 18 inches of water.

Marginals A wide range of plants including many highly decorative rushes and sedges may be grown at the margin of a pond. Plant in about 3 inches of soil in shallow containers with about 3 inches of water above the top of the container. About 10 such plants will do for a pool 9 × 6 feet. *Acorus calamus* "variegatus," variety of sweet-scented flag, green and cream sword-shaped leaves 18 inches or more tall. *Alisma plantago-aquatica* (great water plantain), broad leaves, small pink flowers in summer, reaching 2 feet or more. *Butomus umbellatus* (flowering rush), narrow, sword-shaped leaves, pink flowers in June; 18 inches or more. *Calla palustris* (bog arum), heart-shaped leaves, white column-type flowers, spring to summer, red berries in autumn; 6 inches. *Caltha palustris* "Plena" (marsh marigold), dark-green wavy leaves, rich double golden flowers, 6 to 9 inches; wet soil to 3 inches of water over the crowns. *Cotula coronopifolia* (brass buttons), smooth green leaves, long-lasting bright-yellow flowers, low-growing; wet soil to 3 inches deep. *Cyperus longus* (sweet galingale), rushy leaves up to 4 feet, dark-brown flowers in summer; wet soil to 3 inches of water. *Eriophorum angustifolium* (cotton grass), grass-like tufts, with cotton-wool-like flower heads, 1 foot or more. *Glyceria aquatica* "Vari-

egata" (manna grass, reed grass), thin strap-like leaves striped green and gold, 18 inches or more. *Iris*. This large genus provides many beautiful water plants, some of which should be in every pool. Choose from *I. kaempferi*, of which there are many modern strains with huge flowers of orchid-like quality; *I. laevigata*, which is sometimes confused with *I. kaempferi*, but lacks the pronounced leaf "rib"; *I. pseudacorus* (yellow flag); and *I. sibirica*. All bloom from spring to summer and there are many interesting varieties from which to choose. *I. versicolor*, the North American wine-colored "flag" is another marginal species. Most grow 18 inches to 2 feet; wet soil to 3 inches of water over the roots; some varieties will do well in soil that is merely boggy. *Mentha aquatica* (water mint), fragrant foliage reaching 1 foot with pale-lilac flowers; wet soil to 3 inches. *Mimulus guttatus* (monkey musk), perfoliate leaves, brownish-red-spotted flowers in summer; wet soil to 3 inches. *Myosotis palustris* (water forget-me-not), bright-blue flowers, low-growing; wet soil to 3 inches. *Pontederia cordata* (pickerel weed), heart-shaped leaves and blue flower spikes, 18 inches or more. *Ranunculus lingua* "Grandi-

florus" (great spearwort), narrow leaves; buttercup-like flowers, 2 feet or more. *Sagittaria sagittifolia* "Flore-pleno" (syn. *Sagittaria japonica plena*) (arrowhead), arrowhead-shaped leaves, double white flowers, 18 inches or more. *Scirpus tabernaemontani* "Zebrinus" (zebra rush), contrasting green and white bands make this a striking rush; 4 feet. *Typha latifolia* (great reed mace), rush-like, bearing brown spikes up to a foot-long; 6 feet or more.

Bog plants Most of the above marginals can be treated as bog-garden plants, but *Iris kaempferi* and the marsh marigold are especially suitable for growing in the bog garden. The bog garden can merge with the rest of the garden, linking the water garden with the land garden, with ferns and other moisture-loving plants making the transition. *Aconitum napellus* (monkshood), divided leaves, purple-blue flowers in early summer, reaching 3 feet or more; "Bressingham Spire" is an especially good variety. *Cardamine pratense* (lady's smock, cuckoo flower), pretty lilac or pale-violet flowers spring to summer, to 18 inches; *Cv.* "Flore Pleno" has double flowers. *Gentiana pneumonanthe* (bog gentian), flowers blue with bands of greenish speckles, 6 inches. *Gunnera manicata*, giant rhubarb-like leaves which may reach 8 feet across; only for the large bog garden. *Helonia bullata* (swamp pink, stud flower), rosettes of short, sword-like leaves, rich-pink spikes in spring, 1 foot. *Lythrum salicaria* (purple loosestrife) — there are several cultivars of this beautiful flower with purple to rose-like florescences in July: *Orchis maderensis*, long leaves, tall purple flower spikes in summer, 1 foot to 18 inches. *Osmunda regalis* (royal fern), the fronds can reach well over 4 feet long; conspicuous fertile fronds; russet fall leaves. *Parnassia palustris* (grass of Parnassus), 6 inches, white flowers, summer. *Pinguicula vulgaris* (bog violet), violet flowers, 6 inches, summer. *Primula beesiana*, rosy-purple flowers with yellow eye, May, 2 feet or more. *Primula bulleyana*, flowers buff-orange, April to May, 18 inches or more. *Primula helodoxa* (the glory of the marsh), yellow flowers, early summer, 2 feet or more. *Primula rosea*, rose to carmine flowers. April, 6 inches.

The Calla lily *Zantedeschia aethiopica*, an ideal plant for the waterside, or for planting actually in the water.

Crinum × powellii 'Alba', the white form of the Paradise lily, one
of the largest-growing of bulbs.

Bulbs, Corms and Tubers

No other group of plants can produce such a wealth of color for as little money or effort as this group. This is particularly true of the spring-flowering bulbs such as daffodils and crocuses, many of which, once planted, can be forgotten, to surprise you with their colorfulness year after year.

A bulb is in fact a whole plant, complete in itself, but in embryo and in miniature. It is very like those paper plants that children used to be given at Christmas, which are folded up in small shells and, when dropped into a tumbler of water, miraculously unfurl themselves. An onion is a typical bulb, and if you cut an onion exactly in half you can see precisely how a bulb is constructed. In the middle there is a bud containing the flower and the leaves. This central bud is surrounded by layers of white fleshy scales that are modified leaves. Both the scales and the central bud are attached to a hard lump at the bottom called the baseplate. It is from this that both stem and roots develop once growth begins. The roots are deciduous — that is, they die off at the end of each season's growth — although in a few cases they are perennial. Most bulbs renew themselves each year, the old scales giving their substance to the new scales.

Most bulbs are protected by a further layer of modified leaves known as the "tunic." The tunic may be white, brown, or black. Such bulbs are called "tunicated." A daffodil is a typical tunicated bulb. These bulbs normally reproduce themselves by producing a second, smaller reproductive bud off the baseplate but within the protective layer of scales.

Bulbs that are not protected by a tunic are known as "imbricated." Lilies are typical imbricated bulbs. The scales are usually thick and fleshy. Most imbricated bulbs are increased in cultivation by removing the scales and inserting them in boxes or pans of sandy soil.

A corm is an altogether more solid structure. It consists almost entirely of the fleshy base of the previous year's stem and in effect is a short, thickened stem. As with a bulb, there is a baseplate from which the roots develop, and a bud, but the bud is tiny compared with that of a bulb: it is usually formed beside the old stem. Whereas bulbs renew themselves annually, corms usually wither and die, giving their substance to the new season's growth. As this growth dies, an entirely new corm is formed, usually on top of the old corm. In a few cases (cyclamen, begonias, and gloxinias, for example) the corm does not die but just goes on increasing in size until it degenerates with age.

Tubers are different. They are enlarged underground stems whose function is to store up plant nutrients accumulated during one season's growth to start the plant growing again the following season. Unlike bulbs and corms, they have no baseplate and no tunic. Most have a multitude of dormant growth buds.

Reference is sometimes made to tuberous-rooted plants. Here it is the roots, not the stem, that store up one season's nutrients to begin the next season's growth. There are no buds on the tuberous roots themselves; the buds congregate around the base of the previous year's stem, and from there the roots spread out in starfish fashion.

Rhizomes are also underground stems. They can vary greatly in appearance, but in general they are treated like corms.

In spite of their differences, bulbs, corms, and tubers are all very easy to cultivate. There is only one basic rule that must always be observed: all need a well-drained soil. Without a well-drained soil they will rot.

A light, sandy soil is ideal. Such soils are naturally well-drained. On other soils the aim should be to make the bulb areas as light and sandy as possible. On heavy and moderately heavy soils this can be achieved by working in quantities of leaf mold, well-rotted manure or peat, and sharp sand. On the very heaviest soils bulbous plants must be grown in raised beds contained within low walls of brick, stone, or logs. The bed should be filled with a mixture of equal parts of ordinary garden soil, sand, and well-rotted manure or leaf mold.

The main planting season for many bulbs is in the fall. The earlier in the fall they are planted the better, as this gives them time to start making root growth before frosts make this impossible. Consequently, early planting is invariably rewarded by a better show in the spring.

The planting of bulbs is the easiest thing in the world. However, there are two important rules that must be followed. Bulbs should generally be planted at twice their own depth, and the base of the hole in which the bulb is planted must be flat. It is simply no good to take out a hole shaped like an inverted dunce's cap. The bulb will settle halfway down leaving its roots dangling in the air. The baseplate must be in contact with the earth at the bottom of the hole. With large bulbs, which are more likely to rot owing to the greater depth at which they are planted, it is advisable to place a handful of sharp sand at the bottom of the hole and set the bulb on that. With exceptionally large bulbs, it is also worth encasing the whole bulb in sharp sand before refilling the hole with soil, especially in heavy soils.

In general there are three different ways of using bulbs in the garden: they may be used in formal bedding schemes; in beds and borders among other plants; or allowed to naturalize themselves in lawns, woodland, or selected areas of borders.

Hyacinths and tulips are the most popular bulbs for spring display in formal bedding schemes. Daffodils are used to a certain extent but are better suited to large borders. By careful selection of varieties it is possible to have daffodils in flower from March until May, while by a similarly careful selection of tulip varieties it is possible to have these in bloom from the end of April until early June, or for about 6 weeks from the earliest to the latest. There can be no doubt that for a really striking effect in massed planting schemes, pride of place must go to the tulip. The earliest to flower have an average height of 10 to 12 inches. The early-flowering doubles, which follow next in season, are slightly shorter, while the best of all the bedding tulips, the "Triumph" or early-flowering "Darwin" tulips, are rather taller, having an average height of about 18 to 30 inches. The late "Darwins" or cottage tulips come last in the succession of blooms.

Hyacinths come into their own in formal bedding schemes in small borders. The flowers themselves, even in the double forms, and their presentation above the half-grown leaves, is itself rather formal.

Daffodils, although limited in their range of color, have a glory all their own, and are rightly prized as the harbingers of spring. By and large they do not lend themselves well to formal bedding schemes and are much better planted in bold groups in beds, borders, or lawns. In large gardens the groups need to be of twenty or thirty bulbs each, while in smaller gardens eight to sixteen bulbs to each group is probably sufficient.

In general, where bulbs are being used in formal bedding schemes, it is better to confine each bed to a single genus, be it tulips, daffodils, or hyacinths. In less formal schemes it is well worthwhile mixing the genera, but keeping each genera within its own clearly defined area. Hyacinths should always be planted at the front of any such scheme, while the taller-growing daffodils or tulips should occupy the center. Totally informal schemes can be made by mixing the different genera, but in general these are neither as pleasing nor as striking.

The planting of bulbs should not be confined to the beds and borders. They may also be planted in the lawns, under trees, and, in larger gardens, in the orchards. Where bulbs are used in this way, the general idea is to gain a "natural" effect, as though the bulbs just happened to be growing there. There is only one way to achieve the sort of haphazard effect that is found where bulbs really grow wild, and that is to take a handful of bulbs and toss them into the air in the general direction of where you want them to grow, and then to plant them precisely where they fall. Once planted, they should be left in the ground for several years to increase naturally.

Many daffodils are suitable for naturalizing in this way, and the smaller-growing species such as *Narcissus triandus* (the angels' tears daffodil), *Narcissus cyclamineus,* and *Narcissus bulbocodium* are ideal. All the species mentioned seed themselves freely and soon naturalize in situations that suit them. Crocuses, both spring- and fall-flowering, and snowdrops are also suitable for naturalizing.

It is particularly important never to mow where bulbs have been naturalized until all the leaves have died down — usually about mid-June. The reason for this is that the leaves of the bulbs continue to build up the new bulb for the following season's flowering, right up until the time they turn yellow and die. If they are removed before their natural cycle of growth is over, the bulb is weakened and the next season's flowering is imperiled. Similarly, where bulbs are grown in formal bedding schemes, they must be allowed to finish their natural cycle of growth. It is always best, if possible, to leave the bulbs in the ground until their leaves have withered, but if they have to be lifted before completing their growth cycle they should be replanted immediately in some other part of the garden and allowed to finish their growing season there. Where daffodils are planted in borders it is possible to overcome this problem, provided that the soil is sufficiently well-drained, by planting the bulbs a foot deep. Subsequent cultivations can then be carried out above the bulbs without disturbing or damaging them. The bulbs should be lifted every three or four years, divided and replanted. If they are left in the ground longer they may begin to deteriorate.

Forcing bulbs in bowls for indoor decoration in

winter is now very popular. Cultivation is not difficult: the important thing is to use only the highest-quality bulbs. They may be grown either in soil or in bulb fiber, but if grown in the latter they take a week longer to come into flower and, since the fiber contains no plant foods, they must be either thrown away after use or planted in the garden, where it will take them a year or two to build up their strength. The bowls should have proper drainage holes: it is almost impossible to guage accurately the degree of moisture at the bottom of a holeless bowl.

Bulbs for forcing should be planted three to five in a bowl and placed in water until thoroughly soaked. They should then be allowed to drain for at least 4 hours, before being put away in a dark, cool place. There they should remain until growth is about 2 inches high, when they may gradually be introduced to more light and more warmth. The purpose of storing the bulbs in a dark place is to encourage them to make good root growth before the tops start growing strongly. If no suitable cupboard or cellar is available, the bulbs can be started in the garden, putting them in a sheltered place and heaping at least 4 inches of sand over the top of the bowls.

Daffodils and hyacinths are the bulbs most often used for forcing. If hyacinths are used, they should be what are called "prepared hyacinths." These have been specially treated to bring them into flower early. Other plants that can be forced in a similar way are crocuses and ixias. It is also possible to buy "prepared" tulips, but these are not usually successful in bowls.

A number of other bulbs can also be grown indoors, but they must not be forced. These include Amaryllis, Haemanthus, Hippeastrum, Ismene, Lachenalia, Schizostylis, Vallota, Veltheimia, and Zephyranthes. All should be planted in well-drained pots in a porous soil, with the bulbs buried to little more than half their depth. During the growing season the bulbs should be watered liberally and given an occasional liquid feed; they should be allowed to become completely dry during their dormant season—i.e., for about three months after their leaves turn yellow. In general it is better to err on the side of underwatering than overwatering.

One or two bulbs have the remarkable power of being able to produce their flowers while sitting on a saucer on a windowsill, without either soil or water. Colchicum and *Sauromatum guttatum* are the two best known for this ability. Colchicums produce large pink or mauve crocus-like flowers in fall, while *Sauromatum guttatum,* often known as the Voodoo Lily, produces one of the most curious flowers in the vegetable kingdom. It is more like a reptile than a plant: a long, mauve ribbon spotted with brown and purple, that slowly curls itself around a long, black rod, the whole flower measuring about 2 feet. It flowers in spring. Both plants need to be planted

Narcissus 'Geranium', a delightfully scented, many-headed daffodil.

outdoors to make leaf growth, lifted once the leaves have faded, and washed before being brought indoors to perform their remarkable feat once again.

The propagation of bulbous plants is not at all difficult. The problem is in knowing which bulbs should be increased in which way. Unlike most flowering plants, which have only one or two possible means of increases, the bulbs have a variety of alternative ways of increasing themselves. The simplest way is to raise new plants from seed, and the great majority of plants mentioned in this chapter produce fertile seeds, although it must be stressed that if the seeds come from a hybrid the offspring may not be in the least like the parent plant. Seeds should be sown either in the fall or spring following their collection. Most will take two to five years to reach flowering size.

Alternatively, bulbs and corms can be increased by dividing the offsets and planting them, by means of the aerial bulbils that occasionally form at the point where the leaf meets the stem, or by the removal of stoloniferous bulbils (stolons are underground stems at the end of which new bulbs form). Details of the propagation of various bulbs, corms, and tubers are included in the alphabetical list that follows.

Acidanthera

Gladiolus-like plants, white flowers with a chocolate blotch. They should be cultivated like gladioli. *A. bicolor,* hardier of the two species; highly scented white flowers with a dark, reddish-brown center, 2 feet. *A. murielae,* very similar, less scented, 3 feet. Both flower August from spring-planted bulbs or in May in mild climates when fall-planted. Individual flowers 4 inches across. Excellent for massing. Increase by seed or offsets.

Allium /Ornamental Onion

The genus to which onions, shallots, and garlic belong. The leaves of many species smell of garlic when crushed. Hardy, bulbous plants, thriving in sun. Mostly easy to grow. *A. albopilsum,* flowers deep lilac, 18 inches, May to June. *A. caeruleum,* 18 inches, flowers sky-blue, May to June. *A. cernuum,* drooping pink bells, 12 inches, June. *A. moly,* flowers yellow, May to June, 8 to 12 inches. *A. narcissiflorum,* rock garden, bell-shaped rose flowers, 6 to 12 inches, May to July. *A. roseum,* flowers lilac-rose, 12 to 15 inches, May to July. Increase by seed sown as soon as ripe or by offsets lifted in October.

Alstroemeria / Peruvian Lily

Summer-flowering lily-like plants prized for floral decoration. Avoid breaking the extremely brittle rhizomatous roots when planting. Plant 6 to 8 inches deep, cover with dry straw in winter in cold areas. Winter-hardy to about 15 °F. Full sun, a rich, sandy soil. May be planted outdoors in the spring, lifted in the fall, and stored overwinter in dry peat as for tuberous-rooted begonia. *A. aurantiaca,* 36 inches, yellow or orange flowers spotted brown or yellow. *A. ligtu,* vigorous hybrids, pink, red, orange, or yellow, 36 inches. Increase by seeds sown several to a pot. Do not plant out for a year, then, plant without disturbing the soil ball; also by division.

Amaryllis /Belladonna Lily

Closely related to the indoor Amaryllis, which are strictly Hippeastrums. *Amaryllis belladonna,* leaves strap-shaped, flowers huge, trumpet-shaped, borne 6 to 8 inches in a cluster on top of a stem 18 to 30 inches tall, Fall. Flowers after the leaves. Plant the large bulbs in light, sandy soil. In cold climates store in a cool, dry place over winter.

Anemone /Windflower

A. apennina, sky-blue flowers above pale-green leaves, spring, 6 inches. Likes shade and will naturalize under trees. *A. blanda,* flowers white, mauve, pink, red, or blue, spring, sun. Excellent planted in the same ground as fall-flowering bulbs such as nerine or amarylli. *A.* "de Caen" and *A.* "St. Brigid", both produce large, brightly colored, some rather poppy-like flowers, in red, blue, pink, purple, or orange with a black center. Plant in fall to flower in spring; plant in spring to flower in summer. They reach 9 to 12 inches. A. nemorosa, the wild wood anemone; leaves finely divided, 3 to 4 inches, flowers white or pink, spring, with longer-lasting flowers. Likes shade and a slightly alkaline soil. Plant 2 inches deep and increase all types by division of the roots in fall. For other species, see the alphabetical list of plants for beds and borders.

Begonia

For gardening purposes, begonias are divided into two groups, those known as "tuberous-rooted," and those known as "fibrous-rooted." For the fibrous-rooted begonias, see the chapter on Greenhouses. There is probably no other group of bulbous plants, except perhaps the orchids, that can rival the tuberous-rooted begonia for sheer opulence of flower. In spite of their beauty, they are among the easiest of all plants to grow. The modern types are not species, but hybrids of complex parentage. There are two methods of cultivating tuberous-rooted begonias. They may be grown either in pots or in the open ground. If grown in pots they should be planted in compost made up of equal parts of peat, leafmold, and sand. In the open garden they should be planted shallowly in beds or borders once all danger of frost is over. The concave part of the tuber should be planted uppermost. Plant in a semi-shaded position, sheltered from winds. For the finest flowers the plants should be well-watered at all times — so long as

the soil does not become soggy. Water should be stopped at the first sign of frost and the plants then be dug up in their entirety without damaging either leaves or roots. They should be taken into a dry, frost-proof place until the roots and foliage have withered. Once this has happened the stems should be cut off an inch above the tuber and the roots shaken free of earth. They should then be stored in dry peat in a dark, frost-proof place until the spring. Potted begonias need not be removed from their pots, but watering must be stopped altogether and the plants must be kept in a dark dry, frost-proof place throughout the winter.

Brodiaea/Spring Star flower

Brodiaea uniflora (Ipheion uniflorum, Triteleia uniflora). One of the gems of spring; tufts of blue-green, grassy leaves. Flowers palest porcelain-blue with darker center; April, 4 to 6 inches. "Violaceum," almost white flowers; "Wisley Blue", deeper blue. Increases rapidly by means of seeds and offsets, making dense clumps.

Canna/Canna Lily

Tuberous-rooted relatives of the banana, valued for the subtropical appearance of their large green or bronze leaves and for their flamboyant red, yellow, orange, or pink, often spotted flowers. Modern plants are hybrids. Grown in the greenhouse in large pots or used as bedding plants. Start the tubers indoors in warm temperatures in peat, and increase watering gradually once leaves show. Move plants to a frame in late April or May and gradually harden off. Once the chill is off the ground, plant out, growing tubers in rich, well-fertilized soil when there is no danger of frost. Cannas must have full sun, really rich soil, and plenty of moisture during the growing season. Lift in fall before severe frosts begin, dry off, and store in a cool, well-ventilated but frost-free place until the following season. Increase by dividing the roots or by seed, which must be soaked in tepid water for 24 hours before sowing in a minimum temperature of 20 °C.

Camassia/Quamash

Easy-to-grow plants carrying spikes of starry flowers on 3-foot stems.

Cyclamen neapolitanum, strictly a corm not a bulb, may naturalize itself in any shady corner.

Plant 4-inches deep in good, well-drained soil in sun or semi-shade. *C. leichtlinii,* flowers white, cream, or blue, 3 feet. *C. quamash,* violet-blue flowers. Increase from offsets.

Cardiocrinum giganteum/Giant Himalayan Lily

The most magnificent of all the lilies; also known as *Lilium giganteum.* Bulb large, 6 to 8 inches in diameter, a foot tall; leaves oval, 18 inches long and 16 inches wide, flower stem 10 feet or more high; flowers highly scented, 6 inches long, trumpet-shaped, creamy white tinged green outside, reddish markings in the throat. Essentially a woodland plant. Plant bulbs with crowns at soil level. Flowers once, then dies, but leaves numerous offsets, which take 3 to 5 years to flower. Rarely found in cultivation.

Chionodoxa/Glory of the Snow

Treasured for their brilliant bright-blue flowers in early spring. Perfectly hardy; plant in any fertile soil. *C. luciliae,* bright-blue flowers with a white center, 4 to 6 inches. *C. sardensis,* gentian blue, 10 inches. Increase readily from seed and by division.

Colchicum/Meadow Saffron

The commonly cultivated species produce crocus-like flowers in fall, the flowers appearing out of the bare ground. The massive leaves follow in spring. Plant July or August, 4 to 8 inches deep, in sunny, well-drained soil. *C. agrippinium,* small flowers, pink checkered purple. *C. autumnale,* larger flower, soft rosy-lilac, very freely produced; var. "Album," a striking white form. *C. speciosum,* large goblet-shaped flowers, from pink to purple; var. "Album" is a white form of exceptional beauty. The hybrids "Lilac Wonder" and "Water Lily" have larger flowers than the species; both are striking plants. Increase by seed sown in a cold frame as soon as ripe or by division.

Crinum/Paradise Lily

Massive, highly decorative plants of tropical and subtropical orgin and appearance. Flowers huge, trumpet-shaped, lily-like, scented; leaves strap-shaped, to 4 feet long; bulb enormous, 8 inches in diameter, 2 feet long. Plant 1 foot deep, preferably under a south wall. Winter-hardy to 15 °F. Provide a mulch over winter. Do not manure. *C. bulbispermum* produces a large flower in clusters of up to 20, trumpet-shaped, pale pink, veined purple inside, highly scented; leaves blue-green, early summer. *C. × powellii,* hybrid of great vigor, flowers huge, trumpet-shaped, rose-pink flowers borne 10 to each 3-foot stem, late summer. "Alba," a white form. Grow other species in the greenhouse. Increase by seed sown on the surface in a 70 °F house.

Crocosmia

C. aurea, gay fall-flowering cormous plants. Leaves sword-shaped, flowers tubular, produced in large sprays, yellow, orange, red, or scarlet, 2 feet. Plant 3 inches deep in sun in any fertile soil. In the north plant and treat as gladiolus.

Crocus

Deservedly the most popular of all the spring-flowering bulbs, bringing a flare of color at the end of the winter season. What is not generally realized is that by careful selection of species crocuses can be had in flower from August until April. Most are hardy and will thrive in any fertile, well-drained soil, preferably in full sun. The following is a selection. Other kinds may be found in nurserymen's catalogues. **Spring flowering:** *C. ancyrensis,* earliest of the spring-flowering species, small, long-lasting flowers, deep orange-yellow, January. *C. chrysanthus,* the parent of many of the large-flowered named sorts: among the best named forms are "Blue Bird," large globe-shaped flowers, soft-blue edged white; "Cream Butterfly," soft creamy-yellow, very free-flowering; "Lady Killer," rich purple edged white, pointed petals, very early; "Snow Bunting," white with purple feathering and a golden-yellow throat. *C. tomasinianus,* pale saphire-lavender flowers with an orange center, March; will seed itself freely and make a carpet of color. **Autumn flowering:** *C. ochroleucus,* small, creamy-yellow flowers, October; seeds itself freely when undisturbed. *C. sativus,* the Saffron Crocus, bright lilac with bright-red stigma, October to

November. *C. speciosus,* bright feathered lilac, September to November. *C. zonatus,* rosy lilac.

Cyclamen

The hardy cyclamen are smaller both in leaf and in flower than the indoor sorts. Best planted in bold groups under trees or in light shade, where they will seed themselves. Seed can also be collected as soon as ripe and sown while still sticky in pots placed in the ground and covered with a pane of glass until germinated. Seedlings should not be transplanted until they have completed their first year's growth. Plant shallowly, just under the surface of the soil, except *C. europeaum,* which should be planted 4 inches deep. Cyclamen dislike transplanting, and once planted should be left alone. Mulch with well-decomposed leaf mold and provide winter protection. *C. atkinsii,* kidney-shaped leaves, deep-green spotted silvery-white, flowers crimson, pink, or white, January to March. *C. europeaum,* round, deep-green leaves red underneath, flowers crimson, August to September. *C. neapolitanum,* flowers August to October, the flowers springing out of the bare ground, followed by the leaves; deep pink, pale pink, or white, leaves heart-shaped, deep green marbled pale green and white; worth growing for the leaves alone. *C. repandum,* bright crimson, April.

Dahlia

The biggest, brightest, and most flamboyant of all late-summer-flowering plants. No other group of plants can rival them for sheer vibrancy of color. Natives of the highlands of Mexico, they were cultivated by the Aztecs long before Europeans discovered them. Today there are literally thousands of cultivars, and these are classified into groups according to the size and shape of the flower.

Single-Flowered
Height 1½ to 2 feet; plant 18 to 24 inches apart; flowers up to 4 inches across, daisy-like. "Nellie Geerlings," scarlet; "Orangeade," flame; "Princess Marie Jose," lilac-pink.

Anemone-flowered
Height 2 to 3½ feet; plant 2 feet apart; flowers up to 4 inches across. "Bridesmaid," white petals, lemon

center; "Lucy," purple petals yellow center.

Collarette
Height 2 to 4 feet; plant 2 to 2½ feet apart; flowers up to 4 inches across. "Mrs. H. Brown," flame and orange petals, yellow collar; "Nonsense," creamy-white petals, orange collar; "Ruwenzori," scarlet petals, yellow collar.

Peony-Flowered
Height up to 3 feet; plant 2 feet apart; flowers up to 4 inches across. "Fascination," purple; "Grenadier," scarlet: "Orange Flora," orange.

Decorative
These are the prize of the dahlias, with the largest flowers of all. They are subdivided into five groups:
EXHIBITION Height 5 to 7 feet; plant 4 feet apart; flowers 10 to 15 inches across. "Burgess Ray," yellow; "Crossfield Festival," bright red and white; "Holland Festival," fiery orange petals tipped white.
LARGE Height 3½ to 5 feet; plant 4 feet apart; flowers 8 to 10 inches across. "Bunratty," purple; "Enfield Salmon," pink; "Robert Damp," yellow.
MEDIUM Height 3½ to 4 feet; plant 3 feet apart; flowers 6 to 8 inches across. "Betty Russell," yellow; "Breckland Joy," bronze; "Terpo," crimson.
SMALL Height 3½ to 4 feet; plant 2½ feet apart; flowers 4 to 6 inches across. "Millbank Inferno," red and orange; "Snow Queen," pure white.
MINIATURE Height 3 to 4 feet; plant 2½ feet apart; flowers up to 4 inches across. "David Howard," orange; "Jo's Choice," scarlet; "Newby," peach.

Ball
Height 3 to 4 feet; plant 2½ feet apart; flowers 4 to 6 inches across. The flower is ball-shaped. "Doreen Hayes," scarlet; "Gloire de Lyon," white.

Pompom
Height 3 to 4 feet; plant 2½ feet apart; flowers up to 2 inches across. The flowers are very like those of the Ball dahlia but are smaller and even more ball-shaped. "Little Conn," dark red; "Pom of Poms," scarlet.

Cactus
These dahlias have fully double flowers with spiky, pointed petals. The group is divided into five subsections according to size:
GIANT Height 4 to 5 feet; plant 4 feet apart; flowers 10 to 12 inches across. "Danny," pink; "Gladys M. Reynolds," bronze; "Polar Sight," creamy white.
LARGE Height 4 to 5 feet; plant 4 feet apart; flowers 8 to 10 inches across. "Drakenburg," purple; "Royal Highness," pink; "Royal Wedding," scarlet with yellow center.
MEDIUM Height 3½ to 4 feet; plant 3 feet apart; flowers 8 to 10 inches across. "Apache," bright red; "Autumn Fire," tangerine tinged scarlet; "Rotterdam," crimson; "Topaz," yellow.
SMALL Height 3½ to 4 feet; plant 2½ feet apart; flowers 4 to 6 inches across. "Doris Day," crimson; "Marilyn," pink; "Rothesay Red," crimson.
MINIATURE Height 3½ to 4 feet; plant 2½ feet apart; flowers up to 4 inches across. "Charmer," purple; "Happy Mood," yellow; "Little Ann," pink; "Snip," bronze and orange.

Bedding Dahlias
These are annuals that need to be grown from seed each year. They reach 12 to 20 inches in height and should be planted 12 to 24 inches apart. The flowers, which may be single, semi-double, or double come in many colors; 2 to 3 inches across.
Cultivation Dahlias are easy to grow, but for show-quality blooms give them a little extra attention. Plant in any fertile, well-drained soil in full sun. The ground should be dug thoroughly before planting and enriched with manure or decomposed organic compost. Plant in May or June. The larger sorts should be planted 4 to 6 inches deep. Stakes should be put in the ground at planting time. If they are put in later they are liable to damage the tubers. Once in growth, water plants freely. For really big, handsome flowers pinch out all the buds that form in the leaf axils, allowing only one stem to develop, which means cutting off other shoots at ground level as they appear. At first frost the top growth of dahlias will turn black and wither. The stems should then be cut off 6 inches above the ground and the tubers carefully

lifted with a fork, the earth shaken from them, and left on the ground to dry. Label the tubers at this stage, either by variety, if known, or by type and color. Before nightfall they should be transferred to a dry, frost-proof place and allowed to finish drying-off. All traces of earth should then be removed and any rotten or damaged tubers discarded. Store over winter on slatted shelves or in slatted boxes. **Propagation** Dahlias can be propagated by root-division, by cuttings, or by seed. **Root-division** This operation involves slicing vertically through the old stem so that a number of tubers are detached, each with a portion of the old stem attached to them. New growth can be made only by the buds that occur around the base of the previous season's growth, so it is essential to make sure that each tuber has a part of the previous season's old stem attached to it. **Cuttings** The same principles apply here as to dividing the tubers. Each cutting must have a piece of the previous season's stem attached to act as a "heel." The previous season's tubers are planted shallowly in an earth-filled box and placed in the greenhouse or the home. They are liberally watered to encourage quick growth. As soon as the shoots are 2 to 3 inches high they should be detached from the parent plant with a sharp knife and potted up singly in 3-inch pots, or in boxes and spaced 3 inches apart. They need to be kept growing well, and this means keeping them warm and moist. After 10 to 15 days they will have rooted. They should not be planted out until the weather is warm and danger of frost is past. **Seed** The single flowered sorts, especially the dwarfs, and the annual dahlias are easily raised from seed. Sow seed in March in the greenhouse in pans or boxes in a porous soil mixture and keep at a temperature of between 18 and 21 °C. After germination, harden off and plant out in May or June.

Eranthis/Winter Aconite

Eranthis hyemalis. The harbingers of spring, opening their brilliant bright-yellow flowers in mild spells any time from late December to March, 3 inches. Will naturalize in borders or on the south side of a hedge.

Erythronium/Dog's Tooth Violet, Trout Lily

Spring-flowering bulbous plants of great charm. Flowers have reflexed petals like cyclamen; many have leaves spotted or blotched yellow, pink, or brown. Plant 3 inches deep. Increase by seed sown in a cold frame as soon as ripe or by offsets; some species naturalize readily. *E. denscanis:* "Rose Beauty," pink flowers; "White Splendour," pure-white flowers; both 3 inches, March to April. *E. californicum,* flowers creamy-yellow, several to each stem, 9 to 15 inches. *E. hendersonii,* flowers lilac-mauve with purplish-red markings at the base of each petal, 6 to 8 inches. *E. revolutum,* 10 to 12 inches and one of the easiest garden species, with named forms in various shades of pink, white, and purple, May. *E. tuolumnense,* flowers deep yellow on tall stems, March to April.

Fritillaria/Fritillary

A large group of plants, a few of which are very spectacular in the garden. Increase by seed sown as soon as ripe in a cold frame, or by offsets. *F. imperialis,* the Crown Imperial. Easily cultivated in sun or shade, in any fertile soil that is not waterlogged. Plant the large, white bulb 8 inches deep, slightly on its side, and surrounded by sand. Flowers borne in whorls in 2 or 3 tiers on the upper part of the stem; large, drooping, and bell-shaped; yellow, orange or red. There are several named forms. *F. meleagris,* the Snake's Head Fritillary. Curiously symmetrical, square-shouldered, bell-shaped flowers, maroon-purple color checkered with paler squares. Named forms include colors ranging from pure white to deep black-purple, 1 foot. Plant in damp soil in sun or shade.

Galanthus/Snowdrop

The drooping white bells of the snowdrops are too familiar to need description. *G. nivalis* is the common single snowdrop, but there is a double form, *G. nivalis* "Plenus," which has longer-lasting flowers of twice the size. *G. nivalis* "Olgae," which flowers October to November. *G. elwesii* flowers a little earlier and also has larger flowers. *G. rhizehensis* flowers December to January.

Galtonia/Summer Hyacinth

Galtonia candicans looks very much like a "stretched" version of a white hyacinth. Flowers milky-white, bell-shaped, scented, borne 15 to 20 on a stem 2½ to 4 feet tall, late summer. Plant 6 to 8 inches deep in a warm, sunny part of the garden. Mulch heavily in the north. Increase by seeds sown in a cold frame, or by offsets.

Gladiolus

A large group of highly decorative cormous plants mainly natives of Africa. Although there are some 250 species, most of the plants grown in gardens are hybrids. None is really hardy, the corms needing to be lifted and stored away from frost over winter. The modern hybrids are divided into 3 groups — the large-flowered, the Primulinus, and the Butterfly types.

The snake's head fritillary, *Fritillaria meleagris* is best appreciated from close quarters.

a)

a) A *Gladiolus primulus* hybrid Gladiolus "Archimedes." The yellow hooded flowers show the parentage.
b) An unnamed gladiolus hybrid of a singularly pure pink.

b)

Cultivation. Gladioli will grow in any fertile, well-drained garden soil. Plant the corms 4 to 5 inches deep, 9 to 12 inches apart, in sun, in deeply dug, well-fertilized soil. Water well in the growing season, but never let the soil become waterlogged. Corms planted in late March will flower by the end of June. It is safer to leave planting until mid-April, although this means flowering begins a little later. If the site is exposed, staking may be necessary. Put the stakes in the ground when planting the corms; do not add them later. After flowering, remove the flower spike. Do not lift plants until the leaves have turned brown. Then wash the earth off the corms, and cut the foliage off an inch or 2 above the corm. The corm should then be dried. Once dry, the old corm husk should be pulled away and the corm and cormlets dusted with both insecticides and fungicides before being stored in a cool, dry place, preferably in slatted shelves or boxes for the winter. The winter temperature should be 40 to 45 °F, and the corms must not be allowed to become damp. The different varieties should be carefully labeled before being put away for the winter. Propagation is by means of cormlets planted in the spring in the open garden. Seedlings are easily raised, sown in a cold frame in April. Seedlings will show great variation; most will be inferior to the parent plants, but at least they will be your own and unique. Seedlings take as long as cormlets to reach flowering size.

Hyacinthus/Hyacinth

Hyacinths are of two types, those known as the Roman (early-flowering) and those known as the Dutch (large-flowering). Although among the most popular of spring bulbs, they are not the easiest bulbs to grow well and are far more fussy than daffodils or tulips. They need full sun, very light, sandy soil, free from stones and clay, neither too acid nor too alkaline. Given these conditions, they will be among the loveliest of spring bulbs and will flower in April. Plant 6 inches deep and 6 inches apart. In wet soils they deteriorate more quickly and may be dug after the foliage has died and then replanted in the fall.

Iris

A large genus containing some of the best-loved of all garden plants. The common bearded iris with its creeping rhizomatous root is dealt with in the section on herbaceous plants. The plants dealt with here are bulbous. They are slender and refined plants. There are two main groups: the Reticulata Group, which are dwarf, early-flowering iris; and the Xiphium Group, which are rather larger and later-flowering. **Reticulata Group** Enchanting dwarfs, flowering January to March. Grow in full sun in sharply drained soil. *I. danfordiae,* brilliant acid-yellow flowers on 4-inch stems, February, leaves spiky 12 or 18 inches. The bulb splits itself into many offsets after flowering. These offsets take 3 to 4 years to flower again, so ensure continuity of flower by planting a small number of new bulbs each season. *I. histrioides,* the hardiest and most robust plant in this section; striking royal-blue flowers standing up well to bitter winter weather, 9 inches, February. *I. reticulata,* the best-known of this group; flowers pale sky-blue to a deep purple-blue, the outer segments crested with gold, 6 to 10 inches, February or March. All the plants mentioned may be grown in pots and brought indoors in winter. **Xiphium Group** The irises of the section grow up to 30 inches tall and flower between May and July. Plant 4 inches deep in sun in rich, well-drained soil. They form dense clumps and are very free-flowering. The different species of this group have been freely hybridized to produce the following groups: *Dutch Irises,* flowering May to June, colors include white, yellow, blue, purple, and mauve. Very hardy and easy in almost any soil. **English Irises** Hybrids of *I. xiphioides,* prefer rather damper soil than the others. Large flowers, up to 5 inches across, appear at the top of a slender stem and open in succession, blue, purple, mauve and white, June to July. **Spanish Irises** Blooming earlier than the others, usually in May. Each bulb produces only a single-flowering stem, with a single flower at the top; the range of colors includes yellows, blues, whites, and purples. This group is excellent as cut flowers. Dutch iris can be grown in the greenhouse in the winter.

Ixia/African Corn Lily

Pretty South African cormous plants producing brilliantly colored flowers in June and July. Each corm produces a series of stiff sword-shaped leaves 12 to 24 inches long and a slender but very strong and stiff floral stem bearing 10 to 12 wide-mouthed flowers in the brightest shades of red, yellow, orange, pink, or white, also multicolors. Plant the corms 4 to 6 inches deep in light, sandy soil in October or November in the sunniest position in the garden. Winter-hardy in mild climates. Use as cool-temperature greenhouse plants in the north. The plants normally offered by nurserymen are hybrids.

Leucojum/Snowflakes

Hardy bulbs thriving in sun or semi-shade in ordinary well-drained garden soil. The flowers are somewhat like those of a giant snowdrop. Plant in September 3 to 4 inches deep and 5 to 6 inches apart. *L. aestivum,* the Summer Snowflake, May, 15 inches. *L. autumnale,* the Autumn Snowflake, white flowers with a pink base, 6 inches, October. *L. vernum,* the Spring Snowflake, white flowers with green spots at the edges of the petals, 9 inches, March. *L. vernum* var. "Carpathicum," free-flowering.

Lilium/Lily

The lilies are unsurpassed for grace, beauty, and majesty. Those that can be grown in the open garden have an exotic appearance that no other garden plants can match.

Lilies are capricious plants. It is not uncommon to find that one particular species will thrive in one garden and will simply not grow in the garden next door. On the other hand, there are so many species and hybrids that some of the easier sorts are certain to thrive in every garden. The story that lilies will only grow in shade is a myth. The great majority are found in the wild growing in full sun, but with their roots shaded either by loose rocks or low-growing vegetation. Nor is it true that you can't grow lilies in a lime soil; there are many species and some hybrids that will thrive *only* in limy soils. In general, however, the structure of the soil is more important than its chemical composition. The ideal soil is made up of about equal parts of leaf mold, garden soil, and

sand. The ground should be thoroughly prepared to a depth of 18 inches. Lilies like plenty of moisture at the roots during their growing season, although, like other bulbs, they quickly rot if there is stagnant water in the soil. They are best grown in clearings between shrubs. In general, lilies should be planted 4 to 6 inches deep and given a liberal mulch of peat or leaf mold every fall. Once planted, they should not be disturbed. Many lilies have very heavy flower heads and need staking. Care should be taken not to drive the stake through the bulb. Planting is normally done in late summer or fall, and propagation may be carried out by means of seed sown in a cold frame as soon as ripe, or by scales inserted in sand in pots or pans and kept in a cold frame until established.

Many lilies are also suitable for cultivation in pots. Large pots should be selected, varying in size from 6 to 10 inches, according to the size of the bulb. The bulbs should be covered with about an inch of soil and then plunged in sand or in the cold frame until the stem is about an inch high. They can then either be placed in a shaded part of the garden or brought indoors. Watering should be done with care, the object being to keep the soil perpetually moist without ever allowing it to become waterlogged.

The following list is only a selection of the less capricious sorts. Enthusiasts should consult books on lilies for a fuller list and more-detailed cultural instructions.

L. amabile, 3 to 4 feet, martagon (turk's cap) type flowers, red or orange speckled black, June to July. Lime-tolerant, and flourishes among herbaceous plants; easily increased by seed. *L. auratum,* the Golden-Rayed Lily of Japan, on the loveliest of all lilies, 4 to 8 feet tall, bearing as many as 20 flowers on each stem, each flower measuring as much as 10 to 12 inches across; flowers are white or yellow with purple, crimson, or brown markings, August, September, or October. All named forms are good. *L. candidum,* the Madonna Lily, the floral emblem of the Madonna. The oldest of all cultivated lilies, it will flourish in almost any soil and in almost any garden, but seems to do best in a sunny location with some lime in the soil. The 3- to 5-foot stem produces several large white trumpet-shaped flowers with golden

stamens in June to July. It should be planted in August so that the leaves, which last over winter, can build up strength in the bulb for the following season. It hardly ever produces fertile seed. *L. candidum* "Plenum," a double form, is curious rather than attractive. *L. henryi* bear 10 to 20 martagon-type flowers on each 5- to 8-foot stem, the flowers a brilliant orange, speckled black. Thrives on a heavily limed soil but will not flourish on an acid soil, and peat is virtually fatal to it. *L. martagon,* the Turk's Cap Lily. Sun or shade, lime or acid soils, produces its relatively small flowers freely in June and July, pink to deepest claret, and palest pinks to pure white. Comes easily from seed, but seedlings take 7 or 8 years to flower. *L. pardalinum,* beautiful North American species, completely hardy, one of the easiest to grow. The flowers are of the martagon type but larger, bright orange with brown spots, 5 to 20 per stem on stems 3 to 7 feet high. July flowering. Needs a deep, rich soil. *L. pumilum* (*L. tenuifolium*), Siberian Coral Lily. Charming diminutive species growing scarcely more than 12 to 18 inches and bearing numerous martagon-type flowers of the most vibrant orange in June. Easily increased by seed, seedlings taking 2 to 3 years to flower; most effective massed. Plant in a sunny,

Nerines produce their iridescent pink flowers from the bare earth in autumn after the leaves have died away.

The American 'Bellingham Hybrid' lilies can be left to form ever larger and more spectacular clumps, unlike most lilies which need lifting and replanting regularly.

sandy position. *L. pyrenaicum,* the Pyrenean Lily. This easy lily bears numerous greenish-yellow black-spotted flowers in May or June on stems 2 to 3 feet high. There is also a "red" form with orange flowers. An easy, hardy species, tolerant of most soils and situations. *L. speciosum,* closely related to *L. auratum,* but smaller-growing, producing in August and September 5 to 10 very large, scented flowers with recurved petals on stems 1 to 4 feet high. The flowers have a most exotic appearance and are very variable in color. *L. superbum,* 15 to 20 orange martagon-type flowers produced in July and August on stems 4 to 8 feet high; very like *L. pardalinum.* Easy to grow, but dislikes chalk or lime. *L. tigrinum,* the well-known Tiger Lily. Shares with the Madonna Lily the honor of being one of the oldest cultivated lilies, having been grown as a root crop by the Chinese for the past thousand years or more. The 2- to 4-foot stem produces

10 to 12 orange-red flowers with brown or black spots in the center and flowers between July and September. Easy to grow in moist, peaty soil planted 6 to 8 inches deep in full sun. Seeds are usually sterile, but it can easily be propagated by means of the bulbils produced in the leaf axils. These simply need potting in a sandy soil until established.

Many hybrid lilies are now available, among the best of which are the **Bellingham Hybrids.** These are very robust, growing 4 to 8 feet high and blooming in July. They bear masses of large orange, red, and yellow flowers with reflexed petals. They do best in full sun in a moist, peaty soil. the **Mid-Century Hybrids** are also very robust, easy to grow, and floriferous. Blossoming in July, the 3- to 5-foot stems bear 6 to 10 wide-open trumpet-shaped flowers which are either upright or horizontal, in a wide range of colors from white to deepest purple. They need a semi-shaded posi-

tion, and although they will grow on chalk soils, dislike too much chalk or lime. The "Olympic Hybrids": these have been produced by crossing lilies with the martagon-type flower with trumpet-flowered lilies, and the flowers vary between these two extremes. In the main, these hybrids grow 3 to 5 feet and flower between July and August. Colors range from white to deep pink. They are hardy and easy to grow.

Muscari/Grape Hyacinth

Colorful spring- and early-summer-flowering bulbs valued because they are inexpensive, easily grown, and can be relied on to put up a good show year after year. Planted 3 to 4 inches deep in October in any fertile soil. Increase by seeds or offsets. *M. botryoides,* the Grape Hyacinth, azure-blue, spring, 8 to 12 inches; there are white and pale blue forms. *M. comosum,* the Feathered Grape Hyacinth, late spring, 8 to 12 inches, violet-blue flowers with a tuft of sterile flowers at the top of the stem; a fascinating curiosity. *M. moschatum,* the Musk Hyacinth, spring, 8 to 10 inches, flowers yellow or purple, strongly scented.

Narcissus/Daffodil

The daffodil is by far the most popular of all spring-flowering bulbs, and certainly there are no other spring bulbs that can provide the same quantity or quality of flowers, and no others that come in such a brilliant range of yellows and creams. Today over 10,000 named varieties have been registered, and at least 500 varieties are easily obtainable. This embraces a range of flower color and shape that goes far beyond the normal yellow trumpet-shaped flower or the starry-white pheasant's eye narcissus. Indeed, so wide is the range now that it is little wonder that an increasing number of gardeners are making a hobby of collecting and growing the different sorts. There are flourishing daffodil societies in the United States, Britain, Holland, New Zealand, and Australia.

Narcissi are among the easiest of bulbs to grow. They will tolerate both chalk and acid soils, and grow well in both heavy and light soils — provided they are well-drained. They are equally at home in beds and borders or naturalized in lawns, meadows, woodlands, or orchards. They prefer sun or slight shade and should be planted as early in the fall as possible. The larger bulbs should be planted 5 to 6 inches deep, and smaller bulbs 3 inches deep. The species can be propagated by seed, but the named varieties will come true only from offsets. There are so many named varieties that only a selected list can be given here. Catalogs should be consulted regularly, as new varieties appear on the market every year.

Trumpet Varieties "King Alfred," very large deep-golden-yellow, still one the largest and one of the best; "Golden Harvest," golden-yellow trumpet of enormous size; "Beersheba," magnificent pure-white with broad segments and a very long trumpet of perfect shape; "Music Hall," white petals and deep-yellow trumpet, very striking; "Rembrandt," a uniform deep golden-yellow, even larger than

"King Alfred" and flowers a perfect shape.

Large-Cupped Varieties
"Armada," a very large and outstanding flower, of great substance, golden petals and vivid orange cup; "Carlton," enormous flower of clear yellow, cup frilled; "Grulleman's Giant," a giant indeed, with creamy yellow petals and a huge cup fringed and crowned with orange, withstands severe weather very well; "Red Marley," deep golden-yellow petals and fiery red cup, good in full sun; "Scarlet Elegance," a deep golden-yellow flower with a deep-red cup, an unusually brilliant color combination.

Small-Cupped Varieties "Edward Buston," pale yellow with orange crown; "Jill," white petals and small yellow cup frilled red; "Snow Princess," white petals, cup yellow edged orange.

Pink Varieties These are still relatively new in commerce, and thus relatively expensive, but their unique color makes them well worthwhile, expecially for floral decoration. "Lady Bird," large flared trumpet with ruffled edge, outside pale-apricot, inside orange-apricot, petals white. "Mrs. R. O. Backhouse," the original pink daffodil, and still one of the best, trumpet long and slender, blush-pink with a deep edge, petals white.

Double Varieties "Yellow Cheerfulness," a very popular double creamy white; "Inglecombe," bright lemon-yellow, late-flowering; "Mary Copeland," white intermixed with brilliant orange; "Texas," yellow and orange intermixed. Jonquil Varieties: these are highly prized for their scent, their graceful habit, and their profusion of blooms; charming as cut flowers. "Trevithian," 2 or 3 flowers per stem, pale lemon-yellow, overlapping perianth lobes, and shallow cup; "Golden Sceptre" and "Golden Gleam" are both similar, but of a deeper yellow.

Poeticus Varieties These are the plants also known as Pheasant's Eye Narcissi. The best of these is "Actaea," which is unsurpassed for size of flower; "Pheasant's Eye" is a very old and popular variety.

Species and Miniatures These are all diminutive plants, suited either to the rock garden or to naturalizing in lawns. *N. bulbocodium,* the Hoop Petticoat Daffodil, consists almost entirely of a broadly conical trumpet, the

perianth reduced to a few tiny segments; the typical form is deep yellow. *N. b.* "Citrinus" has pale lemon-yellow flowers; *N. b.* "Tenuifolius" is more dwarf and earlier flowering; *N. b.* "Obesus" has a wider open trumpet; all about 6 inches, and prefer a light, sandy soil. *N. cyclamineus,* rich yellow, narrow trumpet and reflexed petals, 6 inches, likes moist, boggy ground. *N. triandus,* a charming dwarf with reflexed perianth and cup-shaped trumpet, 6 inches. There are various color forms ranging from pure white to deep yellow.

For the lover of the unusual there are also a couple of little-known fall-flowering species, and one even takes orginality so far as to produce green flowers. Neither of these species is very winter-hardy. These are *N. serotinus,* a dwarf plant producing short stems in September, each bearing one or two flowers nearly an inch across, greenish-white with a short, wide-open yellow trumpet. The leaves appear in the spring. *N. viridiflorus,* also a small plant, producing on top of a 6- to 7-inch stem 1 to 5 flowers, rather like those of a small, olive-green narcissus.

Nerine/Guernsey Lily

Beautiful fall-flowering bulbs, prized for their iridescent pink flowers, which appear out of the bare earth in September to October. Plant 5 inches deep (deeper on sandy soils) at the foot of a south wall; give a mulch of well-rotted organic matter after the flowers. They may take 2 years to flower again after planting. Old clumps losing their vigor should be broken up and replanted in August. Leaves strap-shaped. Hardy species include *N. bowdenii,* the one most frequently grown, 15 to 18 inches, deep pink; there are named forms in different shades of pink, the best being "Fenwick's Variety." In the north use as cool-temperature greenhouse plants.

Schizostylis/Kaffir Lily

Only one species, *S. coccinea,* is grown, but there are several forms. Leaves sword-shaped 1 to 2 feet long, flowers bright crimson, disk-shaped on a floral stem up to 2 feet high; "Major," larger flowers; "Mrs. Hegarty," pale-pink flowers; "Viscountess Byng,'' palest shell-pink. Plant shallowly in rich, moist soil in mild climates, otherwise use as a greenhouse plant, flowering September until December.

Scilla

Several species are commonly grown: *S. hispanicus,* the Spanish Bluebell, with 10-inch spikes of bell-shaped violet-blue flowers. *S. non-scriptus,* the wild bluebell of English and French woods, bearing bell-shaped flowers on the inner side of an arching stem. There are white and pink forms, as well as the usual blue form. Both species are May-flowering, easily cultivated in a woody soil in partial shade. The Siberian squill, *S. sibirica,* is among the bluest of blue-flowered plants, producing a pyramid of little flowers on 3-inch stems in March. Plant 2 to 3 inches deep in a sunny spot, where it will seed itself freely. *S. tubergeniana,* lighter blue flowers, taller growing. Increase by seed or offsets. Other species are occasionally offered in catalogs.

Sparaxis/Harlequin Flower

Small, cormous plants closely related to Ixias and Freesias. Plant in well-drained soil in full sun in fall and protect with a covering of dry straw until March in mild climates. In the north grow in greenhouse as Freesia. Flowering May/June. Flowers brilliantly colored, 1 to 2 inches across in shades of reds, yellows oranges, and whites, with different-colored markings in the centers of the flowers. Increase by division in late summer.

Tulipa/Tulip

A genus of over one hundred hardy bulbous plants that have been popular in Europe for at least 350 years. At one time ''tulipamania'' hit Holland, where most of the early breeding was done, and single bulbs were sold for as much as $14,000. each. Most of these varieties have now been lost or destroyed. The species are just as good for garden plants as the hybrids. Modern hybrid tulips are divided into fifteen divisions.

Division 1 *Early singles:* height 6 to 15 inches, plant 4 to 6 inches apart. Flowers outdoors in April, under glass in February. **Division 2** *Early double:* height 12 to 15 inches, plant 6

inches apart. Flowering period as above. **Division 3** *Mendel tulips:* height 15 inches, plant 6 inches apart. Flowers rounded, 4 to 5 inches across. Flowers April and early May. **Division 4** *Triumph tulips:* height 20 inches plant 6 to 8 inches apart. Rather angular flowers 4 to 5 inches across, on stout stems. **Division 5** *Darwin hybrids:* height 2 to 2½ feet, plant 6 to 8 inches apart. Contains some of the largest and most brilliantly colored tulips. Flowers April, May. **Division 6** *Darwin tulips:* height 2 to 2½ feet, plant 6 to 8 inches apart. Flowers rounded 4 to 5 inches across. Flowers May. The most popular tulips for bedding. **Division 7** *Lily-flower:* height 18 to 24 inches, plant 6 inches apart. Flowers long-waisted, petals pointed, 6 to 8 inches across. Flowers May. **Division 8** *Cottage tulips:* height 3 feet, plant 6 to 8 inches apart. Flowers rounded, 4 to 8 inches across. Tall stems. Flowers May. A very late group. **Division 9** *Rembrandt tulips:* Similar to division 6 but different color ranges. **Division 10** *Parrot tulips:* height 18 to 24 in-

ches, plant 6 to 8 inches apart. Flowers usually bicolored, petals often twisted, sometimes fringed, 8 inches or more across. **Division 11** *Late double:* height 18 to 24 inches, plant 6 inches apart. Flowers 4 inches across, peony-shaped. Flowers May. **Division 12** Tulips in this group are derived from *T. Kaufmanniana.* Flowers tall, pointed, usually bicolored. **Division 13** Tulips derived from *T. Fosteriana:* flowers in this group are noted for their brilliant red. **Division 14** Tulips derived from *T. Greigii,* foliage usually maroon or purple brown, sometimes spotted. Flowering April, mainly reds and yellows. **Division 15** *Species.* Among the best are *T. acuminata,* the horned tulip; *T. Kaufmanniana,* the water-lily tulip, and *T. sylvestris,* a native of Europe, which will naturalize itself in many gardens. Flowers yellow. **Cultivation:** Tulips need good drainage and plenty of sun to grow well. Most of the hybrids need to be planted in fall to flower in spring and should not be lifted until leaves have died away. Increase by offsets.

Crotons, botanically known as *Codiaeum,* have the most brilliantly colored leaves of any greenhouse plants.

Greenhouses, Frames and Cloches

Greenhouses

A greenhouse enriches any garden. Besides color in the greenhouse itself all year round, it is also a source of color for the house and the garden, since many of the brilliantly colored flowering and foliage plants seen in the garden later in the year start life in the greenhouse in winter, and those house and pot plants that display such brilliant blooms in the house may be nourished in the greenhouse. A small greenhouse may not be profitable for growing most vegetables or fruit, but what could be tastier than your own freshly picked strawberries out of season? Cucumbers, melons, and tomatoes are other interesting greenhouse crops.

The type of greenhouse you choose depends largely on what you wish to use it for and how much you are prepared to spend on it (both on buying and maintaining it).

The construction of a greenhouse is related to its use. The glass-to-ground-level types are suitable for growing tall plants planted in the greenhouse, such as carnations. They are also good for plants that need maximum light at ground level, such as lettuce. If you want to use the greenhouse for pot plants, one with low wooden, concrete-paneled, or brick walls would be suitable. Some greenhouses combine glass-to-ground on one side with low walling on the other side. The glass-to-ground-level types are more costly to heat, since glass loses heat in winter more rapidly than brick or wood, so for cold or exposed locations the low-wall types are a better buy.

Conventional span-roof greenhouses are available in a variety of sizes. The most popular size is 8 × 10 feet. Larger and smaller ones are also easily obtainable. Modern-looking spherical, curved, or hexagonal greenhouses have the advantage of trapping the greatest possible amount of light, but they must be well ventilated to prevent overheating on sunny days in summer. This usually means using a fan to vent the air.

Choose a well-designed greenhouse that has been built of tough materials. The modern aluminum-alloy greenhouses are good, and high-quality galvanized steel will last a lifetime, but paint it regularly unless you are certain that it is completely resistant to rust. Redwood and cypress are often used in greenhouse construction. Red cedar is tough and very attractive and lasts well if treated with an occasional coat of preservative.

When choosing a greenhouse, see whether it can be easily extended later on, whether it can be easily constructed, and whether a putty or a no-putty system is used to fix the glass.

One of the most economic and convenient types of greenhouse, and certainly the most space-saving, is the lean-to, which can be located against any wall, but preferably not one facing north.

Before buying a greenhouse, check with your local authority to see whether you need a building permit. You probably will not, but check to be sure.

The site for your greenhouse should be as sheltered as possible without being overshadowed. If you erect the greenhouse with its length running from east to west, it will get the benefit of most of the winter sun; if you give it a north to south alignment, all parts will receive the maximum amount of summer sunlight. The east-west alignment is generally best, because you can alter plant positions in summer so that those needing the most sunlight will receive it.

Most greenhouse manufacturers supply comprehensive instructions on the erection of their greenhouses. They can usually be erected by unskilled labor. First make sure that the site is level. Low brick walls may be made with ordinary bricks, a 3-to-1 ratio of sand and Portland cement, and the skillful use of spirit level and measure. Follow the manufacturer's glazing instructions carefully or you may have to contend with a leaking greenhouse. Plastic greenhouses are inexpensive but are less efficient at trapping light, and they encourage condensation.

Greenhouse Heating

Heat your greenhouse according to your choice of plants. For instance, if you wish to grow tropical foliage plants and orchids you should remember that to heat the greenhouse to an intermediate level (never below 50°F or 10°C) costs twice as much as to heat it to a cool-house level (never below 45°F or 7°C); to heat it to a warm-house level (55°F or 13°C) costs three times as much; and to heat it to 60°F or 16°C costs four times as much as to heat it to cool-house level. If you wish to grow tropical plants you will probably select the heating system — solid fuel or oil — that gives you the cheapest running costs.

Another important aspect of modern greenhouse gardening is automation, and it is here that electricity comes into its own. The list of gadgets includes soil-warming cables, propagators, overhead mist units that provide a moist spray for cuttings, electric-fan heaters, electric tubular heaters or heating cables, fans and air extractors, and thermostats. In general, electric heating suits the person with plenty of money but no time to spare, but it is also an economic proposition for the gardener who is interested in running a cool greenhouse.

The third main type of heater is the propane heater. A heater with a "blue-flame" burner, which provides efficient use of the fuel, can hold its own, but buy only the type of heater made of noncorrosive metal. A propane heater is inexpensive to run and install, and the more expensive kinds have extension radiator pipes for heating larger areas. They are excellent for maintaining greenhouses at cooler temperatures. Heaters of this kind need careful attention and maintenance, both in respect to safety and efficiency. Oil heaters and natural-gas heaters increase the atmospheric content of carbon dioxide if they have no outside vents, which plants require, and are sometimes favored for this reason. There is, however, danger of injury to plants if the gas is not properly burned and fumes collect in the greenhouse.

To find out how much heating your greenhouse requires, you need to figure out how much heat is lost and how much heat needs to be put in to overcome that loss and raise the heat to the required level. Quantities of heat are measured in terms of British Thermal Units (BTU) per hour. Greenhouse manufacturers and heating-appliance manufacturers will all help you work out the heating needs of your greenhouse. It is worth bearing in mind though, that an all-glass house invariably needs more heat to maintain it at any given temperature than one that has walls of brick, wood, concrete blocks, or transite.

Ventilation and Shading

Having enclosed plants in a house to keep them warm, it is also necessary to see that they get a change of air to supply them with carbon dioxide. Ventilation also ensures that the plants do not become subject to too humid an atmosphere. Undoubtedly the simplest method of ventilation is to install an electric exhaust fan or fans, controlled by a thermostat. On an automated system it is important to ensure a balance between heating and ventilation to avoid waste of power.

Shading is also important, and the cheapest method of shading a greenhouse is to paint the exterior of the glass with a proprietary lime-solution mixture. When removed in winter, the glass gets a cleaning, which helps to increase the amount of sunlight entering the greenhouse at that time. Unheated greenhouses often become *overheated* in summer, and need shading to avoid scorching the plants.

Automatic Watering and Other Devices

Capillary watering is one of the most important modern advances in greenhouse gardening. It works on the simple principle of allowing plants to draw up water from a layer of fine sand. It is only suitable for watering pot plants and is installed on the greenhouse benches or tables. The bench must be level and covered with polyethylene film. A 2-inch thick layer of fine sand is fed with water by a pipe with small holes covered with glass fiber, running through the sand, and linked to a level-water ball valve system.

Lighting in the greenhouse is essential in winter for those who are not home all day, and it is possible to obtain suitable fluorescent tubes that provide "near-natural" color. More-elaborate lighting will enable you to flower chrysanthemums, carnations, and other plants out of season and to promote rapid growth.

Frames

Frames can be used like miniature greenhouses. Seeds can be propagated in both heated and unheated frames, and cold frames can be used to propagate cuttings of many plants, such as chrysanthemums, azaleas, and evergreens, and for overwintering not-so-hardy plants. They are also excellent for hardening off plants from the greenhouse intended for the garden. Ventilation should be in-

Tomatoes being grown on the straw bale method in a small greenhouse

creased gradually until the plants are hardy enough to go into the garden.

Forcing
A number of outdoor bulbs are worth forcing in the greenhouse for early flowering. These include crocuses, daffodils, Dutch irises, fritillaries, early-flowering gladioli, hyacinths, *Lilium longiflorum, Scilla,* and tulips. All bulbs must be encouraged to form roots before tops, so give them a moist, cool period, either plunged in their pots under peat in the ground or in a cellar or dark room. When the tops are forming, bring them into the greenhouse and increase warmth gradually. Never let the temperature get much above 60°F (16°C). A slightly cooler temperature at flowering will prolong their lasting quality.

Alpines
True alpine plants are simply those that grow between the areas of permanent snow and coniferous tree growth. Such places may occur at sea level in Arctic and in mountainous regions, such as the Alps themselves. In nature, alpine plants are often protected by a thick coat of snow for many months and are spared the wind and rain characteristic of normal temperate winters. If you decide to try alpine plants you should bear this in mind and provide dry (it is dry under the snow), even temperature conditions during the plant's dormant period.

An unheated greenhouse will do for alpines, which need even temperatures in their dormant period, but some heat will prevent too much moisture and freezing roots. It is possible to separate sections of your greenhouse with polyethylene walls to provide varying conditions in different positions.

The following table will provide you with decorative plants at differing seasons. All can be grown in the cool or cold house which is frost-free. Most like sandy, well-drained soil with some stone chips, and they tolerate lime unless otherwise stated.

Cacti and Other Succulents
This large and varied range of plants is characterized by their ability to withstand drought by storing water in their fleshy plant tissue. Some — the cacti — have developed thick, protuberant stems to retain water, and most cacti have dispensed with leaves altogether. Such plants are known as stem-succulents. Others, which include members of the lily and spurge families, have developed fleshy leaves for storing water and are known as leaf-succulents.

Apart from the hardy garden plants, such as the sedums and sempervivums, most of these plants require cool greenhouse conditions, with a winter temperature of about 40°F (4°C) or more. The growing compost should consist of 2 parts (by bulk) loam, 1 part sharp sand, 1 part peat, plus some pea-sized pieces of grit or charcoal to improve drainage, which is most important to succulents. For this reason clay pots are better than plastic. About a quarter of the depth in which the plant grows should have a layer of gravel at the bottom. Succulents generally like to be repotted every two or three years, when all old soil should be removed.

Most cacti, except the popular Christmas cactus, *Zygocactus truncatus,* and the epiphyllums, like sunshine, and their natural ability to store water

Alpine Plant Table

NAME OF PLANT	SPECIES OR TYPE	COLOR	HEIGHT	WHEN TO START	FLOWERING PERIOD	REMARKS
Armeria (Thrift)	*juniperifolia*	lilac-pink	2-4 in.	July or spring	May-June	A sandy soil is preferred
Erica (Heather)	*carnea* cultivars	rose-pink, white, etc.	18 in. or less	October	Jan.-April	A peaty soil, no lime
Gentiana (Gentian)	*sinol-ornata*	blue	6 in.	spring	September	No lime; incorporate peat, leaf mold and stone chippings
Phlox	*douglasii* and *subulata* cultivars	pink, lavender, white, etc.	4-6 in.	August	Feb.-Mar.	Avoid too much watering in winter
Primula	*pubescens* hybrids	rosy-crimson, purple, etc.	3-6 in.	Sept.-Oct.	Apr.-May	Repot annually after flowering
Saxifrage	many species	yellow, pink, white, etc.	1-3 in. or more	October	spring	Cushion plants
Sedum	*spathulifolium*	yellow	3-4 in.	spring	June-Sept.	Plant close together

enables most to withstand excessive dryness of atmosphere. Cacti and other succulents should generally not be watered at all for a month or two after November, and only very lightly, about once a month, thereafter, until the growing season.

Propagation of leaf-succulents is by leaf-cuttings; others may be increased by division or by stem-cuttings. Offsets (young plants that form on their parents, as with Bryophyllums) may be detached and potted.

The following are some easy species to grow, and many produce brilliant flowers: *Bryophyllum diagremontianum, Cephalocerus senilis* (Old Man Cactus), *Chamaecereus sylvestrii* (Peanut Cactus), *Crassula falcata, Echinocatus grusonii* (Golden Barrel Cactus), *Echinocereus regidissimus* (Rainbow Cactus), *Echinopsis tubiflora* (Hedgehog Cactus), Epiphyllum hybrids, *Kleinia articulata* (Candle Plant), *Opuntia microdasys* (Prickly Pear), *Sempervivum* (Houseleek), and *Zygocactus truncatus* (Christmas Cactus).

Orchids

Orchids used to be rich men's hobbies, but not any more. Many can be purchased very cheaply, and many do not require high temperatures. For cool-house orchids, such as cymbidiums and cypripediums, the winter temperature should never fall below 45°F (7°C). Cattleyas, the South American epiphytic orchids, need a minimum temperature of 55°F (13°C) or more in winter.

Like cacti, orchids do not thrive on overwatering, and their roots are liable to rot. The rule is to water well when the compost appears to have dried out, using soft water, preferably rainwater. Damping down the walls, floor, and staging helps create the correct degree of moisture in the atmosphere. In winter, watering is cut down to about once a month, or even less, according to conditions. There is a knack to potting orchids, but it is a knack that any nurseryman will probably be only too pleased to demonstrate.

In winter, light is needed, but in spring and summer, guard against too much sunlight. Good air circulation around the plant is vital, especially in spring and summer, but drafts must be prevented.

Ferns

The accent for ferns is on shade and moisture. A fine atomizing spray can be used for general damping-down, and the plants should be kept out of direct sunlight. A position in the greenhouse on moist gravel or ashes below the bench is satisfactory.

A suitable compost is 2 parts peat (by bulk), 1 part loam, and 1 part sand or very fine gravel. Potting is best done in spring before the new growth begins. Plants may be divided with a sharp knife at this time.

Half-hardy ferns require a minimum winter temperature of 40°F (4°C), and truly tender ferns need a winter minimum of 60°F (16°C). Never allow ferns

to dry out completely.

Some ferns suitable for a greenhouse with a winter minimum temperature of 40°F are:

ADIANTUM (Maidenhair Fern)   The delicate foliage of these ferns and their cheerful pale-green color makes them very attractive.

ASPLENIUM (Spleenwort)   *A. bulbiferum* is the popular plant that carries young plants on its fronds; they can be potted to propagate it.

PTERIS   Another easily grown and popular fern with several different forms, the most well-known being *albo-lineata,* which has a central white line down down the long, narrow fronds.

Annuals and Biennials

Many garden annuals can be sown in a greenhouse in fall to obtain flowers the following spring. These include such plants as cornflowers, larkspurs, nicotianas, and nigellas. In the same way, flowers can be kept in bloom later in the season by sowing in late spring. Early spring color in the cold greenhouse can be obtained by overwintering such plants as wallflowers sown the previous spring.

Perennials

Many hardy perennials can be forced into earlier bloom in heated or unheated houses. Particularly suitable are Belladonna Delphinium, *Primula denticulata, P. veris,* (Foxglove), and *Campanula* species. Perennials that are not so hardy can often be saved by overwintering them in the greenhouse.

Tomatoes are the most popular of all greenhouse crops. They require practice to grow well, but good crops create a great sense of satisfaction.

Key to Greenhouse Heating

Unheated	no artificial heating	(U)
Cold	never below freezing point	(CC)
Cool	never below 45°F (7°C)	(C)
Intermediate	never below 50°F (10°C)	(I)
Warm	never below 55°F (13°C)	(W)
Hot	never below 60°F (16°C)	(H)

Selective Table of Greenhouse Bulbs

*Although one type of greenhouse may be best for a given plant, it is often possible to grow the plant successfully under cooler conditions, often by starting it under heat indoors. The best conditions are given first.

NAME OF PLANT	GREENHOUSE TYPE OR SPEC.	COLOR	HEIGHT	WHEN TO START	FLOWERING PERIOD	REMARKS
Begonia	Tuberous (W, I, C, CC, U)	Red, yellow, pink, etc.	1 ft or more	Feb—Mar	June—Oct	Place tubers hollow-side up, round-side down. Lift and store dry in winter.
Clivia (Kaffir Lilly)	Miniata (C)	Red, yellow, orange	2 ft	Feb	Apr—June	Grow in 6-inch pots and feed well
Cyclamen	Indicum (CC, U)	Rosy-pink, magenta, white, bicolor	10-15 in	Sept—Oct	Dec—Mar	Incorporate leaf-mold and allow tip of bulb to show. Flowers 12 to 15 months from seed.
Freesia	Many hybrid cultivans (C, I)	Pink-red, orange, violet,	1 ft or more	Aug—Sept	Feb—Mar	Plant 1-inch deep in porous soil. Plunge pots to get good roots. Bring inside in Sept—Oct. Dry off outside in summer.
Gloxinia	In variety (W, I, C, CC, U)	Red edged white, purple, etc.	1 ft or less	Jan—Apr	July—Sept	Store dry tubers at a temperature not less than 50°F in winter. Start them in warmth and pot when growth reaches 1 in.
Haemanthus (Blood Lilly)	*Katherinae* (W, I, C)	Red	1-2 ft	Spring	July	After the large onion-like flower and then the leaves die, reduce watering until dry. Pot in porous soil with half of bulb showing. Avoid repotting.
Hippeastrum	These hybrids are sometimes called Amaryllis. (W, I, C)	Red, pink, white	1 ft or more	Jan—Mar	Mar—July	Treat as for Haemanthus. Prepared bulbs are usually available in Oct for Christmas flowering.
Lilium	*Auratum elegans longiflorum* (W, I, C)	White or colored depending on cultivan.	4-7 ft	Oct—Mar	Aug—Sept (earlier if gently forced)	Plant 1 to a 7-inch or 3 to a 10-inch pot. Keep cool or plunge; protect from frost. At 3 inches increase watering and bring into cold house; on budding bring into warmer atmosphere. A rich compost but avoid too much lime.

Nerine	Hybrids (C)	Red, pink, rose, etc.	1 ft or more	July—Aug	Sept—Dec	When growth appears, water well. Dry off after leaves yellow.
Vallota (Scarborough Lily)	*Speciosa* (C)	Scarlet	1-2 ft	June—July	Aug—Sept	Plant with tip just beneath soil level.

General Ornamental Greenhouse Plants

NAME	SPECIES AND VARIETY	GREENHOUSE TYPE	HEIGHT OR HABIT	FLOWER OR FOLIAGE	REMARKS
Acacia (Mimosa)	*A. decurrens dealbata*	(C)	May grow 3-50 ft	Flowers yellow, spring	Start in tubs in March. Prune after flowering.
Allamanda	*A. cathartica*	(W)	Climbing	Yellow flowers, summer, evergreen	Pinch out unwanted growth or train beneath roof. Dormant in winter.
Asparagus	*A. plumosus*	(C)	Some shoots climbing	Light, feathery foliage	Known as the Asparagus Fern, but not a true fern: used in bouquets. There is a good drawf variety, *nanus*. Easy to grow.
Azalea—See Rhododendron					
Begonia (fibrous-rooted)	Many cultivars	(C, I, W)	6-18 ft. or 24 in.		Best from tip cuttings. Keep moist in summer. Shade preferred.
Beleperone (Shrimp Plant)	*B. guttata*	(C, I)	2-3 ft	Beautiful shrimp-pink bracts	Keep moist in summer. Prune for compactness in spring. Propagate cuttings.
Bignonia (Trumpet Flower)	*B. capreolata*	(C)	Freely climbing	Yellow-scarlet flowers, summer	Keep well-drained. Propagate side shoot cuttings in fall.
Bougainvillea	Several species	(C, W)	Climbing	Bright-pink bracts	Prune back in winter. do not overwater them.
Camellia	*C. japonica*	(CC, C)	Evergreen, shrubby	Brilliant red, crimson-to-white winter flowers	Grow in large pots of lime-free compost. Hardy, will stand summer outdoors.
Campanula (Bellflower)	*C. isophylla*	(C)	Trailing	Flowers blue, summer	A delicate plant, at its best in hanging baskets.
Capsicum (Ornamental Pepper)	*C. frutescens (syn. C. annum)*	(C)	Bushy	Ornamental fruits, Aug—Dec.	Grown from seed sown in spring.
Carnations	Perpetual-flowering	(I, C)	Tall-growing	Pink, white, purple, red, bicolor	Must have plenty of light and air. Start with rooted cuttings.
Celosia (Cockscomb)	*C. plumosa*	(C)	1-2 ft	Beautiful yellow, orange, red plumes, late summer	Start from seed under heat in spring. Grow in large pots. Also for garden use.

Celsia	*C. arcturus*	(C)	3 ft	Yellow flowers with prominent purple anthers, spring-summer	Sow seed in March.
Chrysanthemum	Various	(W)	Late-flowering	Decorative, incurved, pompon, etc.	Plants are brought in from outside in September. Keep in light and airy conditions. Disbud.
Cineraria	*Hybrida grandiflora, Multiflora nana, etc.*	(C)	Winter-to spring-flowering, 1-2 ft.	Many varied colors	Grow from seed sown May to Oct. Keep in airy, cool conditions and do not overwater.
Cissus	*C. discolor*	(W)	Climbing	Long, wide, velvety leaves, with white, purple and pink coloring	Keep out of draft in warm, humid atmosphere. More difficult than *C. antarctica,* Kangaroo vine.
Citrus (Sweet Orange)	*C. sinensis*	(I, W)	Shrubby	White flowers, Glossy leaves, orange fruit	Water and feed in summer. Keep in light, air position.
Coleus	*C. blumei*	(W)	12-18 in	Many varied leaf color combinations	Grow from seed in Feb—Mar under warmth. Discard plants and take cuttings in fall.
Erica (Heather)	*E. gracilis, E. hyemalis*	(C)	12-18 in	Rosy-purple, rosy-white flowers, Sept—Dec. *(gracilis),* Dec—Mar *(hyemalis)*	Provide a lime-free, fibrous compost and keep well-watered. Hardier kinds can bring winter color to unheated greenhouses.
Euphorbia (Poinsettia)	*E. pulcherrima*	(W)	2-4 ft. from cuttings, July to Oct.	Bright red bracts, grow at 60-65°F.	Cut back in spring. Really a succulent.
Exacum	*E. affine*	(C)	6 in	Blue flowers, June—Oct.	Grow from seed sown in Mar. Treat as an annual.
Fuchsia	Many named vars.	(C)	Shrubby, some trailing, others better trained	"Ballet-dancer" flowers, spring to fall, red, pink, etc.	Easily propagated by cuttings, spring to summer. Pinch out side shoots on standards, but leave main stem until it reaches the desired height.
Gardenia	*G. jasminoides*	(W)	Shrub	Flowers white and fragrant	With sufficient warmth flowers can be had in winter or summer.
Hedera (Ivy)	*H. helix:vars.*	(U, CC, C)	Climbing	Decorative, interesting leaf shapes and colors	Likes damp, but not too much watering. Many usual vars. are cultivated.
Hoya (Wax Flower)	*H. carnosa*	(I, C)	Climbing	Waxy pink flowers, spring and summer	Dormant in winter. Water and feed well until budding, and in flower.

Impatiens	*I. holstii hybrids*	(CC, C)	12-24 in	White, pink, orange, red flowers	Flowering throughout the year in the greenhouse. Reduce watering in colder weather.
Jasminum	*J. pubescents*	(C)	Climbing	White flowers, fragrant, spring	Light, airy conditions are best. Train to wires, etc. Prune in Feb. Easily grown.
Lantana	*L. camara*	(C, I, W)	Shrub to 4 ft	Pink, orange, yellow, flowers, June	Rich, well-drained compost should be provided. Grow from seed only cuttings.
Leptospermum	*L. scoparium nana*	(CC)	Shrub, dwarf, 1 ft	flowers rose, June	Lime-free, sandy compost suits this evergreen dwarf tree. Prune in spring.
Nerium (Oleander)	*N. oleander* vars.	(C)	6 ft or more	Double white, pink, red flowers, summer	Cultivate in large pots with rich compost. Give only moderate water in winter. Prune after flowers are over.
Oplismenus (Panicum)	*O. hirtellus variegatus*	(I, W)	Trailing	Striped leaves	Suitable for hanging baskets. Provide plenty of moisture and warm atmosphere in summer.
Passiflora (Passion Flower)	*P. caerulea*	(C)	Climbing	Flowers, a striking arrangement of petals, sepals, stamens, and stigmas	Need plenty of room. Prune late winter. Given less water in water.
Pelargonium	Regal, many cultivars	(C, I)	Spring-Flowering	Lavender, pink, and red flowers	Take cuttings in late summer. Buy young plants in pots in early spring. Water well and give light is season.
Petunia	Many kinds	(U, CC, C)	Low-growing, trailing	Flowers tinged or striped, red, pink, yellow, mauve, etc.	Treat as a summer annual in U and CC.
Plumbago	*P. indica*	(W, H)	2 ft	Flowers red, winter	Good perennial pot plant. Use a rich compost in warmth.
Primula	Various hybrids and species	(C)	1 ft	Flowers yellow, pink, Feb—May	Grow from seed sown in mid-summer. Provide well-drained compost and moist shade.
Rhododendron	Azaleas	(C)	Shrubby	Flowers pink, red, salmon, white, etc.	Can be grown in large pots or tubs in limepfree, peaty compost with good drainage.

Rheo	*R. discolor*	(C, I)	Upright	Leaves dark green above, purplish beneath, 1 ft long	A moist atmosphere is essential, but avoid overwatering in winter. Light in winter, shade in summer.
Saintpaulia (African Violet)	Many cultivars	(W)	Low-growing	Pink, violet, white, etc., leaves hairy, heart-shaped	Moist atmosphere and winter sun essential.
Schizanthus (Poor Man's Orchid)	Improved vars.	(C)	1-2 ft	Pink, rose white, etc. large and small flower types, spring	Grow from seed sown in Aug. Prick out into small pots and do not overwater in winter.
Stephanotis	*S. floribunda*	(I, W)	Climber	Flowers white, fragrant. June—Sept	Growth must be trained carefully and thinned. Shade in summer. Provide moist atmosphere.
Streptocarpus	Various hybrids	(C, I)	1 ft	Flowers, pink, mauve, white, etc., summer on	Sow seed on surface in warmth in spring or end of winter. Moisture, ventilation, and slight shade from spring on. Keep drier in winter.
Thunbergia	*T. alata*	(C)	Climber	Flowers, yellow, orange, summer	Grow from seed sown in Mar—Apr. Quick growth. Treat as an annual. Easy to grow.
Zebrina (Wandering Jew)	*Z. pendula*	(C, I)	Trailing	Leaves dark, silver-striped, purple underneath	Suitable for hanging baskets. Pinch back to control. Water well in summer, less in winter. Take 2-in cuttings and root in sandy soil spring to fall.

Growing vegetables can be as satisfying, if not more satisfying, than growing decorative plants. With a little planning the experienced gardener can keep the larder stocked and cut the costs of house-keeping.

a)

Greenhouses come in a variety of shapes and sizes to suit every garden and every budget.
a) A typical red cedar Dutch-type greenhouse, suitable for growing crops that are best grown directly in the ground.
b) A red cedar lean-to-type house. Such houses can be heated from the home heating system.
c) An even span greenhouse. Greenhouses this size are for the real enthusiast.
(Greenhouses of these types are also available in aluminum for easy erection and maintenance).
Courtesy Halls of Paddock Wood

b)

c)

Vegetable and Herb Gardens

Vegetables never taste better than when they come fresh from your own garden, providing you have given attention to promoting good growth and have kept the garden free of insects and disease. There are several reasons your own vegetables taste better: first, they are fresher — usually eaten right after harvest, so no flavor is lost during storage and shipping; second, they are harvested at the best stage for best flavor; and third, they were grown by you and there is your pride of producing them.

The great majority of vegetables are relatively easy to grow: seed is inexpensive, and the economies that can be made (with relatively little expenditure of time) are very considerable. In addition, one can grow some of the rarer and exotic vegetables that are seldom found in grocery stores and which are expensive even when they can be bought.

The site of the vegetable garden should be an open one, receiving as much sunshine as possible. However, if the site is a windy one, low fences should be erected as windbreaks (a windbreak filters the wind rather than blocks it; solid walls, by contrast, may create powerful wind currents, like those encountered between high buildings). Hedges and trees are less suitable as windbreaks than fences, as their shade and roots tend to be detrimental to the plants. However, a row of espalier fruit trees or a neat hedge can be used effectively to separate the vegetable garden from the ornamental garden. The choice of hedge or windbreak really depends on the amount of space available, since, if the vegetables are spaced sufficiently far from the hedge or espalier trees they will not be affected by loss of root nourishment.

The size of the vegetable plot will depend largely on the ambitions of the gardener. A plot 200 by 50 feet could supply the vegetable needs of a small family year-round, but one half that size would be more manageable for someone with less spare time. The vegetable garden can be more demanding than the flower garden. A lazy flower gardener can still achieve an attractive show, but a lazy vegetable gardener is wasting his time. After preparing the soil, sowing, planting, and topdressing, there are operations such as weeding, hoeing, thinning, and watering which are essential if good crops are to be obtained, and, even with the help of modern machinery, these tasks are still time-consuming.

Paths are important in the vegetable garden, because a lot of walking around is involved when doing various jobs. It is best to surround the whole plot with a path wide enough to take a wheelbarrow. Simple paths between rows can be made with straw or peat or any other mulching material. Sometimes it is necessary to work when the ground is wet, and a few boards are very useful for creating "instant" paths across the soil. They also prevent the soil from becoming compacted. The vegetable garden is the obvious site for the compost heap, the garbage bag, frame, and the greenhouse.

The best position for a herb garden is a sheltered one, rather like a herbaceous border, with the tall-growing, shrubby plants at the back. Herbs vary considerably in size, some, such as sage, rue, and rosemary being shrubby, while others, such as marjoram, thyme, and chives are low-growing.

Within the vegetables are included several main groups: fruit crops, salad crops, cole crops, root crops, and legumes. Root crops, such as parsnips, carrots, and beets, like deep, clean soil manured the previous year, not just before sowing, as their roots tend to split in freshly manured ground. The same needs apply to potatoes, which are often planted on a new vegetable plot to "clean" the ground. For potatoes, the ground must be deeply cultivated, and if this is done well they are an ideal crop to start with on any new plot. Cole crops include cabbages, Brussels sprouts, cauliflowers, and broccoli. They need plenty of lime and nitrogenous fertilizers. Legumes, such as peas and beans, have on their roots special nodules containing bacteria, which are part of a system by which the plants convert or "fix" the nitrogen in the air, making it into plant food.

This process illustrates one of the points of crop rotation. The roots of peas are left in the ground after harvesting so that the nitrogen in them remains to feed the following crop, which may lack the ability to make nitrogen for itself. Cole crops and salad crops need plenty of nitrogen, so they usually follow legumes. Another reason for rotation is the prevention of disease. If, for example, cabbages are grown year after year on the same piece of ground they may develop a disease called club root. If they are grown on different soil each year, they will be less likely to develop this disease. So, as well as helping to balance the supply and demand for plant foods, rotation helps to eliminate pests and diseases. A simple form of rotation is to divide your plot into three equal sections and arrange the groups of plants in the following way, as an example:

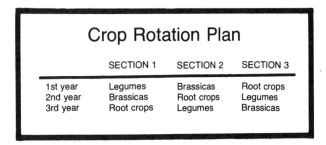

Crop Rotation Plan			
	SECTION 1	SECTION 2	SECTION 3
1st year	Legumes	Brassicas	Root crops
2nd year	Brassicas	Root crops	Legumes
3rd year	Root crops	Legumes	Brassicas

The cycle would be repeated in succeeding years. Separate plots need to be set aside for permanent crops such as rhubarb and asparagus, and yet another for crops such as onions, marrows, and lettuce. If the vegetable garden is too small to make rotation seem worthwhile, or if you prefer to follow your own ideas, it is as well to bear in mind that you should not plant the same thing on the same piece of ground from one year to another. Related plants, such as tomato, potato, eggplant, and pepper, should be rotated, since they are susceptible to many of the same diseases.

Mulching
This is a very useful procedure in the vegetable garden, saving watering by preventing loss of moisture from the ground, smothering weeds, and encouraging the production of humus and plant food. Peat is very useful, especially where young and delicate plants are concerned, but once plants have grown enough not to be smothered, straw is less expensive if available. Lawn clippings and compost are other alternatives.

In recent years a vogue has started for using black plastic as a substitute for these mulches on crops such as broccoli, Brussels sprouts, cabbages, cauliflowers, and tomatoes, the sheets being laid on the ground and the plants set between them. For a row, two lengths of sheeting are used, leaving a narrow gap in the middle for the plants. For potatoes the plastic is simply laid over the ground after the potatoes have been planted. When the shoots appear, the plastic is lifted and slits are made in it to enable the shoots to be gently drawn through. Pieces of thin wire tied to stakes are a neat way of holding the plastic down.

Succession Sowings
Quick-growing plants such as lettuce, radish, and summer spinach are best sown at two-week intervals from early to late spring. This can be done with the same variety or varieties, because their quick-growing properties ensure that they will mature at intervals throughout the season. The great advantage of this method is that by sowing only a small number of seeds at a time it is possible to harvest reasonable

quantities over a long period instead of a huge crop all at once. This practice is limited by the climate of the latitude of your garden.

Intercropping
This is related to successional sowings in that the same quick-maturing plants may be accommodated in between rows of slower-maturing plants. Thus, lettuce may be grown between beds of beans. The only condition for such intensive cultivation is that the ground should have been prepared to provide nourishment for both crops. Where the slow-maturing plants tend to overshadow the quick-maturing ones, it is important that the rows should be on a north-south axis or the smaller plants may be deprived of light.

Catch Cropping
This is rather like intercropping, except that instead of growing two crops at the same time, the catch crop is grown to maturity before the main crop has made much growth. A good example of catch cropping is growing lettuce on the ridges thrown out of celery trenches before it is necessary to start hilling the celery.

Double Cropping
This involves replanting a piece of ground as soon as the previous crop has been taken out. A lot of early crops are harvested by early summer, and the same location can be used for another vegetable such as sweet corn or spinach, depending on the latitude. The ground must be properly prepared between one crop and the next.

Cloche Culture
The advantage of cloches, or plant protectors, is that they enable you to carry on intensive cultivation in a restricted area. In these days of small gardens, cloches have really come into their own in British gardens. There are many types of cloche, but the barn type, with almost vertical walls and an inverted V-shaped roof, is the best-known. Rain falling at the sides of the cloche is absorbed by the ground underneath the cloche. Glass cloches are generally held together by galvanized-wire frames, and the most useful sort are about 2 feet long. By placing them end-to-end and securing a flat piece of glass across each end, they effectively form a miniature greenhouse. Plastic cloches are less expensive and generally as effective, but have different light and heat conducting properties.

There are many ways of using cloches, but perhaps the most useful where winters are long and the ground takes a long time to warm up is to permit earlier planting. The ground is prepared and about 4 ounces of balanced NPK fertilizer are worked into the topsoil a week before planting, and the cloches are placed over the hill. In this way seeds can be sown directly into the soil 2 to 3 weeks earlier than when sown in the open. Beets, Brussels sprouts, carrots, cucumbers, squash, and beans benefit from cloche culture. Other plants that benefit include cauliflowers, endives, parsley, shallots, spring onions, and turnips. Lettuce and radishes may be sown out of season, in late September, for overwintering under cloches in some areas. In the south radishes may be sown even later, and in the north sowing commences again in February. Tomatoes benefit from early cloche protection. By skillful timing, the gardener can get maximum use from his cloches by transferring them from one plant to another. For instance, cloches used to protect early cauliflower can be removed in April and used for protecting tomatoes. Maximum use of the ground is made by intercropping other quick-maturing plants between the cloches.

Frame Culture

The garden frame should be placed in an open position where it will get plenty of light. A frame is in effect a permanent cloche and can be used in the same way. All the various plants mentioned in the cloche section can be grown equally well under frames. It is possible to make a very simple frame at home, without any great knowledge of woodwork, by attaching second-hand windows to a simple wooden, brick, or block frame. A heated frame is usually called a "hot bed"; one without supplied heat is called a "cold frame."

The ground inside the frame may be enriched or improved as needed, or it may be completely replaced with a specially prepared compost. In any case it should be well-drained. More commonly, the frame is used for starting and hardening-off young plants before transplanting to the garden. These might be celery or tomato plants sown in a heated frame. Seeds that germinate easily without heat, such as cabbage and lettuce, might be sown directly in the cold frame and transplanted to their permanent positions in the garden after germination. This is often done to get the plants off to an early start, sowing the seed in late February. Sometimes frames are used for ripening and drying of lifted crops, such as onions and shallots.

Frames tend to be subject to sudden changes of temperature in early spring, when a sunny day may cause them to heat up rapidly, only to be followed by a frosty night, chilling them down equally rapidly. Ventilation and regular watering are necessary to prevent overheating, while sudden frosts should be guarded against by covering the frame with sacks or matting.

Home-grown vegetables always seem to taste better. *Bottom,* Cauliflower "Unwins Snocap," a large-heading, very early variety. *Center,* Cos lettuce "Giant Perfection." *Top,* Cabbage lettuce "Suzan." Lettuce can be had over a long period by growing both leaf and heading types.
Courtesy Unwins of Histon

Using the Vegetable Table

The times and operations referred to under the planting and transplanting column relate to the young plants after germination under glass or in a seed bed outside. Where sowing times are given under glass, but not followed by any entry in the planting column, you can assume the plant will complete its life under glass. Where the time to sow is followed by (HF), this means the seed should be sown in gentle heat, either in a heated frame or in the greenhouse. Where the time to sow is followed by (CF) or (C), this means the sowing should be done in a cold frame or cloche. Where plants like celery, cucumber, lettuce, and squash are propagated by germinating the seed in gentle heat, always harden them off slowly in a cold frame, or in stages by putting them outside in reasonable weather for longer and longer periods, avoiding any violent changes in temperature or humidity. Successional sowings should be made at intervals of 14 days.

Storage or clamping usually refers to laying root vegetables like carrots in dry sand or dry peat, although it is possible to store most root vegetables in clamps, by making a heap of them, covering the heap with a 12-inch layer of clean straw, and covering the straw with a foot of earth. A thick wedge of straw through the earth at the top enables the clamp to "breathe."

The references to NPK, and so on, are discussed in an earlier section of the book, and if in doubt you should refer to that section. For instance, if the entry under "in the open" in the sowing column says PK (BD), reference to the NPK table will show you this means a base dressing of superphosphate before sowing, and a base dressing of sulfate of potash. Generally, dressings around planting time are made about a week before the actual planting takes place. Where an "NPK" application is recommended, a complete fertilizer should be used.

Key to Table of Vegetables

(BD)	Base dressing
(TD)	Topdressing
N	Nitrogen
P	Phosphate
K	Potash
(C)	Under cloches
(HF)	Hot frame or cool, intermediate, or warm greenhouse
(DF)	Suitable for deep freezing (after variety)

Savoy cabbage, with their bold, blue-green leaves, are among those vegetables that could be grown just as well in the flower border as the vegetable garden.

Table of Vegetables

PLANT NAME *TYPE OF SOIL*	TIME TO SEED		SPACING BETWEEN	(inches)	PLANT OR TRANS- PLANT	HARVEST	NOTES & CULTIVARS
	Under glass	In the open	Rows	Plants			
Artichoke (Globe) *Deep, rich*			48	36	Mar—Apr NPK(BD)	2nd yr	Plant offsets with roots. Remove flower heads in 1st yr. After 3rd yr's crop, dig up the plants.
Artichoke (Jerusalem) *Ordinary*			30	15	Feb—Mar NPK(BD)	Oct—Mar	Plant tubes 5-in deep. Best treated as an annual.
Asparagus *Deep, rich, well limed.*			15	15	Apr NPK(BD)	Apr—June in 3rd yr NPK(TD)	Plant 3-year-old male-only crowns in 3 rows on 4 ft (raised) wide beds. Cut 5-in shoots below soil level. Cut down yellowing "fern" in fall. Beds last 10-20 yrs. "Mary Washington" or Washington strains. (DF)
Beans, Lima *non-acid*		In warm soil, May—June PK (BD)	24-30	4-6		July—Sept	Water well. Good crop after peas. "Fordhook 242", "Thaxter" (DF).
Beans Snap *Non-acid*		May—July NPK (BD)	24	2-3		July—Sept	Make successional sowings (14-day intervals). Pick as soon as 4 in. long or less. "Provider," "Top crop," "Tenderette," "Kinghorn Wax" (All DF).
Beets *Light to medium loam.*		Mar—July NPK (BD)	15-24	2-3		July—Oct	Thin out at 1-in high. Hoe. Harvest with care. Gently twist off tops. Store in peat, or pickle. "Detroit Dark Red", "Ruby Queen," "Crosby's Egyptian."
Broccoli *Deep*		Feb—Mar July	24	18	Mar—Apr NPK (BD) Sept—Oct	May—June Oct—Dec	"Coastal", "Waltham 29", "Green Comet", "Gem", (all DF).
Brussels Sprouts *Deep*	Mar	Apr	30	24	June—July NPK (BD)	Oct—Dec	Hoe and water regularly. Firm or stake developed plants. Pick as ready. Not widely adapted. "Jade Cross", "Long Island Improved", "Catskill".
Cabbage (Fall) *Heavy, well drained*		June—July	12-16	24-30	Aug—Sept PK (BD)	Sept on	Topdress nitrate of soda 6 weeks after planting. Use same cultivars as in spring crop.
Cabbage (Over wintered) *Fertile*	July—Aug	July—Aug	12-16	24-30	Sept—Oct NPK (BD)	Mar—May	"Greenback", "Early Round Dutch."

Cabbage (Spring) *Fertile*	Jan—Feb	Mar—Apr	12-16 Less space for dwarf varieties	24-30	May NPK (BD)	June—Aug	Seedlings germinated under glass should be hardened off. Give nitrate of soda 6 weeks after planting out. "Golden Acre", "Stonehead", "Jersey Queen", "Early Jersey Wakefield", "Emerald Cross", "Superette", "Copenhagen Market", "King Cole", "Danish Bal-lhead", "Savoy King", "Savoy Chief-tain".
Cautaloupe *Light, fertile*	Apr (HF) May		36-48	18	May NPK (BD)	July—Aug	Control insects and diseases. "Burpee Hybird", "Harper Hybrid", "Gold Star Hybrid", "Harvest Queen", "Golden Perfection", "Hearts of Gold", "Edista 47", "Saticoy Hybrid".* (*Wilt resistant)
Carrot *Deep, loamy*		Mar—May NPK (BD)	12-30	1-3		July—Oct	Successional sowings in drills and thin out in 2 stages. Use later thinnings. Do not apply manure. "Nantes", "Royal Chantenay", "Danvers 126" (all DF). Store Oct crop in dry sand.
Cauliflower *Well limed*	June—July	June—July	18-24	24-36	Aug—Sept NPK (BD) N (TD)	Sept—Dec	"Early Snowball", "Snowball Imperial", "Snowball Y", "Early Purple Head" (all DF).
Celeriac *Rich, deep*	Mar (HF)	May—June NPK (BD)	18	12	May—June NPK (BD)	Oct on	Root half sits on soil. Water well. Use roots like parsnip (store in dry peat). "Giant Prague".
Celery *Deep*	Mar (HF)	Apr (C)	18-36	4-6	May—June NPK (BD)	Aug—Sept	Trench 18 in. deep by 15 in. wide dig in manure. Embank sides of previously prepared trench for earthing up. Set plants in fine soil. Remove sideshoots when 15 in. high. "Summer Pascal".
Chicory *Rich, deep*		May—June NPK (BD)	15-18	4-5		Oct—Nov	Top lifted roots leaving 1 in. of stem above the crown. Store in cool, frost-proof shed. To blanch, place crowns 1 in. above soil in deep pot covered with another inverted pot. Exclude all light for 1-2 months.

Tomatoes are probably the most rewarding of all crops to grow. A good crop of well-grown fruits are a joy to look at and a joy to eat. Many modern varieties are resistant to the diseases that plagued tomatoes in the past.

Cucumber *Rich, deep*	Apr (HF)	May NPK (BD) N (TD)	36-48	18	May NPK (BD) N (TD)	July—Sept	*Slicing* "Gemini", "Ashley", "Poinsett", "Marketmore", *Pickling* "SMR58", "Pixie", "Pioneer", "Frontier", "Premier".
Eggplant *Rich, friable*	Apr (HF)		36-48	18-24	May NPK (BD) NPK (TD)	July—Sept	Culture similar to tomatoes. "Black Beauty", "Florida High Bush", "Black Magic", "Jersey King".
Endive **(Escarole)** *Rich, well drained*		June—July NPK (BD)	12-24	12		Nov on	Blanching begins Oct. Cover with black plastic, exclude all light for month or more. "Green Curled", "Batavian".
Kale *Loam*		Apr—May, Aug	24	12	May—June Aug NPK (BD) N (TD)	Nov—Apr	Sow in drills. Sometimes intercropped with early potatoes. Mulch. "Vates", "Dwarf Green Scotch."
Kohlrabi *Loam*		Apr—June NPK (BD)	12-18	9		July—Dec	Sow for succession. Thin. Easy to grow. Use leaves for greens and root-stem for turnips (eat when small).
Leeks *Rich, deep*	Jan—Feb	Mar—Apr	18	12	May—June NPK (BD)	Oct on	Plant in deep holes. Flood with water. Leave. In late July mulch or earth up. Store in ground. "Improved Musselburgh", "London or *American Flag*", "Lyon", "Marshall's Colossus" (exhibition).
Lettuce *Rich*	Jan—Feb (HF)	Mar—Apr, Aug	12	9	Mar—Apr, Aug NPK (BD) N (TD)	May—July, Sept—Dec	The season can be extended by use of cloches and forcing. Successional sowings outside after Apr through summer. "Great Lakes", "Bibb", "Buttercrunch", "Salad Bowl", "Grand Rapids".
Mustard and **Cress** *Rich, deep*	All yr (HF)	Mar on (C) Apr—Sept NPK (BD) N (TD)	12-18	3-4		14—21 days after sowing	Sow thickly in separate containers indoors. Mustard 3-4 days after cress.
Okra *Loamy*		Apr—May	48	12-18	In warm soil	July—Sept	Seed in drills after last frost and thin. Harvest pods daily. "Everald", "Dwarf Green Long Pod", "Clemson Spineless", "Perkins Spineless".

Onion *Rich, deep*	Jan—Feb (HF)	Mar—Apr, Aug	12	1-4	Mar—Apr NPK (BD) N (TD)	When ripe lift and dry	Outside sow in drills. Thin or transplant. Plant sets in March. Sow spring onions Aug and Mar. "Ebenezer", "Yellow Globe", "Sweet Spanish", "Early Harvest", "Pronto S", "Bermuda", "Fiesta", "Aristocrat", "Elite", "Beltsville Bunching".
Parsnip *Rich, deep*		Apr—May NPK (BD)	18	2-4		Nov on	Sow in drills and thin. Lift as required. "Hollow Crown", "Model", "All America".
Peas **(early)** *Rich*		Mar—Apr NPK (BD)	8-24	1-2		May—June	Stake with netting or twigs or let trail on ground. "Meteor", "Alaska", "Little Marvel".
Peas **(Main, late)** *As for early*		Mar—May NPK (BD) N (TD)	8-24	1-2		June—July	Sow outside as for early. Use series of varieties for succession. "Thomas Laxton", "Frosty", "Wando", (all DF).
Pepper *Rich, friable*	Apr	(HF)	36-48	18-24	May—June NPK (BD) N (TD)	Aug—Sept	Culture similar to tomatoes. Remove fruit from very young plants. *Sweet* "Delaware Belle", "Calwonder", "Yolo Wonder", "Canape", "Keystone Resistant Giant", "Peter Piper", Ruby King", *Hot* "Long Red Cayenne", "Red Chile", "Red Cherry", "Hungerian Wax".
Potatoes **(Fall)** *As for early*		June—July NPK (BD) N (TD)	30-36	12		Aug on	As for early. Earthing up may be done if desired. Control insects and diseases. Irrigate as needed. "Kennebec", "Katahdin", "Bliss Triumph", "Red La Soda", "Superior".
Potatoes **(Spring)** *Rich, well drained*		Mar NPK (BD) N (TD)	30-36	12		May—June	Each tuber should have 1-3 tough sprouts after exposure to light in frost-proof room. Mulch early foliage. "Irish Cobbler" and same cultivars as for fall crop.
Pumpkin *Rich, deep*		Apr—May NPK (BD)	48-96	24-48		Sept—Oct	Harvest before frost and store. "Connecticut Field", "Small Sugar", "Jack O'Lantern", "Cinderella", "Youngs' Beauty".

Radishes *Rich, well cultivated*	Mar—Sept NPK (BD)	8-12	1		Apr—Sept	Sow thinly and thin out. Sow for succession. "Cherry Belle", "Scarlet Globe", "White Icicle".
Rhubarb *Rich, deep loam*	Mar (HF) NPK (annually)	36	36	Mar	Apr on. Do not harvest 1st year after trans-planting	Forcing under containers which are covered with straw or mulch gives Jan—Feb pulling. Mature roots can be forced in cool planting greenhouse. "Canada Red", "MacDonald", "Valentine", "Victoria".
Rutabaga *Deep*	Mar—Apr July—Aug NPK (BD)	12-18	4-9		July—Aug Dec.	"American Purple Top", "Laurentain.
Salsify *Rich, deep*	Apr—May June NPK (BD)	12-18	2-3		Oct—Mar	Sow in drills, and thin. Water. Lift roots as required for parsnips, boil spring shoots
Seakale *Rich, deep*	Mar—Apr NPK (BD)	12 (seedlings) 18 (cuttings)	6 12	Mar		Take pencil-thick side-growth cutting Nov and 2 in. in sheltered sandy bed. Plant Mar, feed, hoe mulch. Blanch as for forcing rhubarb in open in Nov (exclude light and mulch well). Roots can also be lifted and forced in dark in intermediate greenhouse as for Chicory. Prepare for salad or steam
Shallots *Rich, deep*	Feb—Mar (bulbs) NPK (BD)	12-36	6-8		July	Sit bulbs half in soil. Lift when leaves wither, dry in hot sun, pickle or store.
Southern Peas **(Black-eyes or Cowpeas)** *Well-drained, not rich in N*		36	4-6	May—June PK (BD)	July—Sept	Plant after last frost. Pick 2 to 3 times per week. "Extra Early Blackeye", "California Blackeye 5", "Mekan", "Pink Eye Purple Hall", "Princess Ann", "Mississippi Silver".
Spinach (Spring) *Rich*	Mar—Apr NPK (BD) N (TD)	12-18	3-6		May—June	"America", "Dark Green Bloomsdale".
(Fall)	Aug—Sept NPK (BD) N (TD)	12-18	3-4		Sept—Nov	Pick large leaves only. "Hybrid 7", "Dixie Market", "Hybrid 56", "Virginia Savoy".
(Overwintered)	Sept—Oct NPK (BD) N (TD)	12-18	3-4		Feb—Mar	"Hybrid 7", "Virginia Savoy".
New Zealand *Rich, deep*	May—July NPK (BD) N (TD)	30-42	15-18		Summer	Stands dry conditions.

Squash *Rich, deep*		Apr—May	36-48	24-36	Apr—May NPK (BD) NPK (TD)	When ripe to Sept	Sow in 3 in pots. Water well and liquid feed. "Early Prolifie Straightneak", "White Bush Scallop", "Caserta", "Zuccini", "Table Queen", "Hubbard", "Boston Marrow".
Sweet Corn *Rich*		Apr—July NPK (BD) N (TD)	36-42	6-12		June—Sept	Control insects. *Yellow* "Seneca Beauty", "Spring Gold", "Earlibelle", "Northern Belle", "Butter and Sugar", "Seneca Chief", "NK199", "Buttersweet", "Golden Queen", *White* "White Jewel", "White Dutch", "White Cross Bantam", "Stowell's Evergreen Hybrid", "Silver Queen", "Country Gentlemen Hybrids" (all DF).
Sweet Potatoes *Loose, friable*	small potatoes	Mar—Apr (HF)	30-42	12-18	Apr—June (Rooted sprouts)	Aug—Oct	Transplant slips after last frost. Harvest before frost in fall. *Moist* "Puerto Rico", "Centennial", "Jewel". *Intermediate* "Nemagold", "Goldmar". *Dry* "Orange Little Stem".
Swiss Chard *Loamy*		Apr—May NPK (BD) N (TD)	18-36	6-12		June—Oct	Use white stem like asparagus, green part for spinach. Easy to grow. "Luculless", "Fordhook Giant", "Rhubarb".
Tomatoes *Rich, friable*	Feb—Mar (HF)	Apr—May (C)	36 (staked) 48-60 (bush)	18 30	May—June NPK (BD) N (TD)	July—Oct	Bush varieties easy to manage, just mulch around with straw. Stop another at 4-5 trusses and remove side shoots. Consult local adaptation of cultivars. "Spring Giant", "Campbell 1327", "Jet Star"*, "Campbell 17", "Supersonic*", "Heinz 1409", "Ramapo", "Marion"*, "Manalucie"*, "Better Boy" (*For staking.)

Turnips *Deep* **(summer)**	Mar—Apr NPK (BD)	12	6		June on	Sow in drills and thin. "Shogoin" (DF), "Purple Top", "Just Right", "Seven Top", "Tokyo Cross".
(winter)	July—Aug	12	9		When needed	Moisten soil before sowing.
(tops)	Aug—Sept	18	3		Mar—May	Give cloche protection in cold weather.
Watermelons *Loose, friable*	Apr (NF)	48-96	48-96	Apr—June	July—Sept	Plant in hills. Space ice box types closer than large-vine types. "Sweet Princess", "Charleston Gray", "Jubilee", "Summer Festival", "Crimson Sweet", "Triple Sweet" (seedless), "Sugar Baby" (ice box).

All the vegetables shown here can be grown by the amateur in his own garden. With a little ingenuity the dedicated gardener can keep the family supplied with all the vegetables they need.

Table of Herbs

PLANT NAME	SOIL	PROPAGATION	SPACING (INCHES)		HABIT OR HEIGHT (INCHES)	NOTES
			Rows	Plants		
Basil (sweet)	Rich, light	Sow Mar (HF), Apr—May in open	7	7	12-24	Plant out from heat in June. Treat as an annual.
Borage	Ordinary	Sow Apr—May	12	12	12-24	Once sown propagates itself.
Chives	Rich, deep	Divide Mar or Oct	12	6	Grass-like, 12	Cut regularly, remove flowers.
Dill	Light, well-drained	Sow Mar (HF), Apr—May in open	24	24	Umbelliferous, 36	Rich-flavored seeds. Annual
Fennel	Light, deep, rich	Sow Mar (HF), Apr—May in open	18	18	Umbelliferous,	Treat as annual. Use roots and seed.
Garlic	Light, rich	Plant bulbs Mar	9	9	Like onions	French garlic is finer.
Horseradish	Firm, rich	Set roots deep (Mar)	12	12	24-36	First crop roots after 2 yrs.
Marjoram (sweet)	Rich, deep	Sow Mar (HF), plant June	12	12	12	Treat as half-hardy.
(pot)	Rich, deep	Divide or sow in Mar.	12	12	12	Perennial. Pick before flowering.
Mint	Rich	Divide Oct or Mar	12	12	12-24	Renew bed every 3 yrs.
Parsley	Rich, moist	Sow Apr and July	12	4	6-9	Sow annually. Dig up after 3 yrs.
Rosemary	Ordinary	Sow Apr—July	36	36	to 72, shrubby	Perennial evergreen decorative
Rue	Ordinary	Sow Apr—May	36	24	to 36, shrubby	Perennial needs winter shelter.
Sage	Ordinary	Cuttings Apr, sow May	30	24	to 42, shrubby	Perennial. Cut before flowers.
Savory (summer)	Rich	Sow Mar (HF), Apr in open	9	9	12	Dry in bunches, Aug. Annual.
(winter)	Rich, light	Seed or cuttings Apr	24	24	Low, shrubby	Perennial evergreen decorative.
Sorrel (French)	Rich, moist	Divide Mar or Oct, sow Apr—May	24	24	24, spreading	Perennial, not always hardy.
Thyme	Rich, moist	Sow or take cuttings Apr—May	9	9	Low-growing	Perennial evergreen decorative, pick before flowers.

Rust on *Antirrhinum* Snapdragons. A gardener needs to know his friends and foes, and which chemicals are safe to use on what plants.

All caterpillars are voracious eaters of garden plants. The butterflies into which they turn do very little damage in the garden.

Pests and Diseases

The gardener is most disappointed to see his plants destroyed or damaged by insects and diseases. This is, of course, to a certain extent inevitable. It happens in even the best-managed gardens. Everything that lives is subject to ills and diseases, and garden plants are no exception. The stalwart English Oak is liable to some 600 diseases, yet there are still many healthy specimens standing today. One must be philosophical about these things. Insects and diseases are themselves living creatures, part of the great food chain, and they have to feed. Damage and losses are as inevitable a part of gardening as are flowers and fruits, but with proper garden management and an understanding of the control of pests and diseases, losses can be kept to a minimum.

Insect pests of plants include all those creatures having 6 legs, usually eating the leaves or stems, but sometimes eating the roots. These are mainly small creatures, including most of the gardener's traditional enemies, such as weevils, mites, aphids, and others. There are larger creatures, such as deer and rabbits, that are also pests in some areas. Not all small creatures, however, are pests: many are actually beneficial in the garden, keeping the real pests under control. Among these are ladybirds, centipedes, spiders, many ground beetles, shrews, hedgehogs, and a large number of birds. A considerable amount of care should be exercised in identifying small creatures before deciding whether or not they need to be exterminated.

Diseases are caused by microscopic organisms such as fungi, bacteria, and viruses. These agents of disease are, in fact, themselves plants: they are among the smallest, simplest, and most primitive of all forms of vegetable life.

In dealing with pests and diseases, prevention is plainly better than curative measures. Garden hygiene and correct cultivation are far more important and helpful than spraying the plants with all sorts of prophylactic chemicals. There are certain conditions that tend to promote the incidence of pests and diseases. A plant that is growing poorly is far more prone to disease than one that is growing well. Plants growing in heavy shade are more liable to suffer than plants growing in the open. Overcrowded plants, too, are more likely to suffer disease, especially if they are all of the same kind. Certain conditions tend to lessen the likelihood of disease: good, regular cultivation of the soil exposes many pests to their natural predators; the removal of weeds helps, too, as these frequently act as hosts for pests; good drainage is another factor, as it discourages slugs and millipedes and prevents injurious soil fungi from becoming established. Garden hygiene is of the utmost importance. Weeds left drying on paths are likely to attract fungi and diseases which could spread to growing plants. For the same reason prunings should never be left lying on borders or among shrubs.

In spite of all these precautions, pests and diseases do occur, even in the best-managed gardens. The answer is not to reach at once for the nearest pesticide aerosol: it is to identify the pest or disease. Only when this has been done should the decision be made as to whether or not further steps should be taken, and if so, what steps.

The modern gardener has a whole arsenal of chemicals he can use against plant pests, but the most successful gardeners are those who excercise considerable restraint in the use of these chemicals. Many of these chemicals are known as "broad-spectrum" pesticides — that is, they will kill a very broad spectrum of pests. This may at first seem an excellent thing. In fact, it has its drawbacks: the broad-spectrum pesticides not only kill the pests, they also kill the beneficial creatures. Many broad-spectrum fungicides also kill soil bacteria which are essential to healthy plant growth. For these reasons these chemicals should be used with considerable discretion. In many cases there are specific chemicals for specific pests, and wherever possible these should be used in preference to the broad-spectrum chemicals.

Soil-borne insects and diseases are best controlled by sterilization or fumigation of the soil. Formalin is one chemical for this, being convenient to use, economic, and highly efficient. The soil should be dug deeply and saturated with a solution of 1 gallon of 40% formaldehyde in 49 gallons of water applied to the soil at the rate of 5 gallons per square yard. The soil should then be covered with damp sacks or a plastic sheet for 48 hours to prevent the solution from evaporating before it has had time to do its work, and 4 to 6 weeks should elapse before the soil is used for seeding or planting. Sterilization should not, of course, be carried out in the vicinity of growing plants. Where sterilized soil is required for seeding or potting, the same treatment may be used, piling the soil into heaps before applying the formaldehyde solution. Once sterilized, the soil should be kept in sterilized, airtight bins until used. Unless really large quantities are required, it is usually more economic to buy prepared potting soil.

Under glass, pests are more effectively controlled by fumigation or dusting than by spraying. There is a wide choice of proprietary products available for this purpose, many of them in the form of smokes. Some are exceedingly poisonous, and the manufacturer's instructions should be followed implicitly. Some of these chemicals are poisonous to specific plants, but the manufacturers always list such plants.

The best time for fumigating a greenhouse is the early evening, when the plants are dry. The house should be made as airtight as possible and the work done quickly, starting from the far end and moving toward the door, which should be locked when the work is done. The house should be opened up quickly in the morning and aired for several hours before it is safe to stay in it. On no account should fumigation ever be carried out in a greenhouse or conservatory that leads into an occupied dwelling house. In such cases dusts or sprays must be used.

Considerable confusion exists in many people's minds over the functions of insecticides and fungicides. They tend to use them indiscriminately, regardless of whether it is an insect or fungus that is to be destroyed. With very few exceptions, insecticides kill insects, and fungicides kill fungi.

Insecticides are of two basic kinds: those that kill by contact, either by falling onto the insect itself or by providing a layer for it to walk over; and those that poison when the insect eats some part of the plant to which the pesticide has been applied, or a prepared bait. In addition there are the new systemic insecticides which are abosrbed into the sap of the plant, and which poison the insect when it eats the plant. Many modern insecticides combine more than one principle. This means that the modern gardener does not need to know whether the insect he intends to destroy is one of the sucking or one of the eating types. It is always preferable, however, to identify the insect and use a pesticide designed to destroy that particular creature whenever practicable.

Fungicides are designed not only to destroy the fungus, but also to provide the plant with a thin protective coating that will kill any fungi spores that drift onto it from neighboring plants.

Many of the modern sprays and dusts are not only highly efficient, they are also very expensive. It is therefore important that the equipment used for applying them should be equally efficient, and considerable advances in design and performance have been made over the past few years. The choice is mainly a personal one, but it will depend to some extent on the size of the garden. There is now a variety of pneumatic sprayers, power attachments, knapsacks, bucket types, and small one-hand devices for liquid preparations, while for the dusts there is a similarly wide variety. Whichever type of applicator is chosen, the aim of dusting or spraying must always be the same — to cover the whole plant evenly and thoroughly, including the undersides of the leaves. The work is best done on dry, windless days and preferably early in the morning or early in the evening, when dampness on the leaves will help the dust or spray cling to the plant.

Identification of pests is not always easy. This is particularly true of the largest group of pests, the insects. These have four stages of development — egg, larva or grub, pupa or chrysalis, and adult stage. The grub stage is usually the most damaging to plants, for it is at this stage that the insect has its greatest need for food. The adult stage is usually the least damaging to plants, since at this stage the adult is mainly concerned with finding a place to lay her eggs. Many insects produce more than one generation in a season, and many can lie dormant in the ground through the winter. Different seasons favor different pests. Slugs, for example, are more of a pest in a wet year, while ants, for example, are more of a pest in a dry year. It is difficult to anticipate which pests will predominate in any year, and all that can be done is to identify the pests when they occur and deal with them then. The following are some of the commoner pests.

Ants

Ants are an exception to the general rule that a pest is a creature that attacks a plant, eating its tissues. They do their damage in a more vicarious way. One of the ant's favorite foods is the honeydew produced by colonies of aphids, and in some cases the ants actually keep nurseries of aphids for the honeydew they produce. It is in the nursing and spreading of aphids that ants do most damage. They also cause damage, particularly in rock gardens and raised beds, by their tunneling operations. This not only increases drainage to the point of absurdity, but it can actually leave the roots of plants hanging in mid-air underground. Treatment: Boiling water poured into the nest is most effective on drives, patios, and pathways, but when the nest is situated among growing decorative plants, proprietary ant-killers should be used.

Aphids

These are the well-known Greenfly and Blackfly, which can do an enormous amount of damage to a wide range of plants, both indoors and out. They are small, soft-bodied, and can range in color from black to green, through reds, whites, and blues. They not only do damage in themselves, but also tend to spread fungi. An unattractive, sooty mold (a fungus) often grows on the honeydew created by the aphids, further spoiling the plant's appearance. An aphid colony usually begins on the underside of a leaf and is not usually noticed until the leaf has started to curl. They frequently attack the growing tips of shoots, causing curling and malformation. They should be ruthlessly eradicated as promptly as possible, using a proprietary product.

Club Root

Mainly a disease of garden vegetables, particularly cabbages, turnips, swedes, and radishes, but some ornamental plants such as candytuft, wallflowers, and stocks may be affected. The plants tend to look stunted and sickly, and swellings of various shapes and sizes occur both on the roots and on the stems. These swellings later become slimy as they decay. The disease occurs only where susceptible plants are growing in a soil with too little lime in it for their liking. The treatment is to institute a regime of regular dressings of lime and to avoid planting susceptible crops on the same soil for 2 or 3 years. The disease can often be avoided by keeping susceptible crops as far apart in the rotation as possible.

Damping Off

This is a fungus disease, but a number of different fungi are involved, different fungi attacking different plants. The condition occurs only in seedlings. The fungi attack the seedlings at ground level, the stems collapse, and the plants die. The condition is more easily avoided than cured. Hygiene is of the utmost importance. The soil should be sterile, and so should the pots and flats. The seeds themselves should be clean and, if home-gathered, thoroughly dried and all chaff removed. Excessive moisture, particularly if the seeds are grown under hermetic conditions, should be avoided, and there should be adequate ventilation if grown in a frame or greenhouse.

Mildew

This term is often misused and applied to molds and fungi that are not strictly mildews. The mildews themselves are of 2 types: the Powdery Mildew and the Downy Mildew.
The Powdery Mildews live on the surface of the foliage. They can make the foliage look very unattractive, but they do little harm. They tend to attack roses, vines, apples, *Dianthus,* turnips, strawberries, asters, chrysanthemums, and calendulas, producing a whitish or grayish effect on the leaves. Mild attacks are best dealt with by dusting with a proprietary fungicide; in severe attacks the affected parts should be removed and burned.

The Downy Mildews do far more damage. They live deep within the tissues of the plant and can do permanent harm. They tend to attack melons, lettuce, onions, spinach, wallflowers, and vines, causing yellowish patches on the leaves. The remedy is to spray or dust the plants with a proprietary fungicide, and this should be applied immediately an attack is noticed. Severely affected plants should be burned.

Narcissus Fly

Though usually lumped together, there are in fact 3 Narcissus Flies. There is the Large Narcissus Fly, which attacks only *Narcissi,* including the large-flowered daffodils, and two smaller ones, usually known as Small Bulb Flies, which attack not only Narcissi but also other small bulbs and occasionally root vegetables. All have a similar mode of operation: they lay eggs on or close to the bulbs, and the larvae that hatch from these eggs then burrow into the bulbs and eat out the center. Infested bulbs show weak or distorted growth. If soft, the Large Narcissus Fly is probably the culprit; if rotten, one of the Small Bulb Flies is probably to blame. When planting, it is always advisable to press the bulb gently. If it feels soft and springy it should be discarded, as it almost certainly contains the hibernating larvae of one of these flies. The normal treatment is to discard affected bulbs, preferably burning them. Where really precious bulbs are affected they should be dusted with a proprietary insecticide in accordance with the manufacturer's instructions.

Peach Leaf Curl

A common fungus disease which affects not only peaches but also plums, almonds, and nectarines. The leaves become swollen, curled, malformed, and appear blistered. There are proprietary remedies.

Potato Blight

This is the disease that caused the great Irish Potato Famine of 1846-47. It is most prevalent during warm, moist summers, when it spreads rapidly. It can also affect tomatoes. The fungus attacks the leaves first. Discolored patches appear near the edges of the leaves. These are brownish-black above, and grayish underneath. The spores of the fungus can be washed down into the soil and then attack the tubers. Infected tubers show a brownish discoloration of the flesh. Infected tubers tend to rot in storage and infect sound tubers. In tomatoes, the fruits rot. This disease must be dealt with as soon as it is noticed. The crop should be sprayed with a proprietary fungicide, repeated according to the manufacturer's directions. When the potatoes are lifted, the tops should be cut off with a sharp knife and burned, and only sound potatoes should be put into storage.

Slugs and Snails
Warning

These creatures do an enormous amount of damage in gardens every year, much of it never visible. Some species feed aboveground, but others feed belowground. Since most of the feeding is done at night, the culprit often is not spotted, and its presence can only be deduced by the trail of gnawed-off stems and shoots left behind. Slugs are active all year: snails hibernate in winter, often in rockeries or crannies in raised borders. There is a wide variety of proprietary slug- and snail-killers on the market; all are effective, but some of the older pellet-type slug-killers are highly toxic and should be handled with caution, particularly if used among vegetables.

Warning

Some of the most efficient of the modern pesticides and fungicides are totally unsuited to use in the garden. They are designed for use on farms and in market gardens, where experienced, trained men who wear special protective clothing know how to handle them and how to guard against the dangers of wind-drift. These sprays and dusts are lethal when used in gardens. The sprays and dusts sold for use in gardens are the only ones that should be used in gardens, but even these have their dangers. Many are harmless, but many are not so harmless, either to pets or to humans, and some are really quite dangerous. There can be only one rule: no spray, dust, bait, or fumigant should ever be regarded as safe — no matter what the manufacturers claim. All should be handled with the greatest respect. It is always particularly important to follow the manufacturer's instructions as carefully as possible. It is always dangerous to exceed the stated concentration or to use these chemicals in other ways or for other purposes than those specified by the maker. When not being used, they should be stored well out of reach of children and pets, preferably locked in an outside cupboard. Exhausted aerosols and empty cans and containers should be disposed of immediately. All utensils, such as watering cans, sprayers, mixing tubs, mixing rods, and so on, should be kept out of reach of children: even thorough washing may not rid them completely of toxicity. Any warning that a chemical is not suitable for certain plants should be heeded. Pyrethrum, for example, may damage chrysanthemums and some related genera; malathion may damage sweet peas; and BHC will taint some food parts. Insecticides should not be applied to fruit or ornamental trees when the blossom is open or opening because of the damage it will do to bees and other pollinating insects. Particular care should be taken in spraying, dusting, or fumigating any crops intended for the table at any stage of their development, and care should be taken that chemicals do not drift onto them from the flower garden.

In spite of their dangers, the modern chemicals at the gardener's disposal are a considerable asset and, when used with discrimination and restraint, are an invaluable aid in keeping pests and diseases under control.

Terrariums and Dish Gardens

Terrariums

A Terrarium is a convenient and attractive way of growing plants indoors, especially in our modern homes, where the temperatures are often warm and the atmosphere is very dry. They are not only decorative items, they are also conversation pieces.

A terrarium is essentially a container that allows light to pass through and which can be closed so as to be essentially airtight. Once it has been planted and watered it needs little or no attention for weeks or months. A high level of humidity develops inside, later condenses on the sides, and then returns to the soil. It becomes in effect a self-enclosed rain system. Such high humidity is desirable for many plants.

Many containers used for terrariums are designed to be tightly closed or they may have a small opening. The opening prevents the humidity from becoming as high and may allow a greater number of other plants to be used. Open-topped containers, such as globes, widemouthed jars, or a brandy snifter are suitable for many plants, including the succulents and cacti. The simple protection of the plants by the glass sides allows for protection from drafts and reduces the rate of drying.

A bottle with a narrow neck makes a simple, attractive terrarium, and with the proper selection of plants it remains attractive for an indefinite period.

The first reported notice that plants could be grown in such an enclosed container was made by a London physican, Dr. Nathaniel B. Ward, in a letter read before the Linnean Society of London on June 4, 1833. He had placed the chrysalis of a sphinx moth in some soil in a bottle and observed after some weeks that a young plant of annual bluegrass and of the male fern were growing. He observed these for more than three years. He had covered the bottle with a tin lid and had placed it outside a north window. The grass flowered the second year and the fern developed five or six leaves each year. He continued his experiments for several years, using different kinds of plants.

From his studies and observations he developed larger boxes with glass sides which became known as "Wardian Cases." These were most valuable to plant explorers and to those who shipped plants from one part of the world to another. This made it possible to protect plants for weeks and months on the deck of a ship. In calm weather they could be opened, but they could also be closed during rough, bad weather. The

A large brandy sniffer is easy to plant. This one has a seedling of the Norfolk Island pine, *Araucaria excelsa;* Spider Aralia - Dizygotheca elegantissima; Variegated Ribbon Plant - *Draceana sanderiana;* Baby's Tears - *Helxine soleiroli,* and Mosaic Plant -Fittonia verschaffeltii. This terrarium will require an occasional watering as the top is not covered.

Glass jars with covers make satisfactory small terrariums. The jar on the left has a young *Pteris* fern in it and the larger jar the Gold-dust Dracaena - *Dracaena godseffiana.*

term "Wardian Case" is still sometimes used to refer to an enclosed, glass-covered case used in the propagation of plants, especially for some slow-rooting plants or for certain forms of grafting. These cases were as essential to the sucessful plant explorer of a hundred years ago as the plastic bag is to the modern explorer who ships his plants home by air.

Where displayed

A terrarium is a decorative item in the home and should be given the necessary conditions for the plants to remain at their most attractive. There are two simple but very essential requirements. It must be placed where it receives light, and the temperatures must not be excessive.

Most containers selected for terrariums are simple in design and adapt easily to any interior. They are used in the same locations where flowering or foliage plants would be used.

Plants vary in their light requirements, and this is considered in making the selection. In most cases the plants used are those that tolerate lower light intensities. The light at a window may be quite intense and for a south or west window may be very warm as well. A terrarium, if it is completely closed, may become excessively warm and humid, which might be injurious to certain plants. A curtain between the window and terrarium may be sufficient to break the light intensity. A north window may receive no sun but still have sufficient light for satisfactory growth and maintenance of the plants.

If the location selected is away from the window, where there is little natural light, the daily illumination from a lamp may be adequate. This artificial light should be applied daily for 10 to 14 hours and with an intensity of 100 footcandles or more. This may be from either incandescent or florescent lamps. Specially designed lighting units are sold for house plants—with the lamps and an adjustable stand to regulate its height. These may be operated automatically by a time switch. Where a terrarium receives some natural light each day, the added light from a nearby lamp is desirable even if the lamp supplies only 2 to 3 hours of light daily.

The second requirement for satisfactory growth is temperature. Most homes are kept warmer than would be desirable for most plants. Consequently, avoid locations where the temperature is highest—such as on or near a radiator or heat source. Ideally, plants prefer a cooler night temperature than the day temperature. Native plants from the woods require even cooler temperatures and may not remain attractive for many weeks when the temperatures are constantly much above 65°F.

Plants in a terrarium are protected from rapid temperature changes, but even so, if the temperature change is excessive and frequent, growth may be poor.

Dish garden on an office desk, planted with Nephthytis - *Syngonium podophyllum*, Cardamon Ginger - *Amomium cardamon,* and Gold-dust Dracaena - *Dracaena godseffiana.*

During the summer months, terrariums may be placed outdoors in a shady location if they are covered so that no water gets in. However, since one of the advantages of a terrarium is its minimum care, it is not necessary to take them outside.

Containers

Containers suitable for terrariums are made of glass, clear plastic, or materials that will allow light to pass through. Since the usual concept of a terrarium is that little or no watering is required for long periods of time, the container should have no openings for drainage on the bottom or sides. If a drainage hole or opening is present, provision should be made to collect any water coming through or any moisture that would damage the surface on which it is resting.

Even with these restrictions, there are many containers that may be selected. These include open glass globes, widemouthed bottles, candy jars, fish bowls, brandy snifters, aquarium tanks, and even the common quart jar. With the present popularity of terrariums, diverse styles of plastic containers are being made for this purpose, many of which are separated into two parts for easy planting and care. These are available in many geometric shapes—globes, domes, egg-shaped, cubes, and cylinders with the lower portion for planting and the upper portion of clear plastic.

Large 5- or 10-gallon glass bottles, a gallon-sized glass jug, or other narrow-necked containers may be used, but these will require some patience and extra skill in planting. Plantings in these containers may be referred to as bottle gardens. If the glass of the container is tinted, as are some bottles, then use only those kinds of plants that will tolerate a low light intensity.

Soils

The soil used in a terrarium should be loose and of an

open texture. This usually means that a specially prepared soil mixture is made. Start with a loam soil and add organic matter and an inert material, such as sand. A mixture of equal parts of each provides a loose, porous medium for this purpose. Where a sandy loam is used, little or no sand needs to be added. No fertilizer materials are included in such a mixture. Inert materials such as perlite or vermiculite are often used in commercial mixtures. The soil mixture should be slightly acid.

Small charcoal pieces may also be included. Charcoal chips or pieces may be broken into smaller sizes, or the prepared charcoal that is sold for aquarium filters can be used.

Commercially prepared potting-soil mixtures are sold in plastic bags by nurseries, garden centers, florist shops, variety stores, and other places selling garden supplies. Some of the new plastic terrariums are boxed and include a bag of soil mixture, one of charcoal, one of coarse sand or crushed stone, and perhaps some large bark chips, decorative stones, or a novelty ornament—everything except the plants. The advantage of these commercial mixes is that they have been "sterilized" and are free of injurious insects and diseases. Also, the packages are of varying sizes, so that one may be purchased in a size suitable for the terrarium being planted.

Planting

In planting a terrarium, the first step is to put some form of loose drainage material in the bottom of the container. This may be fine, washed gravel, finely crushed rock, coarse sand, or similar inert material. The amount will vary according to the size and shape of the container. A layer of an inch or two is sufficient. The next step is to place a thin layer of charcoal—enough to cover the drainage material a quarter of an inch or so. Some gardeners mix the charcoal with the drainage material. The purpose of the charcoal is to act as an absorbent material for extra salts and other materials that may accumulate. A layer of dried sphagnum moss, the natural material, is sometimes put over the charcoal and drainage, but this is not always necessary, especially on small sized drainage stone. Where the drainage material is coarse, it helps retard the sifting of the soil into the drainage.

Finally, the soil layer is applied. This should be a layer of at least 1½ to 2½ inches. Altogether, the soil-drainage layer should not be more than 1/5 to 1/4 the height of the container—in order to have adequate space for the plants. If an irregular topography of a miniature landscape is being developed, add more soil to the high spots.

During planting, the material should be damp so that it will not cause dust to collect on the inside of the container. A funnel made of a rolled piece of paper is useful in adding these materials to narrow-necked containers like a bottle.

An aquarium makes an ideal terrarium, large and easy to plant. Note the layer of gravel to provide drainage, the layer of soil, and after planting, bits of bark have been used to cover the soil. A piece of glass covers the top. As plants grow some pruning will be necessary.

The next step is to develop the planting scheme. Remove the plants from the pots in which they are growing, and outside of the container place them together to obtain the most attractive appearance. Before planting, inspect each plant carefully to be sure that they are all clean and free of insects. Wash the plants so that the foliage is clean, and remove damaged leaves. Once this has been done, begin to plant, putting the tallest, most dominant plant into its position, and then plant the others. If the soil and root volume is excessive, then reduce this carefully to a size that can easily be planted in the shallow soil. The smallest, ground-cover kinds of plants would be planted last.

If a rock or a large piece of wood is included as a part of the landscape and is to be partially buried, this is put in place before any planting. The smaller rocks, wood, or other decorations are added after planting. Small evergreen cones, acorns, or pieces of wood covered with lichens are effective for a woodland setting, especially when used with native plants and moss. Interestingly colored rocks may be appropriate with cacti and succulents, or even some bleached, weatherworn branches may be used. A ground cover of gravel, attractive pebbles, or bark chips is effective. Avoid the use of bizarre or highly colored objects that are not in keeping with the setting.

Finally, when the planting is finished and all material is in place, sprinkle lightly with a mist sprayer and cover, if that is the plan.

Bottle gardens with small openings are time-consuming to plant. Long-handled spoons, heavy bent wire with a loop at the end, a mechanic's pick-up tool, and a straight dowel are useful tools to use in planting a narrow-necked container. In addition, it takes patience—much, much patience.

Care and Maintenance

A primary feature of a terrarium is the easy maintenance required—just a periodic check to see that the soil is moist. Even this is probably not necessary if the terrarium has a complete cover to prevent any water loss. Excess water is difficult to remove from a terrarium. Keeping it open will help, or even a slow draft of air from a fan will allow for some natural drying.

If insects or diseases become a problem, handpicking is the only practical solution. The use of pesticides is hardly possible. Ventilating the terrarium may help if mold develops.

Dish Gardens

A dish garden is an attractive arangement of small plants in a container. It is in effect a mini-garden. The plants selected are young: often seedlings or recently rooted cuttings planted together to make a pleasing effect. Plants of varying textures are selected, some with broad leaves, others having narrow or finely cut

leaves. The gardener has a wide choice in selection, but take into consideration the general growing requirements of those selected.

Plants in a dish garden are out in the open, without the protection of a terrarium, and must be able to withstand the temperature and low humidity of the room.

The soil for a dish garden is prepared as for terrariums. A mixture of equal parts of loam, peat, and sand or perlite is satisfactory for most kinds of plants. If it is prepared for cacti and succulents, a higher percentage of sand may be included.

The containers used for dish gardens depend on where they will be used. The size and depth may determine which plants will look attractive. Dish gardens are usually made in containers without a drainage hole. Ceramic ware is frequently used. Select those with an attractive color, plain in design, and at least 2½ to 3 inches deep. Containers made of copper, brass, pewter, aluminium, glass, or plastics are also used. The interiors of the metal containers should be coated with a plastic or waterproof material so they do not corrode.

In planting a dish garden, put a little soil in the container and then put the most prominent plant in place and add the others around it. In deep containers a layer of gravel can be put in first, as for a terrarium. Sometimes a slab of wood with bark or a heavy branch is used to form support for a vine.

The care of a dish garden is similar to that for foliage plants. They will need watering and light conditions according to the kind of plant. Since many of the containers used for dish gardens do not have openings for drainage, care must be taken to see that they are not overwatered. If there is a drainage hole, provision should be made to catch the excess water that may drain through. Fertilizers are not necessary for the first few weeks, but after that time use the kinds sold for house plants.

As the plants grow, they may need some pruning to keep them within bounds; if this is not possible, seperate them and plant them into large pots.

A cake carrier used as a terrarium. Stones are built up around a mound of soil with pieces of moss planted between and over them and young ferns planted at the top.

The Plants

There is a wide selection of plants that may be used in a terrarium or dish garden. Plants from the tropics are perhaps best suited to the high humidity and warm temperature of the terrarium. Desert plants, the cacti and succulents, are tolerant of the high temperatures but not of high humidity

or excess water and are suitable for open-topped containers such as "dry" terrariums or in pottery bowls or pots. Native plants from the woods, seedling evergreens, mosses, lichens, and ferns will tolerate the high humidity but require cooler temperatures than normally found indoors and should not be expected to last for many months.

With these three general groups of

plants it is easy to see that plants should be combined by using together those that have similar growth requirements. Some plants may have a wide tolerance to growing conditions but are best when grown under more moderate temperature and moisture. For example, the Jade Plant, *Crassula argentea* or *Sansevieria,* will tolerate the humid atmosphere of a closed terrarium before it becomes soft and spindly, but it really does best with a lower humidity. When a terrarium is first made, it would be suitable to finish it with some bits of woodland moss, although with high temperatures this is not likely to last for many weeks and will need to be replaced, or perhaps by that time the other plants may have grown and filled in the space.

General Plants

The plants listed below are suggested for terrariums and/or dish gardens. Larger-sized plants are suitable for general indoor decorations when grown with the proper cultural requirements. Flowering plants are not included in these lists, although they may be suitable, such as *Begonia sempervirens* (Everblooming Begonia), *Saintpaulia* (African Violet), or dwarf forms or species of *Sinningia* (Gloxinia), *Achimenes, Columnea* and *Streptocarpus.*

Acorus gramineus (Miniature Sweet Flag). A dwarf grass-like plant, requires moderate light and temperature, propagated by division. *Aglaonema modestum* (Chinese Evergreen), and *A. commutatum* (Silver Evergreen). These tolerate a low light intensity and warm temperature and require moist soil. The Chinese Evergreen may also be grown in water. Propagate by cuttings. *Aphelandra squarrosa* (Zebra Plants). White-veined foliage; requires warm temperature and moist soil. Several cultivars; small plants. Propagate by cuttings. *Ardisia crispa* (Coral Berry). Glossy foliage; requires moderate light and warm temperatures. Seedlings and small plants useful in dish gardens. Older plants flower, followed with red berries that last for months. *Asparagus plumosus* and *A. sprengeri*. Seedlings suitable for terrariums, although they may need pruning to prevent overcrowding; tolerates changing temperatures; propagated by seed. *Aucuba japonica.* Small plants of either the green or yellow variegated form suitable for terrariums; moderate temperatures and moist soil; propagate by seed and cuttings. *Begonia.* Many species tolerate low to moderate light. Use the leaved kinds such as *B. foliosa* or plants of *B. rex* for terrariums. Large-leaved kinds and flowering forms such as *B. semperflorens* require moderate to full light indoors. Propagate by cuttings or seed. *Brassaia*

actinophylla (Scheffleria). Seedlings of this familiar foliage plant add interest to a dish garden or terrarium. The light to moderately green, palmately divided leaves blend well with other plants to make attractive gardens. Give moderate to full light and cool temperatures. When too large, transplant to a single container; avoid excessive water.

Bromeliads

BROMELIADS. Members of the pineapple family, mostly stemless plants, with broad or grasslike leaves, many brilliantly colored, especially when near or in flower. Young plants suitable for terrariums; use in bright light; propagated by offshoots and seed. Several genera: *Aechmea, Billbergia, Cryptanthus, Uriesai,* and *Vriesea. Buxus* (Boxwood). Rooted cuttings or young plants of the *B. sempervirens* (English Box) are used in dish gardens and terrariums; they tolerate low light intensity and moisture.

Cacti and Succulents

CACTI AND SUCCULENTS. The plants considered in this group are not related botanically but have similar cultural requirements. They will grow in sandy soils, low in organic matter. These plants will stand high temperatures, bright light, and low humidity and are best used in open containers and in dish gardens. They grow tall and become spindly with low light. Water sparingly, as these plants will not tolerate wet soils for long periods and are subject to rots. They vary in their methods of propagation depending on the kind, but mostly by seed, cuttings or offsets. Seedlings and young-rooted cuttings are best for dish gardens and the larger sizes as house plants. Some representative kinds of several genera are mentioned. *Agave stricta* (Hedgehog Agave) and *A. Victoriae-Reginae* (Queen Agave), symmetrical rosette, a symmetrical rosette of narrow leaves; dark-green heavy leaves with a narrow white margin. *Aloe arborescens* (Tree Aloe), upright, tree like; *A. variegata* (Tiger Aloe), sturdy upright, triangular-shaped leaves. *Ceropegia Woodii* (Rosary Vine), a creeping plant with heart-shaped leaves and little tubers developing at the internodes. *Crassula argentea* (Jade Plant), tough and long-lived; *C. fal-*

cata, wide sickle-shaped leaves; *C. lycopodioides,* small scale-like leaves, multi-branches; *C. perfossa* (String-O-Buttons), leaves in pairs, clasping the stem. *Echevieria glauca,* (Blue Echevieria), a rosette habit of growth with broad glaucous gray-green leaves. *Euphorbia lactea* (Candelabra Plant), many variations with broad-crested branches; *E. splendens* (Crown of Thorns), spiny growth becoming tall, with scarlet-red flowers. *Ferrocactus,* many species of this dwarf cylindrical cactus with large spines. *Haworthia fasciata* (Zebra Haworthia), tough upright leaves, warty in appearance; other Haworthia species upright or rosette, excellent for difficult situations. *Kalanchoe,* many species, broad leaves, glabrous or pubescent, some with showy flowers. *K. tomentosa* (Panda Plant), erect, spoon-shaped leaves covered with white or brown felt-like hairs. *Mammillaria* (Pincushion or Wart Cacti), typically small or cylindrical in growth, with fine spines. *Opuntia microdasys* (Bunny Ears), similar to the Prickly Pear but with tufts of small, tiny brown bristles. Other species cylindrical and branched or with pad-like leaves. *Sansevieria trifasciata* (Snake Plant), a familiar plant with variegated leaf forms and the dwarf cultivar "Hahnii." *Sedum,* both winter-hardy and tender species, succulent leaves, some with limber stems, vine-like in growth. *Sempervivum* (Hen and Chickens), typically winter-hardy plants but suitable indoors if grown in bright light. *Stapelia* (Carrion Flower), leafless, stemmed succulents, low-growing, and very durable in a dish garden; flowers occasionally, with large, 5-pointed grotesquely shaped blooms having an offensive odor.

Calathea. A tropical American genus of ornamental plants, both upright or spreading, with striped or mottled leaves, bluish-green, silvery, or maroon. *C. ornata* is a popular kind, similar to *Maranta* in appearance, propagated by cuttings or division. *Carissa grandiflora* (Natal Plum), an evergreen shrub with white flowers; use seedlings or rooted cuttings in dish gardens or terrariums, best in the strongest light available. *Collinea elegans* (Dwarf Palm), seedlings suitable for terrariums, and larger sizes as

An unglazed pottery bowl planted as a desert garden using young cactus and succulents. Fine gravel covers the soil and larger stones are included to add interest.

decorative plants; slow-growing, tolerates low light but must not lack water in the soil. More commonly known in the trade as *Chamaedorea elegans*. *Chlorophytum elatum* (Spider Plant), young plants suitable for terrariums or dish gardens, older plants as hanging baskets; white-striped leaves, best grown in moderate light. *Cissus,* several species of vines. *C. rhombifolia* (Grape Ivy) is most common; use rooted cuttings or small plants in dish gardens, but in a terrarium they may grow very rapidly and require frequent pruning. *Coffea arabica.* Seedlings of the coffee tree are excellent in a terrarium with its higher humidity, or larger sizes in dish gardens. *Cycas revoluta* (Sago Palm), a slow-growing plant; seedlings useful in terrariums or dish gardens and large plants in pots; tolerates low light for weeks, as well as variable temperature above 45°F, and variable moisture. *Cyperus alternifolius* (Umbrella Plant), a grass-like plant requiring an abundance of water; young plants suitable for a tall terrarium; requires a warm temperature; propagated by division, seed, or by leaf cluster. *Dieffenbachia* (Dumcane), typically with rather large leaves, generally mottled or variegated; only very small plants useful in terrariums; larger plants excellent in dish gardens and as indoor plants; will tolerate low light intensity and low humidity; propagated by stem-cuttings or side branches. Familiar kinds include *D. picta* (Spotted Dumbcane) and several cultivars such as "Rudloph Roehrs" and "Superba," kinds with more white in the foliage than the species; and *D. amoena* (Giant Dumbcane) for a

large, decorative plant. *Dizygotheca elegantissima* (Spider Aralia), a graceful, woody plant with a palmately divided leaf with narrow segments, leathery texture, also known in commerce as *Aralia elegantissima.* Partial shade, propagate by seed on air layers. *Dracaena.* Durable foliage plants that tolerate low light intensity and variable temperatures. For terrariums and dish gardens use small-leaf kinds such as *D. Godseffiana* (Gold Dust Dracaena) or *D. Sanderiana* (Ribbon Plant), while *D. fragrans* (Cornstalk Plant) and its variations are excellent indoor plants with large, tough foliage. *Episcia* (Flame Violet). Relatives of the *Saintpaulias* with a creeping habit of growth requiring moderate temperature, partial shade, and uniform moisture. *E. cupreata* and its cultivars have leaf patterns of silvery or metallic shades on a green or coppery leaf; flowers brilliant pink, scarlet red, or yellow; propagated by cuttings or runners. *Euomymus.* Rooted cuttings of evergreen species are satisfactory in dish gardens and terrariums. The white or yellow variegated species are usually selected; these generally belong to *E. japonicus.* *Fatshedera* (Ivy Tree). An interesting botanical variation, a bigeneric hybrid of *Fatsia* and *Hedera,* leaves similar to English Ivy but larger; moderate light and cool temperature; propagate by stem cuttings.

FERNS. Ferns grow best in a soil mixture high in organic matter or even in it alone, such as peat. They grow well in the high humidity of a terrarium, and the heavy-textured kinds are suitable in dish gardens or as decorative

plants. They prefer a warm temperature and diffused light. Ferns from the woods require cooler temperatures and may not live more than a few weeks in an enclosed, warm location. Propagation is by division or spores. The following are a few tropical and semitropical kinds for dish gardens and terrariums. *Adiantum cuneatum* (Delta Maidenhair), *Cyrtomium falcatum* (Holly Fern),*Davallia bullata* (Ball Fern), *D. fejeensis* (Fiji Rabbit's Foot Fern), *Nephrolepis exaltata* (Sword Fern), and dwarf finely divided foliage types of the Boston Fern such as cv. "Fluffy Ruffles" are suitable for terrariums or bottle gardens; *Pellaea rotundifolia* (Cliff Brake); *Polystichum tsussimense; Pteris cretica* (Table Fern with many cultivars); *P. ensiformis V. Victoriae* (Silver Table Fern). *Ficus.* An important genus of plants with many suitable as decorative plants, including *F. elastica* ("Rubber" Plant), *F. benjamina* (Small Leaf Fig), or *F. lyrata* (Fiddleleaf Fig). Small-leaf kinds such as *F. diversifolia* (Mistletoe Fig) or *F. pumila* (Creeping Fig) are suitable for terrariums or dish gardens. The decorative figs tolerate low light intensity and cool or variable temperatures; propagated by cuttings or air layering. *Fittonia Verschaffeltii* (Mosaic Plant), a creeping plant with oval leaves with deep-red veins and *F. Verschaffeltii f. argyroneura* with white veins. Require a warm temperature, high humidity, and moist soil; excellent in terrariums; propagate by cuttings. *Geogenathus undata* (Seersucker Plant), low-growing with broad, quilt-like leaves; best in warm temperatures, partial shade, moist soil; propagated by division or cuttings. *Grevillea robusta* (Silk Oak). Seedlings of this lacy-leaf plant tolerate partial light and warm temperatures; useful in dish gardens. *Hedera* (Ivy). The small-leaf and variegated-leaf forms of the English Ivy, *H. Helix,* are useful in terrariums or dish gardens. The large-leaf types and *H. canariensis* (Canary Ivy) are useful in dish gardens. Ivy tolerates low light and low humidity but is best at moderate light and an abundance of water; propagate by cuttings. *Helxine Soleirolii* (Baby Tears) is a rapid-growing plant that is best grown with moderate light and temperature in a soil with much organic matter; excellent in the humidity of a terrarium. *Hoya* (Wax Plant or Wax Vine), a heavy-textured foliage plant with green or variegated leaves, small plants for terrarium or dish gardens, excellent as a house plant; keep warm and moist when growing, cooler and drier in winter. *H. carnosa* and cultivars are most commonly grown; propagate by cuttings. *Iresine* (Bloodleaf), a herbaceous plant, generally with bright-red or variegated leaves. *I. herbstii* is the most common species used outdoors. Used to provide color in a dish garden or terrarium, but grows rapidly and requires frequent pruning; propagated by cuttings. *Ligustrum* (Privet). Rooted cuttings, young plants, or evergreen species such as *L. japonicum* or *L. lucidium* satisfactory in dish gardens, in moderate light and cool temperatures. *Liriope Muscari* (Lily Turf), the variegated-leaf form with grass-like foliage, useful in dish gardens in low light intensity and varying temperature; propagate by division. *Malpighia coccigera* (Miniature Holly), a small-leaf plant with woody stems that requires bright light and moderate temperature; useful for dish gardens. *Maranta* (Prayer Plant), attractive spreading plants used in terrariums and dish gardens for their attractivly patterned foliage; they require warm temperature, medium light, and soil uniformly moist; propagated by division or cuttings. *M. leuconeura* is most commonly grown. *Osmanthus.* Small plants of this woody plant are suitable for dish gardens or as specimens in moderate to low light intensity and cool temperatures. *O. fragrans* (Sweet Olive) and *O. ilicifolius* are both useful because or their dark-green foliage; propagated by cuttings. *Pachysandra terminalis* (Japanese Spurge). Plants of this familiar ground cover, including the variegated cultivars, are satisfactory in dish gardens; grows in low light with moderate temperatures; propagated by cuttings or division. *Pandanus Veitchii* (Variegated Screw Pine). Young plants in a terrarium or dish garden will tolerate extremes in light and temperature. Larger plants are excellent for general decoration; propagated by suckers. *Pellionia,* Herbaceous creeping plants. *P. Daveauana,* green or gray centers in the leaves; *P. pulchra* (Satin Pellionia), with oval leaves arranged

A plastic dome shaped terrarium planted with small ferns, Prayer Plant - *Maranta leuconeura* and variegated English ivy - *Hedera helix.*

shingle-like with grayish color and dark veins. Useful in terrariums and dish gardens, with warm temperatures, moderate light; propagate by division or cuttings. *Peperomia.* Plants with somewhat succulent leathery leaves, some with silvery variegated foliage; require a warm temperature and moderate to full light; avoid excess water as they are subject to stem rot. Excellent kinds for dish gardens or terrariums include the following, which are propagated by cuttings or division: *P. caperata* (Emerald Ripple), heart-shaped leaves with corrugated or quilted effect; *P. Sandersii* (Watermelon Peperomia) with green leaves with bands of silver; and *P. obtusifolia,* with either green or variegated-green and milky white. *Philodendron.* A familiar group of excellent decorative plants, most of which have foliage that is too large for terrariums, but rooted cuttings of the common philodendron, *P. oxycardium,* are often used in dish gardens, as they tolerate low light intensity and warm temperatures. Excellent large decorative kinds include Velvet Philodendron (*P. Andreanium*), Silverleaf Philodendron (*P. sodiroi*), Velvet-Leaf Philodendron (*P. micans*), Bird's-nest Philodendron (*P. wendlandi),* Fiddleleaf Philodendron (*P. panduraeforme*), and Lacy Tree Philodendron (P. selloum). *Pilea.* This genus has many attractive plants that are rapid-growing. In terrariums they are effective but need frequent pruning. They thrive in warm temperatures and an abundance of water. To

keep them from overgrowing, water sparingly; propagate by cuttings, or the creeping types by division. Familiar species include *P. cadierei* (Aluminium Plant), with leaves that have a silvery area between the veins; *P. involucrata* (Panamiga), a compact-growing plant with deep quilted leaves; *P. microphylla* (Artillery Plant), with small light-green leaves and a bushy habit of growth. *Pittosporum tobira.* Small plants of this attractive broadleaf evergreen shrub are useful in dish gardens, and larger plants as specimens for indoor decoration. The variegated form has creamy white along the margins of the leaves. It will withstand low light and warm temperatures. Propagated by cuttings or seed. *Plectranthus.* Plants of this genus are mostly creeping or vine-like in growth. They grow rapidly in warm temperatures and an abundance of water. Propagated by cuttings. *P. australis* ("Swedish" Ivy), with metallic green, almost round leaves, *P. coleoides marginatus* (Candle Plant), with ovate leaves, hairy, with a white margin. *Podocarpus.* Coniferous evergreens from the tropics. Small plants, especially of *P. macrophylla V. maki* ("Southern" Yew) are excellent as house plants or in dish gardens; they tolerate low light and a cool or moderate temperature. Propagate by cuttings or seed. *Polyscias.* Plants with evergreen leaves and a much-branched habit of growth; some species with broad, somewhat heart-shaped leaves and others with pinnately divided leaves, often variegated. Indoors provide moderate light and moist soil; propagate by tip cuttings. *P. Balfouriana*, also with several variegated forms; *P. filicifolia* (Fernleaf Aralia) and *P. fruitcosa*, with divided leaves and purplish midribs or dark petioles. *Pothos*. See Scindapsus. *Sarcococa ruscifolia* (Sweet Box). Young plants or rooted cuttings of this winter-hardy plant are used in dish gardens. The dark-green foliage adds variety to a plant arrangement. Useful in low light intensity and cool temperature. *Saxifraga sarmentosa* ("Strawberry Geranium"). This familiar plant propagates by runners that terminate with a small plant. It is used in terrariums, dish gardens, or as a hanging vine. Use in moderate light and a moderate temperature. The cultivar "Tricolor" has variegated leaves with an ivory-white and pink margin or even a rosy pink in the youngest leaves. *Schefflera*. See *Brassaia*. *Scindapsus* (Ivy Arum or Pothos). These are tough, durable vines with heavy-textured, broad ovate leaves. They withstand high temperatures and moist to somewhat dry soil. Propagated by tip or single-node cuttings. *S. aureus* (Devil Ivy) with gold variegation; several cultivars with white to golden variegation; and *S. pictus* (Satin Arum) with

somewhat heart-shaped leaves and silvery blotches. *Selaginella*. These fern relatives are tropical plants with finely divided fern-like leaves and creeping stems. Best suited in terrariums with a warm temperature and high humidity. Propagated by division or rooting of creeping stems. *S. Emmeliana* (Sweat Plant), *S. uncinata* (Blue Selaginella), and *S. Kraussiana* all have lacy foliage and a creeping habit of growth. *S. Kraussiana V. Brownii* (Cushion Moss) is a dwarf, cushion-like in its habit of growth. *Syngonium*. Plants of this genus are vines with leaves that are arrowhead-shaped on young plants and often with silvery marking; leaves on older plants become more divided and generally green. They grow best in moderate light, warm temperatures, and uniform moisture. Propagated by tip or node cutting. *S. podophyllum*, also known as Nephthytis, has medium-green leaves and several cultivars with varying degrees of silver markings or leaf variations; *S. wendlandii*, with trilobed dark velvety green leaves with white veins on young foliage. *Tolmiea Menziesii* (Piggy Back Plant). Native to the west coast from California to Alaska. Bright green leaves, lobed and toothed, covered with hair. Suitable for terrariums or as a decorative plant

in moderate light and cool temperature. Winter-hardy in protected areas. Propagate by plantlets from adventitious buds developing at tip of petiole. *Tradescantia* (Spiderwort). Creeping or vine-like plants, rapidly growing, ovate to lanceolate leaves with variegation in some forms. Grows best in moderate light but tolerates low light, warm temperature, and abundance of water. Often confused with *Zebrina*. Best for dish gardens, as it overgrows quickly in a closed terrarium. *T. fluminensis* (Wandering Jew), tolerates wide range of growing conditions; *T. multiflora* (Tahitian Bridal Veil), a free-branching kind with small ovate leaves, purplish color on the back and small, white flowers; *T. albiflora*, leaves striped with white, otherwise similar to *T. fluminesis*. *Zebrina*. Vine or trailing plants. Varying from *Tradescantia* in technical details. Also called Wandering Jew, with similar cultural requirements. Useful in dish gardens and hanging containers, requiring pruning to keep in bounds; propagated by cuttings. *Z. pendula*, with ovate leaves, deep green to purple with silver bands and cultivars with more silvering; *Z. purpusii* (Bronze Wandering Jew), broad ovate leaves olive to purplish brown, darker in strong light.